A PASSION FOR

WILDERNESS

To the members
of the Colorado
Mountain Club 1
the readers 2
Trail of Timberline.

See you in the
wilderness.

My best,

Dick Winslow

OTHER BOOKS BY
CLAYTON KLEIN

Cold Summer Wind   1983
One Incredible Journey   1985

WILDERNESS ADVENTURE BOOKS

A PASSION FOR
WILDERNESS

THE CALL OF
RIVER AND MOUNTAIN

EDITED BY
CLAYTON KLEIN

Library of Congress Catalog Card Number 86-50271

ISBN 0-9611596-3-4

Cover photograph by Darrell Klein

Typesetting by Tom and Pat Boufford
Okemos, Michigan

Published by
Wilderness Adventure Books
320 Garden Lane
Box 968
Fowlerville, Michigan 48836

Manufactured in the United States of America

G
10.5
Kl

To all people who have a love

of nature and things wild and free

CONTENTS

"In God's wildness lies the hope of the world —
the great fresh unblighted, unredeemed wilderness."

— *John Muir*, **Alaska Fragment** *1890*

"Each man's necessary path, though as obscure
and apparently uneventful as that of a beetle in
the grass, is the way to the deepest joys he is
susceptible of. Though he converses only with
moles and fungi, and disgraces his relatives,
it is no matter, if he knows what is steel to his
flint."

— *Henry David Thoreau*

KEY TO MAPS

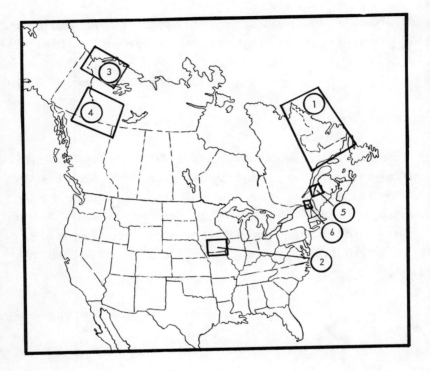

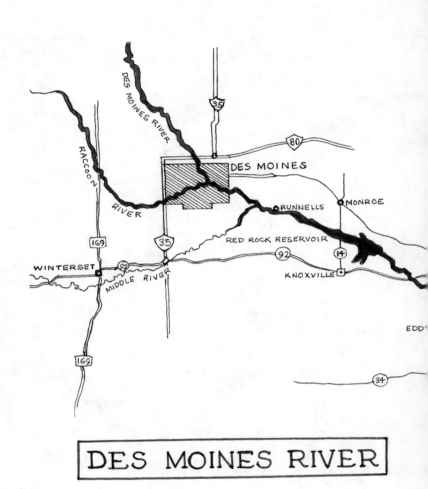

DES MOINES RIVER

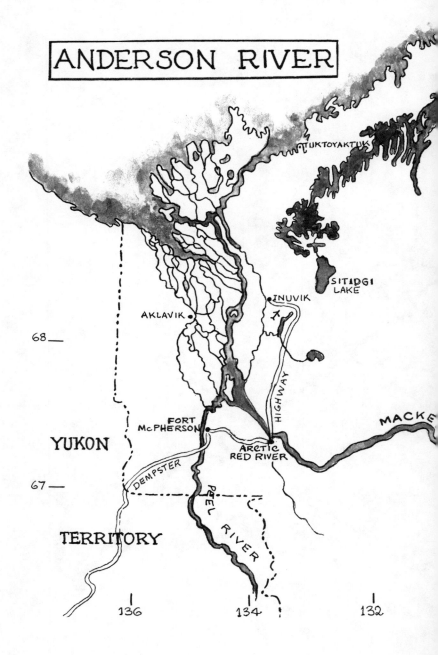

ANDERSON RIVER

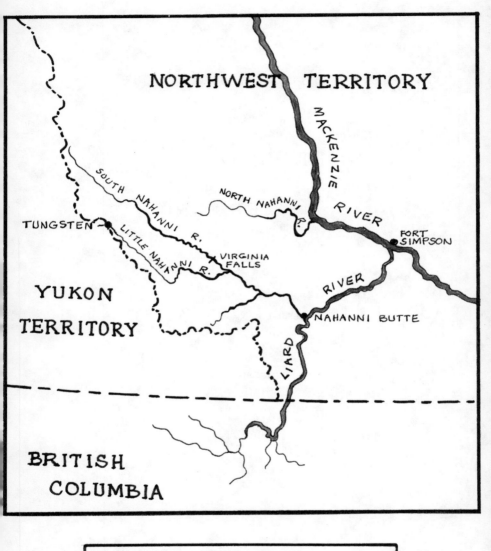

SOUTH NAHANNI

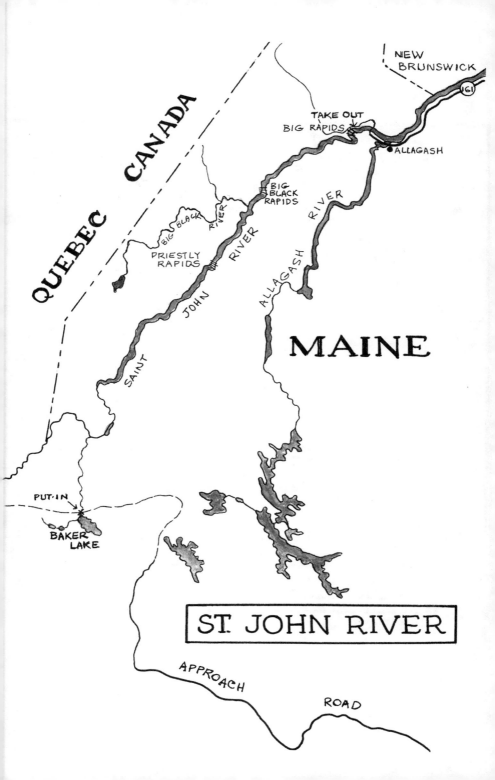

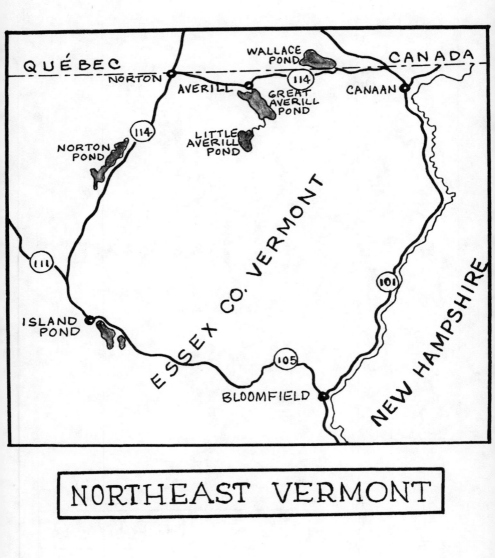

NORTHEAST VERMONT

• • •

ACKNOWLEDGMENTS

A Passion for Wilderness was made possible due to the work and cooperation of many people. First of all, a special thanks to the authors for their prompt replies to our numerous questions.

We would like to express our appreciation to Bern Will Brown for supplying the information on Colville Lake, Northwest Territories.

Thanks to George Thomas, Managing Editor of **Canoe,** for granting permission to reproduce the Lawrence Abrams poem, "Reminiscence."

Thanks to Vaughn Short of Tucson, Arizona, for permission to edit and reproduce "A Canoeist's

Prayer" from his book, **Raging River — Lonely Trail.**

Special thanks to Bernice M. Chappel for her most valued counsel and assistance.

We are grateful to Tom and Pat Boufford of Okemos, Michigan, for their excellent assistance in the word processing of this volume.

Many thanks to Marjorie Nash Klein for the fine cartography and cover design.

We are also appreciative to Jenifer Cowger of Urbana, Illinois; Sally Fahey of Mendota Heights, Minnesota; and Karen Pick of St. Paul, Minnesota, for their reports on the expedition of the six young women to the Arctic Ocean during the summer of 1985.

● ● ●

INTRODUCTION

Many of us enjoy nature and have a built-in desire to learn more about things wild and free. Some of us are satisfied only when we can obtain this knowledge first-hand, out in the field. Most people are born with an inherent passion for wilderness and continually seek out those natural places which are undisturbed by people and their machines.

The dictionary defines the word **'wilderness'** as an uncut forest or trackless waste in an unin-habited region. There are many methods of filling one's needs for the great out-of-doors. Some people find their wilderness in a city park or a zoo, or in their garden plot. The vast majority, however, satisfy their desire for wilderness by visiting a national, state or provincial park, or by taking scenic drives through the countryside or forests. Still others satisfy their wilderness desires by hunting or fishing, by skiing, sailing or canoeing.

There is a smaller segment of the population who, when thinking or speaking of wilderness, mean what is often referred to as true wilderness. True wilderness is a roadless area, well out of reach of any type of motorized conveyance other than the occasional aircraft. To visit the true wilderness, one usually paddles a canoe, backpacks in, or climbs a mountain.

In true wilderness one can pause and listen, hearing only the sounds of nature. Silence and the music of the birds are a part of it. So is the gurgle of a mountain stream, and the roar of a rapids or the beauty of a waterfall. If a person is near a lake or an ocean, it can be the sound of waves beating against the rocks or lapping or splashing upon a sandy shore. One may also listen to the animals and insects, or hear the reverberation of a distant thunderstorm in the night as it moves ever closer and finally strikes the tent with a terrific gust of wind, followed by an hour-long downpour of rain.

For this book we have selected writings of true wilderness experiences about rivers, lakes and mountains. Let's start at the top. Hiking along on a high mountain trail, one is certain to sense the presence of the great forces of nature.

Looking across a valley at another range, while listening to the gurgle of a nearby brook and watching a bald eagle glide on currents of air, a person may feel inconsequential and of little importance. Yet in the mountains, one often rises to a kind of magnificence of his own. Who can stand in the presence of a mountain and remain unchanged?

We love the mountains for their pines and spruces, their cool fresh air and their whitewater streams. These are the birthplaces of rivers. We go to them to find change and isolation, and grandeur. But more importantly, it is what happens inside of us that matters. It is the emotions and the feeling of a nearness to God that draws us back to the mountains time after time.

Rivers, lakes and streams are equally interesting and important to all of mankind. Their cool, sweet waters quench our thirst and nourish our forests and fields. Rivers are the living arteries of our land. The lakes, ponds, and marshes temper the climate and shape the landscape. In centuries past, it was the streams, when flooded, that carved the valleys. The silt they carried down from the hilltops became the rich meadows and fertile soils. There, grasses and trees grew to make a more hospitable land. When people first traveled, they followed streams and rivers. These arteries thus became the original highways of the continent.

Now modern-day adventurers are re-exploring these old river highways by kayak and canoe. In true wilderness areas, with these conveyances, one may visit areas unseen by human eyes for many, many years.   It is a delightfully thrilling experience to hike an old portage trail, knowing you are treading where only native Americans, and an occasional white man, walked in years long past. A greater thrill is to leave a seldom used trail to explore on your own, finding areas where, in all probability, no white man has ever before walked.

These are the things **A Passion for Wilderness** is all about.   Each section contains the writings of authors and poets who cherish the time they can spend in true wilderness.

You are invited to join us in our travels.   The first journey takes us to the rugged, scenic east coast of Labrador.

●   ●   ●

A publisher of wilderness books is certain to receive many inquiries and manuscrips from would-be outdoor writers and authors.   Such is the case at Wilderness Adventure Books.   From our collection of prose and poetry, and upon the suggestion of Richard E. Winslow III, we have chosen previously unpublished selections from the works of five authors.   The section by Elmar Engel is an exception, however, as it contains excerpts from his best-selling book, **Abenteuer Labrador**, which was published in the German language in 1976.

Part 1

THE WORLD'S END:
THE EAST COAST OF LABRADOR

SHIPWRECKED IN LABRADOR

RANGER MERCER IN
THE TORNGAT MOUNTAINS

TRAPPER ON THE KECARPOUI

By

Elmar Engel

ELMAR ENGEL

Elmar Engel with Hund Ruppes

Elmar Engel was born and raised in West Germany. He and his wife Brigitte have traveled extensively in Northern Europe by car and kayak. In 1968 they were invited to Canada to promote tourism from Europe. After driving across the continent, they paddled down the Muskwa, Nelson, Liard and Mackenzie Rivers. Then it was down the Bell and Porcupine Rivers before returning to West Germany.

The following summer was spent canoeing rivers of Labrador and Quebec. Their third summer saw them as immigrants in Atlantic Canada. They bought an old fishing boat in Newfoundland, crossed over to the mainland, and built a log cabin near the shore of Kecarpoui Bay.

The Engels are full time writers and have more than twenty published books, all in the German language. Each year since 1968 they have spent their summers in Canada and winters in West Germany. In addition to writing, the Engels work in broadcasting and TV for German networks. Presently they are doing a series of historic novels. "We are only too happy to share our lives between two continents, two cultures, and between an old-fashioned and urban lifestyle," they say.

• • •

The works presented in this section are excerpts from Elmar Engel's book, **Abenteuer Labrador**. This is the first time any of the Engel writings have appeared in the English language.

Brigitte Engel adds a few words to explain the name, 'Schnubbel': "My German nickname is Schnubbel. That's what Elmar calls me. It has no meaning at all. A British friend of ours felt 'Honeybunch' was the equivalent, but that sounds utterly foolish to me."

3

Elmar   Engel

THE WORLD'S END:
THE EAST COAST OF LABRADOR

In my personal opinion the east coast of Labrador is more the beginning of the world, the real world, than its end. For me, the end of the world is to be found in places like London and New York and Frankfurt. Be that as it may, The World's End nonetheless reflects current North American opinion and geographical reality.

Goose Bay, however, is something else again. If one were to deposit the passengers of a mystery tour

A Passion for Wilderness

in Goose Bay, none of them would be able to say with certainty whether they were in Labrador, Nebraska, Saskatchewan or Iowa. Provincial North American towns are the same wherever you go on the continent. The dusty Main Street, the little white churches, the huge supermarkets, the gas stations, the two or three hotels and the colorful and yet identical plywood and clapboard houses. I often wonder whether the inhabitants of these buildings ever end up in the wrong house late at night, confused by alcohol and the fact that the only difference between their home and the neighbors' is a shade of pastel.

Like so many things on this earth, Goose Bay owes its existence to the war. Among other things, it boasts one of the longest and widest runways in the world. One has the impression that the original American plan was to cover the entire surface of Labrador with a thick layer of asphalt. Luckily, a turn in the tide of the war in their (and Labrador's) favor put a stop to this. The Americans are long gone now, and if it wasn't for the regular monthly welfare payments few of the residents of Goose Bay would have any reason to stay there. As it is, they lead a pleasant and carefree existence.

For the time being, however, I didn't have any time to brood about this sort of thing. The oil company plane was due to take off for Saglak Fjord at six the next morning. Although I had a reserved seat on the flight I had to sign a paper saying that I wasn't allowed to sue the company in the event of an accident. The paper also stipulated that the oil camp itself was strictly off limits for me, and that I was responsible for my own food, lodging and transport home. I signed the form gratefully and without the slightest hesitation. How else could I have got to Saglak?

There was only one catch in the whole plan: I had a light nylon tent and a sleeping bag, but no food or cooking gear. Nor did I have a gun, an axe or fishing gear, and by the time I had finished all the formalities for my flight it was half past five in the afternoon. Luckily, the taxi came quickly.

"Hudson's Bay store, as fast as you can, it's urgent!" I shouted breathlessly as I leapt into the cab. This was obviously an opportunity the driver had been waiting for for years — we shot off down the road like a rocket.

At twenty to six we screeched to a halt in front of the store. I sprinted into the food department where the girls at the cash registers were adding up the day's bills. I grabbed flour, sugar, coffee, salt, sardines, canned chicken, lard, spaghetti, matches and corned beef from the shelves and threw it all into a cart which I left in the care of the astonished checkout girls.

Five to six. Tools and dry goods department. The clerk was combing his hair, the checkout girl was refreshing her lipstick.

"Wait!" I shrieked. "Give me a small pot, a small light frying pan, rope, plates, a spoon, a fork and an axe, quickly!" The clerk stared at me in horror, and the checkout girl dropped her lipstick. At five past six the clerk let me out of the locked store, and I hurled my packages into the back seat of the taxi.

"Liquor Board, and cane it!" I choked in desperation. The driver stepped on the gas, the tires screamed, and we shot off in a cloud of dust and flying gravel. He threw the Pontiac into the corners, striking terror into the hearts of the passersby. One man shook his fist at us. When we arrived at our destination the driver slammed the brakes on so hard that I nearly went through the windshield.

It was too late, alas.

I shrugged my shoulders in resignation and told the driver to take me to the Goose Hotel, which turned out to be a dump, to put it mildly.

"Thirty dollars a night," said the girl at the desk sweetly.

"Damn pricey," I snarled at her, and paid, reminding myself inwardly that it was only for one night. Then she saw the axe.

"Waddaya need the axe for?" she asked in horror.

"Oh, cutting down trees, firewood, what else?" I answered innocently.

"Mister, we got heating and we got air conditioning, and you can't take no weapons into your room."

"Okay, okay, I'll leave the axe here and you can give it back to me in the morning." I gave her the axe.

The room was even worse than the lobby. It was filthy, it stank, and the last occupant had obviously been a marauding vandal. At least it was possible to open the window, which was a small consolation.

A Passion for Wilderness

The garbage dump known as the Goose Hotel had a bar — I had noticed it on my way in — and after I had stowed my things in my room I decided to pay this haven of refreshment a visit. As was to be expected, it was on a par with the rest of the hotel, as were the customers. I walked up to the bar and ordered a beer. The barkeeper ignored me.

"Listen buddy," I growled with feeling, "I assume you don't lose money when you sell beer, so you might as well sell me one." The man looked at me expressionlessly and pointed to a sign, upon which was inscribed: No Service in Work Clothes — No Credit.

I had a look at myself. I was wearing a cord shirt, jeans and leather shoes. The shirt and jeans were clean, and the shoes were as clean as could be expected in the muddy streets of Goose Bay. I had a closer look at the other customers. They were all wearing flowery short-sleeved shirts with flowery ties. Their trousers didn't appear to be subject to the stringent dress code. One of them looked at me pityingly and shrugged his shoulders. "Son of a gun!" I muttered angrily, and stamped out of the bar.

The lady at the desk sold me half a dozen cans of Blue Star, a local Newfoundland brew, which went quite a long way towards reconciling me with Goose Bay. However, the evening was far from being over.

As I was climbing into bed a drunken racket erupted in the rooms on either side of mine. Two parties appeared to be in progress, or perhaps it was one party spread over several rooms. In any case, my room was right in the middle of the action.

A Passion for Wilderness

Judging by the noise it was some kind of wild tribal celebration; Indians perhaps, or Eskimos, or both. Ladies were also present, as far as I could tell from the higher-pitched voices which I could hear.

There was much coming and going between the rooms. Suddenly a shadowy form appeared at my window and climbed into my room. I turned on the light and was confronted by a large Indian, who simply stood there swaying slightly and staring at me expressionlessly. I couldn't tell whether he was drunk or simple-minded or both.

"Get out of here, you rascal!" I shouted at him shakily, and he lurched out of the window into the night again. In less than a minute a fresh salvo of Homeric laughter erupted from the room on my right. My visitor had obviously climbed into the wrong window and was now recounting his adventures. I locked the window, despite the stench.

I tried to turn on the TV, but the vandal before me had removed both the power cable and the wall socket. As far as I could tell from the noise, the party was nearing its climax. I threw one of my shoes at the wall and shouted "Quiet!" There was an astonished silence for a moment, but a few seconds later the party was in full swing again. I tried again but I was only rewarded with even louder laughter.

I nearly missed the plane. My request that I be wakened had, needless to say, fallen on deaf ears, and then I had to go back for the axe, which I had forgotten. But I made it, and just before takeoff I was standing under the wing of the Goose flying boat with my cardboard boxes and a silent group of oil men.   The wing kept most of the pouring rain off us.

Saglak is situated 58°30' North.   My plan was to meet the **Groais,** a British sailing boat, and to sail south along the Labrador coast.   Saglak is one of the deepest and longest fjords in Labrador, cutting into a cold, rocky, mountainous and bare landscape well north of the timber line.   Even the Eskimos have migrated away from the area.

We flew into a broad valley between two round, brown mountaintops.   The fjord was before us, the sea behind us.   The men who had been on the plane with me disappeared into an ugly and dilapidated barrack-like building, leaving me standing on the runway.   I felt a little sorry for myself there, alone in the wilderness, all forms of human habitation off limits to me.

I lugged my rucksack, camera bag and the cardboard boxes from the Bay store the five hundred yards down to the beach in several trips.   The most remarkable thing here was the biggest collection of junked vehicles I have ever seen: trucks, pickups, mobile cranes, snowplows, motorboats, bulldozers, fork lifts, tracked vehicles and others.   The really strange thing was that there weren't more than two miles of road in the whole area.

There were a few buildings there as well, in varying stages of decomposition, and the landscape was full of junk.   Even so, the roofs of the buildings appeared to be intact, and I made myself a nest in a small room next to the entry of a kind of porter's lodge.   I wedged one of the sheets of plywood which were lying about across the broken window, cleared the rubble from the doorway and laid a clean sheet of plywood on four bricks — that was to be my bed at night and my table during the day.

It would probably have been more like 'proper' camping if I had slept in my tent away from all the garbage, but my tent was little more than a thin nylon dog kennel, and I wasn't sure it would withstand a Labrador cloudburst. My porter's lodge wasn't exactly warm, but it was a dry and cozy cave, and it had the added advantage that there was plenty of wood lying around. I hadn't seen a single piece of driftwood on the entire beach.

The sun was shining. I wasn't quite sure what I should do next. What I usually do in situations like this is make a pot of coffee, so I wandered out into the blinding sunlight to collect some wood. Suddenly there was a puffing and snorting and the thundering of hooves, driving shivers up my spine. A herd of caribou charged out of the shade of the building opposite and rushed past me up the hill. I watched them go with my mouth hanging open, and they stopped and turned round to survey me curiously with their typical caribou stare. They seemed to find this gaping figure with the axe in his hand extremely unusual.

When I had recovered my breath and the caribou had finally trotted off I collected some wood, got some water from the stream and made myself some coffee. A shot of rum in the coffee would have been very welcome, to restore the inner man who was a little shaken by the combination of the overpowering mountains, the decrepit results of human efforts and the utter aloneness. Even so, this kind of depression isn't something that happens to me often, and it never lasts long. I've learned to adapt to all kinds of unusual situations, and in this situation I didn't have any other choice — I had neither rum nor anybody I could tell my troubles to.

The sun blazed down from a sky which was now completely cloudless, but even so it was chilly. The light had an intensity which I have never experienced anywhere outside the Arctic. The clarity of the air made even the distant rocky leviathans seem closer, revealing at the same time a multitude of details which made them less menacing.

The bright weather finally drove the last shadows out of my soul — it simply wasn't possible to be depressed in this light and in the cool, fresh air. I climbed to the top of the nearest hill, and discovered that there was another hill behind it. Behind the second hill was a proper mountain. I couldn't see any further than that as the shadows were getting longer and the day was already drawing to a close. My stomach started to remind me that I hadn't eaten anything all day apart from the coffee.

The night wasn't exactly peaceful. Boards creaked everywhere, and I heard sighs and groans and bumps and bangs all over the place. I managed to convince myself that it was the wind playing tricks in the old building, and the sun came up before I had time to change my mind. Daylight drove the giant torngat, the misshapen stallos and the donkey-tailed huldras back where they belonged.

I warmed my naked skin in the morning sun in front of my house, mixing flour, water, baking powder and a pinch of salt to make dough for bannock. The bannock was soon sizzling crisp and brown in the well-greased pan, and the hot, strong, sweet coffee was steaming invitingly.

I felt like a king. I decided to explore a little; there was an old radar station a mile or so up the hill, more than two thousand feet above the cold Labrador sea. Huge scanners loomed up on the hilltop, and behind them was a gigantic white ping-pong ball which housed the station itself. This abandoned relic of the Cold War and of an increasingly perfect and gigantic military technology is the only landmark far and wide. The landscape is arid and monotonous, despite its huge grandeur — there is nothing for the eye to rest on. It's a landscape which doesn't care whether human beings like it or not.

Around the radar station are the buildings which housed the three thousand people needed to operate it, connected by an unbelievable labyrinth of completely enclosed walkways: the winds here can reach speeds of over a hundred and twenty miles per hour, enough to knock over the strongest soldier.

The cliff by the pingpong ball is a murderously sheer drop of nearly two thousand five hundred feet. Several American soldiers who couldn't endure the isolation jumped to their deaths there, hopeful young men broken by the North. Strangely enough, by the same North which gives others of us a new lease on life.

Even though one is usually unaffected by the technology and buildings which other members of our race have constructed, there is something threatening and terrifying about a huge installation like this when it's completely empty. It has a clammy,

The Old Radar Station

deathly atmosphere that sends shivers down the spine. And this is what the entire world would be like if the neutron bomb was ever used, that charming weapon that 'only' kills living beings, leaving buildings and machinery undamaged. It's a terrifying thought; all the people who are prepared to consider the use of such weapons should make a trip to Saglak to get a better idea of what they are talking about.

I stood on the ruins of this modern fortress and looked down at the sea. It was peaceful, but very much alive. There was something comforting about the sea, stretching out calm and blue below me. It was blue for many miles, only turning to grey just before the horizon. I couldn't see a single boat, although the visibility was at least thirty or forty miles.

On the way down the mountain I encountered a huge caribou bull. He simply stood and stared at me, not making the slightest attempt to run away. This was very foolish of him — if I had been an Eskimo with a rifle it would have been the last thing he ever did. Feeling very sure of myself I took a couple of pictures of him and told him to go about his business, as severely and convincingly as I could. I comforted myself with the thought that there was plenty of room for maneuver. Since the caribou obviously didn't feel like moving out of my way I cautiously started to go around him. The caribou, however, had no intention of allowing me to go around him. At least it's not a black bear, I thought nervously, reminding myself that caribou aren't carnivores. I wondered whether they regarded humans as rivals; I knew that elk did. If that was true then this huge beast might be planning to go for me with his huge antlers or, worse, to trample me to a pulp beneath his broad hooves.

Whatever his motives were, he started to circle me. I walked downhill slowly, within the circle. I estimated that he was about ten yards away from me. Perhaps he thought that I was after his harem, or perhaps he had already lost his harem and was convinced that I was somehow responsible.

I started to find the situation very unfunny. When I tried to shoo him off by shouting and throwing a stone in his direction he stopped in his tracks and glared at me angrily.

"You can't possibly think I've been fooling around with your wives," I told him in desperation. "I only arrived yesterday." He continued to circle, unimpressed by my pleas of innocence.

I remembered that one is supposed to speak to wild animals gently when threatened by them. It couldn't hurt to try.

"My dear caribou," I said as gently and politely as I could, "please be so good as to let me pass. I neither wish to shoot you nor do I have the slightest desire to mount any of your wives. I have nothing but the most peaceful intentions." I held my open hands out towards him, which I considered to be a universal sign of good will, and continued my words of peace.

"Oh why don't you get out of here you stupid bastard!" The beast obviously had a low opinion of the Geneva convention, and he was equally unimpressed by the sound of my voice.

A Passion for Wilderness

A terrible possibility dawned on me. Was it possible that he was attracted by the fact that I was only wearing my underpants? The vision of a tabloid headline flashed through my mind: "Explorer Violated by Caribou Bull." That's simply not possible, I told myself, not feeling very convinced. The bull circled in closer. I pulled on my jeans in confusion, my mind full of the most ridiculous and irrelevant thoughts. I remembered the reindeer roundup I had taken part in many years before, in Lapland. Caribou are nothing but a kind of reindeer, I said to myself, and the reindeer had been harmless. I had gone right through the middle of a huge herd of them on foot. On the other hand, that had been in early summer, and now it was much later, practically mating season! Besides, that was Lapland. And this was Labrador. "Could these Canadian caribou be so much more forward and sexy?"

With my trousers on I felt a little more composed. This, I said firmly, is a situation which cannot be tolerated. I took my courage in both hands and walked towards the bull, bending down to pick up a stone as I did so.

My aim was better this time and I hit him in the flank, intensifying the effect by waving my arms wildly and shouting "Shoo! Beat it, you horny devil!" and other less comprehensible war cries.

Just at that moment a herd of caribou appeared upon the bluff, distracting the attention of my suitor, who ambled off to join them. I was free. I walked on down the hill, shaking my head in wonder and more than a little glad to be free of my deviant caribou friend.

17

Those curious caribou

At the bottom of the mountain, not far from the runway, I discovered a simple concrete monument with a cross on it. I had just been beginning to see the funny side of the encounter with the caribou; now the monument and the story behind it suddenly brought me back to the more serious side of life again. The plaque beneath the cross bore the following inscription:

Dedicated to the unfortunate crew of the B-26 which made a forced landing near this spot in December, 1942, in commemoration of their heroic attempt to survive.

18

A Passion for Wilderness

I later managed to get hold of a copy of the plane's logbook, which is a record of an unusual tragedy:

30 November, 1942

Takeoff for Goose Bay at last. (From Greenland). Clouds enveloped us at about 13.15. I changed course in order to get out of the clouds, and instructed the rest of the formation to do the same. One plane emerged. I lost contact with the others as I dived to get below the clouds. We found a hole 600 yards wide to the south, and then we broke through the clouds, but soon afterwards we had to climb back to 13,000 feet again. Lt. Josephson gave me the new code so that we could return to the old course, but we knew we couldn't correct the course any more. At what we estimated to be about the halfway point we picked up the Goose Bay radio beacon, but then we lost it again because the radio broke down.

Now it was too late to fly back, so we tried to orientate ourselves by compass, but we didn't succeed.

At last we reached the coast. We thought we were south of Goose Bay so we flew north. Then we realized that we were actually north of Goose Bay after all. The fuel was almost finished so I had to look for a place to land. I wanted to

find a spot with trees, but then the en-
gines started to sputter so I went down.
The crew was completely calm when I told
them that we were going to have to make a
forced landing.

It was a good landing. We rammed a
rock and ripped open the bomb bay, and one
of the propellers pierced the fuselage
behind me, but apart from that the plane
was intact. The plane had made a 90° turn
as we landed and lay in a good position to
protect us from the prevailing wind.
After eating cold rations we went to bed
in the plane.

We slept very well. Lt. Josephson
shot the stars, and calculated that we
were about 300 minutes from Goose.

Their calculation was more or less correct. They
were also fully aware of the fact that they weren't
very far from Hebron, and they also knew that Hebron
lay to the south.

On board the plane they had the following equipment and rations:

17 wool blankets, 1 eiderdown, 1 pillow, 7
cans of meat, 3 cans of peanuts, 8 cans of
chicken, 2 cans of pineapple, 3 cans of
fruit salad in syrup, 2 cans of dateloaf,
1 can of rye bread, 3 packets of choco-
late, 28 bars of chocolate, 4 packets of
dates, 1 pound of crackers, 4 packets of
figs, 1 pound of cheese biscuits, 1 bottle

of Coca Cola, 2 cans of salmon, 3 pounds of coffee, 20 packets of caramel candies.

The last entry in the log was made on 3 February 1943, two months later:

We've been wrapped up in the blankets without getting up for a week now. Way-wrench died today — he had been delirious for a while. We're all very weak, but we can probably hold out for a few more days.

In the first days they had been full of relief at having survived the landing so well, hopeful when they saw their first seals, hopeful that search planes would find them. They made an attempt to get the transmitter working, but they failed. On the 23rd of December three men set off in an inflatable boat to try to paddle to Hebron. They disappeared without a trace, victims of the sea, the wind and the cold. After the departure of the boat the first cases of frostbite are recorded in the log. This was followed by this entry:

It's amazing how important a man can find one caramel candy. The first fear of death. Food is the only subject of conversation. The men get weaker, and storms and the cold make them weaker still. They pray, but they make no attempt to hunt seals. Instead, they spend their time playing rummy.

A Passion for Wilderness

All the men have bandaged wounds, results of frostbite and lack of care with the rest of the kerosene and methylated spirits. The rations get smaller and smaller. They catch a small bird and make a stew out of it. They say Mass. It gets colder. On the 16th of January they still have some dried soup and a few sticks of chewing gum. The engine oil freezes solid and won't burn any more. They get weaker and weaker.

Some Eskimos from Hebron found the wrecked plane and the bodies of the crew at the beginning of March, one month after the last log entry.

These airforce men had been taught how to obey and how to shoot and drop bombs, but nobody had thought of telling them to use their own intelligence in unusual situations.

I sat on my plywood table in the nude, eating my breakfast and warming myself in the sun, just as I had the day before. A barely noticeable breeze stroked my body, and the sun shone down out of a cloudless sky. The caribou stood in the shadow of the opposite buildings, fascinated by the spectacle of a breakfasting human.

Every now and then I had a look out over the fjord. Then, at last, there she was — the **Groais**, with her unmistakable cutoff hull and rust brown genoa. I packed my things together in a hurry, pulled on my clothes and started waving with my bright orange tent. The boat changed course and headed towards me.

A Passion for Wilderness

A Zodiac inflatable dinghy — a kind of bent rubber sausage — came and picked me up, at the same time depositing the friend I was replacing on the shore.

Clouds started to pile up over the mountains in the west. A strong breeze picked up and whistled in the shrouds. Waves started lapping against the hull of the boat. We weighed anchor and set off to look for a better place to spend the night. We started up the diesel and motored into the wind and the waves, up Pangertok Fjord, a side channel of the great Saglak Fjord, which runs between the mountains for a good twenty miles.

The fjords here can stand comparison with those in Norway; here too, mountain faces rise up towards the sky on both sides, making the tiny human feel very tiny indeed. But compared with Labrador the Norwegian fjords can almost be described as mellow, despite their roughness. Here at the northeast corner of North America the landscape is much more elementary and powerful. One has the feeling that it is no place for mere mortals. The fact that I, the skipper Chris, and his wife Anny and a small dog named Mutty had the temerity to sail about in this cyclopean landscape in a 31-foot sloop called **Groais** felt almost like hubris.

Elmar   Engel

SHIPWRECKED IN LABRADOR

Schnubbel and I had to reach Ungava Bay before the end of September if we wanted to avoid having to spend the winter there. Between us and our goal lay about a thousand kilometres of the unknown with wild stretches of water, the first part of which led through one of the last blank spots on a map of Canada. Actually, this part had been charted just like the remaining stretch of our trip, but the maps hadn't been published by the time of our departure.

A Passion for Wilderness

That didn't bother us very much. Rivers are one way streets that always lead to a destination.

We had already inspected the tricky, malevolent rapids not far from the camp, at the end of Jamin Lake; traversing them now provides the foaming, frothing, chaotic introduction to our river trip. Then we are alone — alone except for the De Pas River, the rocks and the Labrador forest. Not that we have any chance to take a peaceful look at the landscape; we have to cross an entire series of roaring rapids dotted with rocks. High, hard breakers curl over us. Then short, flat and fast stretches where we can catch our breath.

The kayaks lie deep in the water and are hard to steer. The high waves don't bother us; the problem is getting around the boulders. When we scrape past the white frothing holes that have been ripped open by underwater rocks, our hearts stop beating for a split second. After about five kilometres the river slows down so we can take a look around.

The De Pas lies relatively flat, the banks are rocky, the countryside hilly. Sparse forest on either side. A marmot scurries along the rocks to our right, disappearing into a crack. We decide to land and to wait for the return of the marmot. We know that its curiosity will soon get the better of it. And, sure enough, two or three minutes later, its funny face with the snub nose and the polished black button eyes reappears. It scrambles over to us, changes its mind, races back to the crack. Then it reappears, apparently fascinated by the two red kayaks, but still cautious.

We set up camp early; the white water of the

first part of the river had used up a lot of our strength. We aren't in shape yet. but that will come, after three or four days of paddling.

At the mouth of a nearby brook I catch a couple of two pound speckled trout. We eat them along with mashed potatoes from a package and onions fried in bacon fat. For each of us there is a bottle of beer cooled by the river, the last beer for God knows how long. We sit around the fire for a while until the sun sets and the mosquitoes drive us into the tent.

When I stick my head out of the tent the next morning, I catch sight of a brownish black porcupine waddling by. I slip out of the tent to approach the animal; it raises its quills and squeaks angrily at me. Then it clumsily climbs a low fir. I don't think that it was exactly charmed by our encounter.

In the afternoon we travel along a series of rapids which we find easier than those of the previous day. Nevertheless, there is a big difference between doing white water canoeing as a sport on rivers in the Alps or in some other mountain range, and doing it where the kayak is the only transportation necessary for an adventure. In the wilderness you yourself have to bear the consequences you incur through insufficient preparations, carelessness, bad planning or bad luck.

After a few days, the standing waves appear to have become lower, the speed of the water more acceptable, the river more familiar. We have gradually gained self-confidence and even feel that we've made some sort of deal with the De Pas, a deal born of mutual respect. The distances we cover each day are relatively short, maybe thirty kilometres,

Schnubbel shoots a rapids

maybe less. We always stop after about four or five hours in the kayaks, set up camp, go fishing and tramp about the woods, shotgun in hand, looking for grouse and porcupine. Once we observe a magnificent caribou. On the rainy days, we sleep a lot, wasting time and feeling good.

But then it happens, brutally, without warning or escape! Our kayaks have just shot through some rapids, the water cold and hard but presenting no real problem when suddenly we are faced with the backwater and another lower level. Our vision is restricted and the water is incredibly fast. To the left of us is a veritable stone garden of black rocks surrounded by surging white foam, to the right of us, high breakers. And Schnubbel ahead of me is going to the left, directly into the stone garden! I yell, "To the right, for God's sake, to the right!" But my shouting can't be heard over the roaring of the water. Besides, I'm having problems myself in the churning waters. I anxiously follow her progress; she is almost through, but only almost ... I see how the kayak gets stuck on a big black boulder, how the angry water towers above it. Then I'm through, I'm in the backwater, the tip of my kayak pointing upstream. Schnubbel has wormed her way out of the seating hole of the kayak and has taken refuge on the boulder. In a couple of seconds I'm on the bank behind the stone garden. I run upstream and discover that the De Pas has wrapped the kayak around the boulder as if it had been a damp washcloth.

Everything lost! That is, that means ... I can't bear to face the consequences yet. I must try to salvage the contents, the supplies. "Hold on!" I cried through the roaring. "I'm coming with the rope!"

The kayak has capsized upstream, the wreck is in the current, water has shot into the cockpit and twisted the kayak around the boulder. I wade into the tearing, ripping current, the water ripping at my legs. My boots are full of water and heavy. I've only gone about two metres from the bank, am wading knee deep when I come to a hole, not particularly deep but deep enough to make me lose my precarious balance. I'm swept down to where the kayak is, manage to crawl to land. I run upstream and wade into the De Pas again. I am powerless against the force of the river; it sweeps me again past Schnubbel and the kayak. I try to throw the rope around the kayak, but it's too short. I get closer, try again, but again it's too short.

I see that there is no sense in trying further. Even if by some miracle I could fasten the rope to the boat, we don't have the necessary strength to pull the wreck away from the boulder. The De Pas is simply too strong for us. "Come out of there!" I yell over to Schnubbel. "Try to bring something with you!"

Schnubbel is able to get the camera from the stern, and to extract a pullover that she had stuffed into the cockpit of the kayak. She slides into the water and allows herself to be washed to the bank. And then we're standing there beside each other, shivering, frightened to death, wet, freezing, bruised and scraped.

The sky is full of fat grey-black clouds. We now

"Everything lost!   Hold on!"

start frantically to build a fire, a blazing and warming fire from wood we collect along the treacherous river bank.   We are lucky that the matches in their waterproof packing had been in my kayak.   On the slope above the bank, we rapidly set up the tent.   There is thunder to the northwest.

"And now ... ?" Schnubbel asks.

"I'll give it another try.   But I don't think that there's any point — even if we do get hold of the wreck ... "

There is occasional lightning in the sullen

skies, but the storm is taking its time. I walk fifty or sixty metres upstream, wade into the water as far as possible, and try to swim into the middle of the river so that it will drive me towards the boat. But the current is tricky and there are boulders and backwaters. I simply can't get close to the wreck. I feel frustrated and am covered with bumps, bruises, scrapes, and failure.

And then the thunderstorm breaks and the gusting wind brings whipping rain and hail along with it. We crawl into the tent, dry ourselves off as best we can, cover ourselves with the remaining sleeping bag and sit there shivering, trying to warm each other.

"Now what?"

"Tomorrow — then I'll be able to see better — then I'll give it another try." I talk myself into believing that it isn't totally pointless. Gradually I gather my thoughts and the situation becomes clearer, albeit no more positive. Two people and a boat that only seats one. The nearest people? Two fishing camps: one about a hundred and fifty kilometres upstream and the other — God knows how many kilometres — downstream. But somewhere between them is an empty fishing camp — and in this camp there are probably cans of food from the previous year.

Except for two pounds of oatmeal, we have nothing edible. No pepper, no salt, no plates, no pots, no pans, no spoons, cups, or forks. All that was, and still is, in Schnubbel's kayak.

And Schnubbel only has what she is wearing. We're left with the tent, shotgun, fishing tackle, axe, and the matches. What if my boat had been wrecked?

A Passion for Wilderness

We're not only missing the food but also Schnub-bel's sleeping bag, her ski jacket, her warm clothing, her sturdy shoes. Fortunately, she still has her rubber boots and has managed to salvage her sweater.

I have only a vague idea of where we are. There are still no maps of this part of Canada — "We'll try again afterwards, when it stops raining."

Maybe it's a hundred kilometres, maybe only sixty, downstream to Fritz's empty De Pas camp. That would be our other possibility — we would try to reach it! We think we remember Fritz saying that they would be flying in caribou hunters around the end of September. It is now the end of July. We hope that by then ...

Towards evening, the rain stops and the thunder rumbles at a greater distance. We climb into our wet clothes, figuring that is better than jumping naked into the water because there would still be a bit of body warmth between the skin and the clothing that would help mitigate the shock of the cold. We could have saved ourselves the trouble! We don't make it to the boat and give up at last, bruised, scraped, exhausted and depressed.

I make another roaring fire to warm us up. We turn our pants and shirts inside out and place them close to the fire where they emit large clouds of steam. They are drying gradually. I empty the contents of my boat and find some instant pudding, a frying pan, and the bag of oatmeal, about two pounds of porridge. "Oh well, that's not too bad; the frying pan is worth its weight in gold!"

"And tomorrow morning everything will look

A Passion for Wilderness

better, you'll see!" I say, trying to lift Schnub-bel's spirits (and my own!). "We're bound to catch something tomorrow!" I console her. "And besides fish, there is always beaver, porcupine, duck, goose or grouse. And at any rate, there's muskrat!"

Despite our exhaustion, we sleep poorly. The next morning the situation doesn't look different at all despite the fact that the sun is shining and the sky is a brilliant blue.

The first thing I do is take a look at the kayak. It is an even more hopeless venture to try to reach the wreck. Apparently it has rained even more upstream and the De Pas has risen twenty or thirty centimetres. All that is left to be seen of Schnub-bel's kayak is a red shadow under the churning waters. I can feel my stomach rumbling, but it's not hunger or normal pain — it's the brutal clarity of the situation that we are experiencing first hand. We are not armchair adventurers caught up in an exciting movie or a suspenseful book. This is the real thing, and it's happening to us. Two pounds of oatmeal, some instant pudding — but we are sure to catch some fish or shoot some animal. Of course, we would ...

I break off a couple of thin dry twigs from a solitary fir and start the fire, adding some drift-wood to get the fire really going. Now would be the time to put on water for coffee, hot, sweet coffee that we always drink after getting up, coffee that would warm us and wake us up. . . . Nonsense, as if my life depended on coffee! I suppress all thoughts of coffee and throw more driftwood on the fire. It's silly to make a low fire for cooking seeing as we have nothing to cook. At least we should be able to warm up!

Schnubbel crawls out of the tent and I ask her how she slept.

"Well, actually ... "

"We should make our way slowly downstream until we hit Fritz's camp. We've got to ration our strength, try to catch or shoot something underway. We should keep the oatmeal and pudding — for emergencies."

"That's what I thought too. Not that there's any other possibility. Okay, down with the tent! Who takes the kayak?"

"I thought that you should. I'll hike along the bank with the shotgun, try to get something. If there are more rapids, I'll take over until you're feeling more confident. Are you hungry, by the way?"

"No, not at all. I've lost my appetite because of all this."

If we had only managed to save the bacon! Twenty pounds of smoked bacon that we had brought over and smuggled into Canada.

"Maybe we should eat some oatmeal, a handful each? We could heat water in the pan and then mix the oatmeal and the pudding —"

Schnubbel maintains that she isn't at all hungry. I don't feel like eating anything either, to tell the truth.

"We're bound to catch a fish, a pike. I saw a huge one yesterday. Or I'll get a grouse or a beaver or a porcupine, you'll see! Then we'll both be feeling better."

A Passion for Wilderness

"Do you have any idea where we are?"

"Barely. But we should be able to find Fritz's camp — must be able to."

"Tell that to the Marines," Schnubbel replied dryly.

"And we're sure to catch something; why, we've never had a day without a fish, a bird or a muskrat."

"Oh, your optimism! Finally it's coming in handy!" She grinned tremulously. I guess it was supposed to be a confident smile.

I grab hold of the axe, shotgun and fishing rod and traipse along the side of the river while Schnubbel paddles the kayak through the calm waters below the rapids. She is spunky, admirably so. After being capsized so brutally, you're always afraid of the most harmless current, of each wave, of paddling in general. The shock and the fear don't totally disappear for days. Fortunately, the De Pas turns very quiet after the rapids. Calm and consistent, it winds its way northeast to meet the George River.

The bush of Labrador shows me who is the master in this land and who the guest, at best and the invader, at worst. The grass, leaves and shrubs are dripping wet. After only a few minutes, I am as wet as they are. Sometimes I can see the traces of muskrat or beaver trails in the shoulder level willow saplings. The axe is hindering me; I give it to Schnubbel to take along in the kayak.

I often stumble over gravel and pebbles that have been hidden by the vegetation. But worst of all are the willow thickets in the marshy hollows at the mouths of the brooks and tributaries. Taller than I, pressed tightly together, and springing back like a rubber band at the slightest contact, they make it near to impossible for me to penetrate their defense. I bushwhack my way through and have trouble keeping my orientation. We work out a system to help me: I shake the branches of the trees and then Schnubbel gives me directions from the water — left, right, straight ahead. Between the thickets there are marshy and deep holes of water that I don't see until the last minute, brooks which I can hear but not see. Often it is easier to walk through the water right next to the bank; doing this I scare away a couple of plump pike that have been sunning in a small cove.

We try to fish for our noonday meal, but without any success. The fish simply won't bite. In the clear water we can see them following the lures — but not biting on them. When we had enough to eat, there were always more fish than necessary to be had. But now, when we desperately need one, we can't even catch a minnow. It would have been enough to make me sick — if I hadn't already been feeling so sick at heart. Most of all, I would like to spring into the water and grab one with my hands. Or maybe my shotgun might come in handy? Enough of this fantasizing. Onward!

I notice that I'm drinking water at increasingly short intervals. Water weakens. I remember this North Shore bit of wisdom too late. Fortunately the weather is good. The shining sun dries the grass and the willows and finally our clothes. Onward!

In a clearing I catch sight of porcupine marks on

several firs. I poke about with the butt of the gun in mounds of grass and piles of brush; I shake the branches — nothing. I do this systematically, my circles increasing in radius. Nothing. Onward!

There is no change in the countryside. Low rocky hills poor in vegetation, relatively sparse woods of small slender firs, reindeer moss, lichen, rocks, hellish willow thickets in the hollows. I have to cross a heavily flowing, ripping brook. First I leap from stone to stone and then have to wade up to my hips in the icy water. A grouse whirs directly above me but disappears into a thicket of firs before I can take the gun from my shoulder and aim. While looking for my feathered friend, I scratch my face and tear my pants, but all to no avail. No luck. It's enough to drive us crazy.

Pretty early we set up our tent on a flat and sandy strip of bank and make a fire. "A fire makes any wilderness a home," Schnubbel says. Ah, yes, Charlie. Our guide on the Porcupine in the northern Yukon and in Alaska. This was his motto that he said every evening after we had set up the tent and were sitting around the flames under the Northern Lights. This man, who loves fires so dearly, was canoeing this summer through the Canadian Barren Grounds. From Great Slave Lake to Hudson Bay — and he'll be seventy in September! Over a thousand kilometres through a treeless countryside. First he'll have to go upstream, conquering the waterfalls and rapids, enduring the damp and the cold. Without a fire to warm him up in the evening — only then when he can find some dry roots on the treeless tundra.

A Passion for Wilderness

I try to catch a fish in the last light of the day, normally they are biting most then. But in vain. I'm beat, dead beat. Too beat and tired to even be hungry. A muskrat is swimming along the bank, but far from us; it looks over towards us and dives under the water. "Should I?" I ask, reaching for my gun. Schnubbel merely shrugs her shoulders, says she's not hungry. She's probably telling the truth. The muskrat remains invisible. It has most likely let itself be driven downstream and will only emerge again in the safety of the bulrushes.

We sleep a long, deep sleep and feel better the next morning. But now we can sense our hunger. Then I take off; I'm a lot slower on foot than Schnubbel is on the river. The leaves and grasses are dry, the hiking less unpleasant. My muscles only ache at the beginning, the result of yesterday's exertions.

Downstream I can hear a roaring. I hope it is the wind. No, the roaring isn't an angry wind, but rapids. After two hours, we're there. Fortunately, there are no great difficulties. A few waves and then a wide open passage. Schnubbel handles it by herself.

The countryside still hasn't changed. Nothing special or distinctive that would help us figure out where we are. But the weather is good, there's a bit of a wind and only a few mosquitoes are pestering me. There, on the river bank above me, is a rustling, a sound of escaping. I clamber hastily upwards, shoving as I run a slug and a shell into the double barrel of the gun. But once up there, I can't see anything, can't hear any more noises. It was probably a stray caribou that I had startled and that then leapt into the refuge of the bush. Onward!

Schnubbel persistently fishes. Again and again I can see the lure glittering in the air but don't hear any shout of success. This evening I'll go hunt muskrat along some grassy spot. Schnubbel shouts over to me that she had felt a tug on her rod but had lost contact with the fish. Maybe the fish aren't biting because the weather is so good. Our catch was always best in rainy weather.

Another of those horrible truculent willow thickets is in my path; I force my way through. Twigs slapping in my face, I begin to reproach myself: Why hadn't I been traveling in front? Why didn't I bother to bring along a fish net? Why didn't I at least bring some salt along? Why hadn't I packed any emergency supplies in my kayak? Shouldn't we have tried again to salvage the wreck of a kayak? Had we really exhausted all possibilities? — But I banish these recriminations from my head. What use were the "should haves" and "would haves" in our present situation? I had to cope with the reality of it; not with what could have been. Or should have been.

We've come a good way, about ten to fifteen kilometres, I judge. I cross yet another brook and stop to make a fire on a spit of land between the mouth of the brook and the De Pas. I dry my clothes by the fire. Will my rubber boots ever totally dry out again?

Schnubbel tries her luck again at fishing. Nothing. It's as if we're jinxed: we don't see a trace of a fish, no quick movement of a tail, no shadow gliding noiselessly under the water. If there are no trout here in the mouth of the brook, then I'd like to know where they are. We kneel down and drink fresh cold water from the brook. The oatmeal is to be eaten only in a real emergency. Should we stay here for a while, to save our strength, to wait? If I only had an idea how far away we were from that darn camp!

The steady rain the next morning relieves us of the necessity of making a decision. The wind shakes the walls of the tent, big drops of rain patter on the fly. It's not weather for any kind of trip. There are sudden breaks between the gusts, the wind must be catching its breath. Schnubbel is still sleeping when I crawl out of the tent, get the fishing rod, and go over to the extreme edge of a pebbly bank that is only partially flooded. A grey dripping gravy has been produced from the marvelous blue, white and green ingredients of yesterday, a gravy sprinkled liberally with wind-driven gusts of rain. It's cold.

When the wind dies down somewhat, I cast the spoon where the current of the brook meets that of the De Pas, where whirlpools circle crazily, where the pebbly bank suddenly drops off. I let the lure sink and then reel it back in. Nothing. I try again, but this time the wind blows the lure too far downstream, and again, nothing. I have to wait, have to retreat a few steps because the De Pas is getting ready to spit water into my boots. Another break in the wind, another cast. Nothing. I try again further upstream, let the spoon be driven somewhat downstream, and reel in more quickly than before. Still no luck. Then I try further downstream and reel in more slowly. There! A tug — my heart almost stops beating. But then I feel nothing more — it's gone! But something is there — and that something is a fish, probably a grey trout! When the wind dies down again, I cast further downstream, reeling in slowly. Nothing. But there had been a bite, there had been a fish nibbling on the lure!

Then suddenly, after I've cast at right angles to the current, I feel a tug and off she goes — my line. I quickly release the brakes, still keeping close contact to my prey, for something is on the line now, something has bitten. It tries to escape; I brake carefully.

And then it leaps out of the water — a salmon — a fantastic salmon! I'm biting my lips in apprehension and excitement and regain lost ground by reeling in more quickly, the fish has got to be played out. It leaps up once again; for a split second, it looks as if its standing in the air but then it splashes back into the water. Careful, I've got to be careful, despite the twenty pound test line.

I'm not fishing for fun now, this isn't a pleasant sporting event with nothing to lose. A ravenous hunger is giving me new strength. I'm not going to give the fish a chance! And I can tell that it's weakening; its next leap into the air isn't as high as the preceding ones. It will soon be leaping into my frying pan — my mental promise to Schnubbel!

I reel it in closer. In the shallow water at the

gravel bank it makes one last attempt to escape, but I pull it in hard, knowing I can depend on my rod. It gains a couple of metres but appears to be exhausted. Now I close the brake, reel it in, and run up the bank, pulling the still fighting fish behind me way up onto the gravel. Then I reel in the wildly writhing salmon so far that there is only a metre of free line between the lure and the tip of the rod. I grab it firmly behind the gills and kill it with a stab of my knife in its neck.

I squat in front of my prize fish, looking it over, barely feeling the wind and the rain. A fish — and a big one at that! A good ten pounds, a ten pounder salmon! Ten pounds! A new hard shower interrupts my triumphant musings.

Then I go back, cast a couple of more times, and soon have another bite, one as hard and stubborn as the first one. After a minute I land salmon number two! I don't give him a chance, landing him by pulling him up over the wet gravel. It is only somewhat smaller than the first fish. I kill it and also hang it on one of the dead stubs of an old upturned tree. It won't be doing any more biting now.

I clean the salmon and eat a piece of the red, raw meat. With the exception of the liver and the roe, I throw its insides into the whirling back waters. The grey trout are attracted by the insides and within a short while I've caught two of them. Six more pounds of fish! They won't have a fraction of the salmon's nutritional value, nor will they taste as good, but nevertheless, six pounds of fish!

A Passion for Wilderness

The rain is whipping my face and my hands are clammy. I make a fire behind a large chunk of rock from birch bark, brushwood from the dense stands of fir, and twigs. I cover the fire with a large piece of bark to protect it against the wetness and against the drafts behind the rock. I span a tarpaulin diagonal to the direction of the wind, fastening it securely onto four firs and hacking away the extraneous and bothersome twigs. We won't exactly be having a comfortable picnic, but we'll make out fine. At this point, eating salmon anywhere relatively dry would be a culinary delight. The rock serves as the back wall, the tarpaulin as the roof, the firs as the side walls, and in front of us we have the fire. Two bleached driftwood stumps are our chairs. But I don't mind.

I wake Schnubbel up and take her into the living room, our refuge from the rain. Her eyes widen in surprise and delight as she sees the four fish; she kisses me quickly on the cheek before rushing over to inspect the fish more closely. We both feel tremendously relieved. We both feel that we've overcome the worst of it all, or at least that's what we tell each other.

We fry the pieces of salmon, sprinkling them with some charcoal to spice them up. We eat pieces of salmon every possible way that our limited kitchen will permit: baked on a hot stone, steamed, smoked, and of course raw! Salt — if we only had a handful of salt. Every now and then I go down to the spot where the nameless brook flows into the De Pas. But I don't get another bite, not one. I give up, I'll wait till evening, maybe the fish will be biting then.

But they aren't. The next morning it's blue sky and brilliant sun. The whole scene looks like a page ripped from a scenic calendar. As if it hadn't been raining yesterday, as if no foul weather could ever stain this natural beauty. We take down the tent, remove the tarpaulin from the living room, and move on our way. The grass and the undergrowth are wet and clinging; I console myself with the thought of the salmon and the trout that still remain.

In the afternoon I shoot a grouse fluttering above me; it only manages to flutter a few trees further. Unfortunately, to be on the safe side, I have aimed too low and hit the breast of the bird, thus almost ripping it to pieces. Schnubbel plucks the bird while I make a large fire. We let the fire burn down and then roast the bird on a green stick over the coals. And again we rub some of the ashes into the meat to spice it up.

Somewhat later we hear an airplane and then catch sight of it flying far off to the north, much too far off. Our supply of fish is exhausted. Then worry settles down on us like a sticky spider's web and we can't shake it off. After the worry, the first doubts come creeping — and then fear sidles in.

By now, I'm pretty used to the hiking. The De Pas is showing us its best side: a mild current, wide, flat banks, and only a few easy rapids. The weather seems to have stabilized. And just in time for dinner, Schnubbel catches a four pound pike!

During the day now, I move farther away from the river, up to where the land is higher and dryer and the vegetation less profuse and bothersome.

And — oops! I almost step on a porcupine! It squeaks in surprise and anger and raises its quills. I hesitate for a minute before hitting its head sharply with the butt of my rifle. I simply must save ammunition. And I simply couldn't let fifteen pounds of meat waddle off! I run down to the bank and tell Schnubbel to put up the tent — I was calling it a day.

With the tips of my boots I turn the dead animal on its back and carefully begin to peel it out of its pin cushion skin. The quills have tiny hooks that spring away from the skin of the animal at the slightest touch. And if they get stuck in your skin, they can cause long-lasting and bad infections — every sled dog from the bush country of the Canadian North can testify to that.

Now we have meat, lots of meat, good, nutritious and delicious meat, and on top of that we even have fat which I have scraped out from under the skin. We melt the fat in the frying pan and pour it into a tobacco tin which I had used to store worms for fishing. And with the porcupine insides we lured and caught a large pike that evening. Our dinner? Roast porcupine spiced with ashes and pike fried in porcupine fat. And to make our happiness even more complete, a big fat muskrat was swimming directly towards our tent in the last light of the day. Together with the remaining pike, it comprises our breakfast the coming day. We take the rest of the porcupine meat along with us.

This morning I have to go through a most unpleasant swampy lowland area which is bisected by a deep river too wide to jump across. At last I find a tree that has fallen; I hack away at the trunk and improvise a bridge. After crossing, I go upstream a while, winding my way through the under-growth. I catch sight of a beaver lodge, and then of the architect himself. The beaver is swimming directly towards me; I carefully and slowly load the shotgun. I don't need to take aim, shooting diagon-ally down toward the water. The beaver literally leaps out of the water and then tries to dive back in again, his flat tail slapping against the water, his short legs kicking about. The shot has pretty well blown in its head. Then it lies there quietly with blood gushing out of its head, dyeing the water red.

I had never shot a beaver before — and never have since. It wasn't exactly a pleasant thing to do but I had no choice.

Schnubbel has heard the shot. She too has a weakness for beavers, and her joy at the idea of more meat is considerably dampened by the thought that it was a beaver. But the beaver has assured us of survival, at least for the time being. There are at least thirty pounds of meat there, not including the fat. We immediately set up camp, frying out the fat from the back and tail sections. The fat has a penetrating taste peculiar to itself but the meat, on the other hand, is fine and tender. If only we had a handful of salt — after all, it would only have cost us a few cents ...

Darkness once again creeps over the Labrador wilderness, but now it does not seem so daunting. At last we have regained our self-confidence.

Schnubbel contemplates

A Passion for Wilderness

Schnubbel on the water — and myself as far as hunting and fishing is concerned. Now there is no need to stay hungry, we have proved to ourselves our ability to "live off the land." Now we only look for the fishing camp that maybe lay around the next bend in the river ...

Days are passing. It sounds unbelievable, but we are happy. Schnubbel now has her good humor back, and she even makes plans for our next summer's kayak trip down the George River, with more men in the party!

Once more with our ability to "live off the land" we do not worry so much. Always we move on down river, partly paddling, partly walking. The days slip by and we do not count their passing. It matters not which day this is of our involuntary trip. If we economize on our matches, we can wait in the safety of the fish camp if need be until September when the caribou hunters will fly in for the hunting season.

Then, on a clear and sunny day, Schnubbel as usual paddling, and I walking along the river bank, we suddenly hear a well known noise, a noise from the modern world that does not belong to such a wilderness as this. That should be, that could be, that only can be AN AIRCRAFT!

It is the turboprop "Beaver" that had brought us into Jamin Lake, with bush pilot Tim Cole at the controls! Unfortunately I am stuck in the willows again, but manage somehow to free myself to race down to a clear stretch of water. Both Schnubbel and I are shouting and waving — surely he must see us? Tim flies low over the river, the wings wave

A Passion for Wilderness

from side to side — Yes. Oh my God, he has seen us!

It is more good luck that at this point, the De Pas is wide and still. I run into the water as Tim dives once again low over the surface, no doubt looking for any rocks. Another circle, and he is sending up clouds of spray as the pontoons of the aircraft race over the water. Cautiously, Tim brings the plane to rest in shallows just a few yards away. Still a little breathless, I grab the pontoon.

Tim opens the cockpit door. "Ran out of luck, eh? I've seen you from the air — only one kayak, and I remembered that I brought two of these crazy things in to Jamin! Everything else okay?"

Schnubbel grins and giggles, and in some short words I describe the wrecking, the start of the ordeal, try to describe the more or less hopeful days after we had caught some fish and ...

"Well, we've got a load now, but I'll come back tonight and pick you up. Just in case you want to get out of here ... "

For heaven's sake, yes, we want!

Thus we survived a wrecking in the wilderness. It could be the end of a story which left us so much more to experience in this "Land God gave to Cain." For another day we waited, until Tim was finally able to get us out, but still Labrador seemed stacked against us.

When we flew north along the George River with its white water, to reach the Eskimo village of Akisakudluk (Port Nouveau-Quebec), we hit a snow storm. Tim had to follow the deep-cut river valley, tried an emergency landing, but this proved impossible due to the narrow canyon-like valley and rock-strewn stretches of the river.

Finally we arrived at the settlement, where we had to land far out in the bay so as not to drift against the rock cliffs. The plane bounced like a ball on the water for almost half an hour until a small Eskimo boat with an outboard fought its way to take us off. Again, this was almost swamped on the run to shore!

What followed was an incredible Indian summer on the tundra; some marvellous weeks with the Inuit and an Inuit wedding the night before we left this "land made of dreams." It was Northern lights, Eskimo songs and dances and then an original Eskimo parka lined with wolf-fur, traded for the kayak, which we had to leave anyhow. Schnubbel was happy.

And always there was the question of our new-found friends: "Coming back?"

Yes, we would be back.

And that's what we did the follow summer ...

E l m a r   E n g e l

RANGER MERCER IN

THE TORNGAT MOUNTAINS

The Torngats are like the head of a spear projecting north into the ocean between the Labrador Sea and Ungava Bay. East of the Rockies, they are the highest mountains on the Canadian mainland. They are a collection of cold, bare, rocky colossi, many of which rise up sheerly out of the icy sea without even the hint of anything like foothills. The highest peaks are over six thousand five hundred feet above sea level, and they are usually hidden in the clouds or cloaked in fog.

Nobody lives here, and only a very few courageous Eskimos dare to make the trek through the passes leading to the George River valley: the Inuit believe that the giant Torngat and other unfriendly spirits live in this desert of stone and ice.

It's true that most of the Eskimos are good Christians now, and that the missionaries of the Anglican, United, Moravian, and Pentecostal churches have done their utmost to convince them that these heathen giants and ghosts don't exist. Even so, the Eskimos are a cautious folk. They're not willing to take the risk of going there, just in case the power of the Christians doesn't reach all the way into the chasms and gullies of the Torngats after all. And in any case, the giant Torngat and his band aren't the only danger — there are the Tlingits too. Maybe they're not quite as big as Torngat, but they're still much bigger than a normal human being.

Even the few Kabloonas (whites) who sometimes come up here to hunt and fish find these mountains a little eerie. They are usually Christians too, but that doesn't prevent them from worrying about all the resident ghosts and giants and spirits — they often light a candle in the evening so that the great black dog doesn't appear at midnight to tell them that someone in their family is going to die.

This was probably the sort of thing that went through Ranger Mercer's mind in January, 1936, as he set off with the Eskimo Zacharias Ikkusit and his dog team. Their mission was to travel north to Okak Bay and bring the Eskimo Mark Kennitok, or rather, Mark Kennitok's body, back to Cartwright for an autopsy. It was suspected that Kennitok had been murdered, and his mortal remains were believed to be in a trapper's cabin.

Cartwright is near Goose Bay. Okak Bay is more than six hundred miles from Cartwright, and sixty miles from Nain, the last human settlement. Okak Bay is also at the foot of the wildest section of the Torngats.

The Eskimo and Ranger Mercer battled their way through the never-ending storms — calm weather was a rarity — and finally found the cabin, which was almost completely buried in the snow. Kennitok's body was inside, with a ghastly gaping wound in the forehead.

Mercer and Zacharias nailed together a coffin, or rather, a wooden box, and lined it with reindeer moss to protect the body from further damage. Then they loaded the body into the box and started off on the long journey back to Cartwright.

Their plan was to replace the moss with salt in one of the next settlements. Since salt preserves fish, they reasoned, why shouldn't it preserve dead Eskimos? For the time being, however, Kennitok's body was in no danger of decomposing; at temperatures between minus thirty and minus forty centigrade he was literally a block of ice.

At the foot of the Kiglapit Mountains (one of the Torngat mountain chains), they encountered such a violent storm that it was impossible to enter the pass. Zacharias built an igloo, and they spent the next few days there, waiting for the storm to blow itself out. Mark Kennitok shared the igloo with them — he was a silent companion, but one who was difficult to ignore. Mercer was afraid that the dogs might break open the box and eat the body if they left it outside.

Rested, but not in the best of spirits, they harnessed the dogs to the sled and set off up the Kiglapit Mountains. At four o'clock it was already dark, but it was a clear night, the moon was full, and the trail through the pass was easy to see between the steep cliffs. They reached the top of the pass around midnight, at an altitude of four thousand three hundred feet. They stood there with the dogs, a tiny handful of tiny creatures, dwarfed by the cold, moonlit backdrop of cliffs, ice and snow.

The descent was steep and icy. Zacharias was torn between praying to the heathen gods and the Christian God for help and support. Mercer cut the dogs loose, so that they wouldn't be killed or injured if the heavy sled got out of control and ran over them — without the dogs there was no way out of the mountains.

The two men struggled to get the sled down the mountain, but Zacharias was too terrified to be of much help by this time, and it wasn't long before he lost his grip. Mercer couldn't control the heavy sled on his own, and it slid off down the slope, gathering speed rapidly. It hit a rock, somer-saulted twice, knocked the lid off the makeshift coffin, and catapulted the body a hundred and fifty feet through the air in a cloud of flying reindeer moss.

In the eerie moonlight all this would have made stronger men than the superstitious Zacharias lose their nerve. He fled into the night, screaming Torngat's name at the top of his voice.

There's nothing at all in Mercer's report about what he felt at this point himself. Nor does he say anything about his feelings as he clambered down the steep slope, shouldered the frozen body and carried it back to the sled. In any case, he managed to catch some of the dogs and harness them to the sled again — just like their master, they had fled in panic as the sled had gone out of control.

Then Mercer got one of the huskies to follow Zacharias' scent. They found him crouched behind a boulder, muttering unintelligible heathen incantations. The only word Mercer could make out was 'Torngat.' Zacharias was completely beside himself, and nothing on earth would have enticed him to go anywhere near the sled and his dead countryman.

Somehow, Mercer managed to get the sled back onto the trail and down into the valley. Zacharias was still a long way from coming back to his senses, and he followed the sled at a respectful distance. Mercer was lucky enough to chance upon an Eskimo winter camp, and doubly lucky in that the chief of the camp, Hammer Punniguniak, was an old acquaintance of his. After a long palaver Hammer said that he knew what to do, but that Mercer must promise not to say a word about it to the missionary.

After Mercer had agreed to this, the old Eskimo started to dance as if he was in a trance. He murmured incantations and brought out a piece of big medicine, a crow's foot, which he tied round the neck of the now completely apathetic Zacharias. Then he danced again for a while and pulled out some

A Passion for Wilderness

even bigger medicine, the bladder of a seal, which he inflated and tied to the foot of the dead Eskimo. Then he demanded a couple of pounds of flour and packets of tea as payment, and assured the still skeptical Zacharias that the anger of the giant Torngat had now been appeased, and that he could set his mind at rest and continue on his journey with the sled. And just as Hammer promised, the rest of the twelve day journey to Cartwright went without a hitch.

Dr. Lionel Forsythe, who carried out the autopsy, discovered that the cause of Kennitok's death had been a fall, and not a murderous blow with an axe. He also determined that the fall had been preceded by the consumption of huge quantities of alcohol. The investigation which followed revealed that a white trapper had distilled a few gallons of moonshine which he had then consumed in the company of his Eskimo friend. The trapper had to spend the next six months in the relative warmth and comfort of a prison cell — moonshining was, and still is, illegal in Canada.

The effect of Mercer's accomplishment was dramatic: It demonstrated to the Indians and Eskimos that the law had an arm which not even the giant Torngat and his band could keep back. This demonstration also impressed many of the older white residents of the Canadian wilds, whose lifestyle hardly differed from that of the continent's original inhabitants.

Elmar   Engel

TRAPPER ON THE KECARPOUI

Entrel Belvin brought along our mail and with it the news that an editor had printed our pictures. The editor wrote that the money was already being sent. I must admit that our joy did know limits: with money we could now buy plane tickets, and that meant that our best reason for not returning to Europe was blown. Nevertheless, we were still free until the end of October. That gave us enough time to go with Entrel into the interior, to the source of the Kecarpoui River. Entrel wanted to use this occasion to prepare for the fall trapping.

The hinterland of the North Shore is the reflected image of the coastal area. There the sea is dotted with thousands of islands and rocks while the land here is sprinkled with an equal number of lakes, ponds and bogs, which, together with the portages, furnish the only "roads." The trails, which have been chopped out of the northern forest, are just wide enough that a man with a canoe on his shoulders can make his way through. Absolutely nobody lives in the interior; only in the fall does a handful of trappers venture in for four to six weeks to do some trapping.

In winter, when the ice is good, a few hunters speed noisily along on their snowmobiles in search of caribou. But other than that, nothing else disturbs the dignified silence of the wilderness.

Entrel's trapline covered the upper lake area of the Kecarpoui, "our" river. Schnubbel packed the following provisions for our two week trip: 1 bag of flour (25 pounds), 1 bag of sugar (10 pounds), 1 jar of instant coffee, 50 tea bags, 1 pound of baking powder, 1 tin of shortening, 1 side of bacon fat, 1 pound of salt, and 1 large shakerful of pepper. Our kitchen utensils consisted of 1 fry pan, two pots that fit into one another, the lid of which doubles as another fry pan, two tin mugs, two spoons, two forks. Our knives were attached to our belts.

At first glance, it didn't seem as if we had much quantity or variety. But Entrel assured us that something edible was bound to run or swim along our

A Passion for Wilderness

way. And when you have to carry everything your-self, you think pretty carefully about what and how much. Entrel had an axe, a shotgun, a homemade tent about four square meters big, and a little tin stove with him. The stove pipe peered jauntily from the rectangular stove. In addition, sleeping bags, oil cloths, a change of clothing for everybody, a fishing rod, cosmetics in the form of toothbrush and toothpaste — and that was it.

We set off at high tide and are able to paddle about five hundred meters upstream. Then Schnubbel walks along the trail, carrying a light load while Entrel and I each tow the canoe. The water is low, making our work easier.

The rapids at the mouth of the river are just about a mile long. For the most part, the current is fast; only a few deep pools make it easier for us. In high rubber boots, we wade through the water, simultaneously holding onto the canoes and pulling them upstream. The bottom of the river is stony, uneven, slippery from the slimy beds of algae. The current is pulling and tearing at our legs. Sometimes we have to pull the canoes over high barriers of rocks. Looking back, I can see red fibreglass spots dotted on the stones. Whenever we approach one of the deep pools, we climb into the canoes, paddle as far as possible, land in the back waters behind a group of rocks, crawl to the front of the canoe and get out again.

I try to keep pace with Entrel. The guy is fast and agile, used to paddling a canoe alone. I'm better with a kayak and fall behind. But after an hour, I'm at the end of this tricky stretch, too.

A Passion for Wilderness

Entrel is sitting on a rock grinning, his pipe wedged between his remaining teeth. Schnubbel is waiting on the other side of the river, sitting on a dead, split birch.

Entrel and I paddle over to her and trim the canoes there. Entrel packs his gear in the bow while we store ours in the middle. It is warm with scarcely a breath of wind to ripple the surface of the water. There is as good as no current in the river on the kilometre-long stretch to Kecarpoui Lake. The bank to the right of us rises rocky and abrupt; yellow-leaved birches and dark red pine have clawed their way into the crevices of the rock. To our left, the land slopes up gradually; a few metres behind a line of scraggly pines the tundra begins.

We pass by two small islands and a large rocky overhang cracked by frost and leering grotesquely over the water. Then we round a cape and find ourselves on the Kecarpoui Lake. It is eight kilometres long and ranges in width from one quarter of a kilometre to one kilometres. It is ringed by stands of red spruce interspersed with yellowing birches, and dwarfed by massive, mossy granite hills.

To our right is a deep bay with a golden red fine sand beach; a big rocky hill thrusts up above it. Entrel paddles parallel to the shore, keeping a constant distance of five canoe lengths from it. He later explained to us that he has sometimes caught sight of animals on the shore and has been able to shoot at them from the canoe. Now we understand why his canoe isn't red like ours, why it is an inconspicuous olive green.

A Passion for Wilderness

Entrel's slow tempo gives us lots of time to look about. We peer behind every rocky point and into every cove. The components are essentially the same, the spruces and the birches with various stunted growth and higher up the heather, moss and the stones. But the arrangement is constantly new and surprising.

An insane shriek of laughter tears us from our observations — a loon. Entrel imitates its cry, luring it nearer. But the big bird is cautious, remaining out of gunfire range. A pair of fish hawks is circling above us and begin to scold. Suddenly, a whirring sound — both birds plummet down towards us to stop only one or two metres above our heads. They want us out of their territory.

"They must have young ones," says Schnubbel. Their nest lies across from us in the top of a particularly high spruce.

After an hour and a half, we've reached the end of Lake Kecarpoui. The river is roaring towards us over an impassable barrier of rocks. Entrel fills his pipe, assessing the situation. "The portage is short, we can tow the canoes and Bridschitt can Walk." To the right, where a half-overgrown portage trail begins, is a trapper's cabin. A tiny structure, maybe four square meters big and one and a half meters high, scarcely larger than a roomy dog house. And like a dog you have to crawl in on all fours through a low, narrow door.

"Why don't you build your cabins bigger?"

"Why should we? A little cabin is easier to heat. We're almost always alone anyway, and we're only inside nights and on days when it really rains or snows."

We pull the boats over a stretch of gravel, paddle again, pull again, and after ten minutes we are on top.

"Dhingy's Lake!" announces Entrel. Two ducks fly off to the side of us. Entrel watches them, commenting reflectively, "For dinner I'd prefer trout."

With my very first cast, there is a powerful pulling and tugging on the line — it must be a hell of a trout! The fish tires quickly, although it tries one last desperate time to get away as it feels the presence of the bottom. I land it on the gravel shore, a two pound, beautifully marked speckled trout. Taking out the hook, I see that the trout has already conferred a similar fate on a smaller fish. I pull the spoon and fish out of its mouth and kill it by breaking its spine. Then I catch another trout, a half-pounder.

"That should be enough for dinner," says Schnubbel.

At that moment Entrel points to a series of long, swimming shadows whose sides occasionally glitter silver. "A whole school of grilse!"

Grilse are three- to four-year-old salmon weighing between three to six pounds which swim upstream to the brooks where they were born, to spawn. In contrast to the Pacific salmon, which only spawns once and then dies, the Atlantic version swims up the rivers and lakes as many as five times, in order to preserve its species.

I, who have never caught a salmon in my life, am now seeing a good dozen of these magnificent fish swimming about in front of me! I cast the spoon

A Passion for Wilderness

over the school, let it sink for a minute, and then reel in the line tight. No luck. Wait, yes — a curious little trout that has bitten right near the shore. I let it go again. Another try. The salmon couldn't care less about the red and white lure. Again and again I can see their silvery sides shimmering in the oblique light. I pass the rod on to Entrel. First of all he ties an artificial fly about ten centimeters in front of the lure so that for the fish it looks as if a younger brother is chasing the artificial insect. A double incentive to bite. But either these young salmon aren't in the biting mood or else they are vegetarians. At any rate they are paying just about as much attention to Entrel's efforts as they did to mine. Finally I pack the rod back into the canoe and throw a stone at the sliding shadows.

"Oh well," says Schnubbel. "There should be enough for breakfast, too!" For Entrel had caught a half dozen smaller trout in his salmonish endeavors — and kept them. Once he even had a double bite: a trout on both the lure and the fly on a single cast!

Dhingy's Lake is only three kilometres long. With a light wind on our backs, we cross it in half an hour. Far ahead of us, in a narrow forest gorge, we can see the cascades of the "Wild Rapids," as Entrel calls them. We land on a flat, narrow, pebbly beach behind a sandbank. In front of us, the lake is glittering in the setting sun and the wind has almost totally died down.

We look for a camping spot. We find one and I level it as best I can. Entrel sets up a few poles, and our white canvas house is erected within ten

A Passion for Wilderness

minutes. With the back of his axe, Entrel hammers four green pegs into the ground in the tent itself and places the stove on top of them. Schnubbel cuts small pine twigs and spreads them on the floor.

We eat outside. Entrel has made "Country Cake"; that's what he calls the bannock. I clean the trout, cutting up the bigger ones. Schnubbel fries the pieces in fat. It quickly grows dark. As the evening enfolds us in its dark arms, we remain sitting around the fire.

Entrel tells a little bit about himself: "Fourteen I was when my father took me along with him to the trapline for the first time. We came along this way. He stayed with me for eight days, showin' me the best places to lay traps, and then took off. When I got home four weeks later, I only had a few muskrat furs, nothing else." He filled his pipe. "Since then I've gone to the line every October and stay there until just before Christmas. Then I want to be home 'gain with my wife and my kids; besides, then there's the Christmas party."

He throws a couple of logs on the fire, sucking on his pipe. "Trappin' is a gamble. You never know if you'll only get your stake back, or if you'll win anythin'. The prices change from season to season. Right now fox is bringin' in a lot, lynx is good too, muskrat doesn't bring much. Sometimes I make two hundred dollars, sometimes five hundred, last year, it was even eight hundred."

"And you always go alone?" Schnubbel asks. "Don't you get bored?"

"Everybody goes alone. Anyway, I'm so busy most of the time that I don't notice the time. Well, there was once, four years ago, there was already a lot of snow on the ground. So I took off for the line with my snowshoes and mocassins and just got to Salmon Hole cabin when the weather changed and it rained and thawed for two weeks. The water was knee deep over the ice. I sat there for fourteen days and couldn't get out. But other than that I've never been bored."

"Why do you go trapping for two months here and not the whole winter, like they do in the West?" I wanted to know.

"There are two reasons. First, we don't got as many fur-bearin' animals here. There are only woods in the valleys. Higher up there's rock but not much else. So there are less fur-bearin' animals than in the West where you get lots of woods. And we can't trap too much 'cause we want to have somethin' left for the next year. And the second reason, well, in December the seal hunt starts. There, if the goin' price is good, we can make lots of money. Later, in February and March, we hunt for caribou. Eighty, ninety miles up the St. Augustin River. Then there is the second season of seals, the beaters, half-grown seals, and then before you know it, the geese and ducks."

"And what comes after that is cod fishing and then it's trapping season again," I interjected.

"Ya, and another year's gone by. It's a hard life but a good life. Better to earn two thousand dollars a year in St. Augustin than twenty thousand in the mines of Schefferville," Entrel said.

At daybreak the next morning we go on. "We can leave the tent behind. I got a couple of cabins on the line," says Entrel.

Ahead of us lies the "Wild Portage." We are able to paddle the first two hundred metres but then the river gets shallow. Entrel shows Schnubbel the trail and we line the canoes along the other bank. At first there are no particular problems, until I suddenly see a rocky chaos of huge boulders, some the size of rooms, towering up before us. The river is surging and raging over and between them. Entrel fills his pipe and assesses the situation. He jumps from boulder to boulder and finds a kind of natural staircase. "It's O.K. here, throw our stuff up to me!" he shouts.

I throw and push first his and then our gear up to him; he piles it all on the level surface of a boulder. Now for the canoes. I throw the rope up to him, he leans way back and pulls; meanwhile, I heave and push from underneath. And it works!

Entrel swears as his stove comes clattering down to me; fortunately, I'm able to catch it before it can get away and throw it back up to him. Schnubbel is watching us from the bank and calls something out to us. But through the din of the crashing water we can't understand a word. But it can't be important because she waves and then continues on her way.

I have a left boot full of water, empty it and put it on again. I have to pull hard to get it on over my wet socks. The canoes scrape and scratch loudly when we pull them over to the other side. We squeeze our way through the boulders, hoisting ourselves up and slithering down, climbing over fallen trees, slipping on patches of moss. Entrel still has his pipe clenched firmly between his

A Passion for Wilderness

scanty teeth.

The going then gets easier but we still have to exert ourselves, springing from one boulder to another, balancing on slippery stones, and sometimes jumping quickly into the canoe in order to cross a deeper pool of water. After two hours, we're on top; I'm all shaking. And — wouldn't you know it — at exactly this moment a big salmon jumps out of the water! I let him jump, and even Entrel isn't particularly interested. "We'll be able to catch thousands." Even Schnubbel is pretty worn out from her march through the woods.

"What's coming up now is nothing compared to the Wild Portage," Entrel promises us as we load up again.

The lake is only two hundred metres long while the rapids after it are shorter and we can easily tow the canoes. "Clifford's Lake," comments Entrel. After about a kilometre we turn left, carry the canoes over a small rocky path, and then slide them down the other side of a steep bank. We cross a pool ringed in by birches and ashes, carry the canoes around a small waterfall, and tow them further upstream. "Now I'll catch a salmon for sure," Entrel assures us.

"That's what you think!" says Schnubbel teasingly when Entrel, trapper and fisherman, gives up after twenty futile minutes. He hasn't even managed to catch a trout. As for me, I don't bother to try my hand, preferring to stretch out and relax on the white gravel shore.

We continue on our way and come across an extremely narrow pass just before Lake Mishwap and that almost makes me change my plans. Every time that I want to go up the rapids, holding the bow and stern lines in my hands and pulling the canoe, my trusty vessel gets stuck on a boulder that is sticking out of the water, turns sideways, and threatens to turn over completely. I have to give rope immediately and pull the canoe from the rock. And after I have completed this maneuver, the canoe gets stuck again. I give a number of repeat performances. After four or five times, I finally get the canoe past the boulder. Entrel, obviously enjoying the spectacle, is sitting on a stone grinning at my efforts and smoking on his pipe. His next words aren't exactly consoling: "Only two more rapids for today, and both are child's play!"

Lake Mishwap — Mishwap, the Montagnais word for "teepee," leads first to the north and then to the west. Six kilometres of free water without any rapids, enough time for my lungs to regain their strength.

The mountains around us have become higher, steeper and more jagged. We stop for lunch at an abandoned cabin. The door isn't bigger than the bottom of a Coca Cola crate; mushrooms are growing on the decaying floor.

"This is where my trapline begins!"

"Don't tell me that you sleep in this hole!" asks Schnubbel in horror, whispering in German to me. "At the most, a comfortable coffin ... "

"Sure; why not?" asks Entrel in genuine astonishment. "For a night the cabin is good enough!"

After lunch, he whips us into activity, "Only three more hours to Salmon Hole Cabin, don't got

A Passion for Wilderness

Middle Cabin Lake

much time!"

The rapids at the mouth of Mishwap Lake are short and easy to cross; nevertheless, I'm exhausted. And in the stream that connects Little and Big Beaver Lake, my canoe gets so badly stuck between two rocks that Entrel has to come and help me. The setting sun is blinding us, turning the rapids into a flowing silver ribbon where vital details like back waters, boulders, the swellings caused by sunken stones, and above all, the shallow stretches, are visible only at the last moment. The light hurts my eyes. I'm slipping a lot now and scrape rather than pull the canoe over the rocks. I slip, trip, and finally fall totally into the water, but I don't let go of the line! Entrel laughs until the tears roll down his cheeks.

"Only one more hour!" the trapper gasps out in the middle of his laughter. I grit my teeth and, wet as I am, continue. I do allow myself the luxury of emptying the water out of my boots. I barely manage to stagger up the last set of rapids before the Salmon Hole cabin. My wet clothes weigh like lead on me and I feel totally done in by the cold. All of me is clammily cold except for my feet, hot and steaming appendages in squeaky rubber boots.

"Well, that was a nice little day's trip," says Entrel, contentedly slurping on the sweet hot coffee.

"A nice little day's trip ... " I moan in German to Schnubbel. "It was a hell of a march that would have done in any normal, sensible person!" According to my estimate, we probably hadn't even covered twenty kilometres; with the help of a map, I later calculated it to be fifteen. It must have been that Wild Portage that took so much out of me!

I can hear Entrel busying himself at the stove; it is still dark. Sleepily I ask him if he needs any help. "Don't worry about it; I'll just try to catch a couple of birds." I turn over, and when a noise from the cabin awakens me again, it is already bright daylight. Entrel was sitting in front of the cabin skinning three muskrats. I awaken Schnubbel.

"Strange looking birds!" I say jokingly.

"Well, still a meal for the three of us..."

A Passion for Wilderness

"Afterwards I'll catch you a dozen fat fish!

"Okay, fish for dinner! And muskrat for supper!"

It is positive chaos around Salmon Hole cabin. Arriving in the dark the evening before, I hadn't noticed that — although, exhausted as I was, I probably couldn't have cared less. Rusty traps are hanging on desolate tree stumps and on nails on the sides of the cabin. Under an eave of the moss-covered plastic roof is a pile of "moulds," stretching frames in all shapes and sizes, small ones shaped like the flat tail of a beaver for the muskrat, somewhat larger ones for the mink and marten, and "ironing boards" for lynx, fox, otter, and wolf. Some are split in the middle so that Entrel, after stretching a fur over them, can enlarge them by shoving a wedge in the split. Beside the moulds are a pile of bones, half a skeleton of a beaver, mink and otters, some still with meat on them. The whole area stinks to high heaven! The final aesthetic touch is given by the scattered rusty tin cans, the old used tea bags, a torn up net, and a homemade fishing rod, consisting of a peeled stick, a rope, and a bent rusty nail for a hook.

"Not exactly a spic and span household," comments Schnubbel.

After breakfast, I pack up the fishing rod. Schnubbel wants to stay to straighten things up since we were intending to stay for a few days in Salmon Hole. Entrel and I paddle around Salmon Hole, a little lake squeezed in among steep rocky mountains. Entrel has the shotgun and is sitting in the front of the canoe. I am doing the steering.

A Passion for Wilderness

In front of us, we can hear a small waterfall rushing and surging among the ashes, birches, and willows. We are at the source of the Kecarpoui. Behind it is Middle Cabin Lake, big (ten kilometres long) and branching out in many directions, it collects water for the Kecarpoui and spills it over a small fall in the direction of the sea.

We get out at the foot of the falls. Within a few minutes, I have caught six trout, sufficient for dinner. But I haven't caught sight of even the trace of a salmon.

"Maybe they are up in the lake," says Entrel. Whereupon we dutifully climb up a fifty metre trail leading through a stand of crippled, scrubby spruce. Then we can see the enormous surface of Middle Cabin Lake shimmering through the overgrowth, dull as an old tarnished mirror. The sun has just disappeared behind the clouds.

I try my luck, Entrel his. The outcome is two inquisitive and greedy trout that we throw back in again. We now begin to fish systematically from the shore towards a bay, wading as far into the water from the spit of land, as our boots will let us. I cast the lure as far as I can and reel it in. A hard tug, and whoosh! A large fish rises from the water, flipping backwards on its tail. "A Oouananiche!" shouts Entrel. "A fresh water landlocked salmon!" I know he must be excited because he almost lets go of his pipe.

The fish rushes to the right and then to the left — I release the brake, give line, hold contact, and whoosh! there it is again! After I play the fish it lets itself be brought in a bit. It springs high

A Passion for Wilderness

again, I bring it in closer, but eventually have to let it go a second time when it senses the presence of the shore and panics, trying to escape into deeper waters.

But a fish, once it has bitten and is attached to the hook, hardly has a chance of getting away if the right line and rod are being used. It's not exactly what you would call a fair fight between the fish and the fisherman. For the fish, it is a question of life and death; for the fisherman it is a question of fun and food, admittedly very exciting fun and extremely good food. I reel the salmon in closer. It springs up once more, but it is too late. I have it behind the gills and throw it onto the land. I reckon it to be between four and five pounds.

The fresh water salmon is like its Atlantic cousin to the last detail, or rather to the last scale, except for the fact that its back is dark, almost black, and its belly a yellowish color that sometimes shimmers violet. As its name indicates, it never ventures into salt waters. Since we aren't only fishing for our own pleasure, it is important for us that its meat has more calories than that of the trout.

Along with the trout and muskrat, we actually have enough by now. But in October, it is already cold and so possible to store the catch up to eight days in cool, damp moss, or in the sand of a river. This fact justifies for us the pleasure in continuing the hunt, a pleasure which in such situations comes out even in us. And we consider ourselves to be civilized. Entrel can hardly wait to get the rod in his hands. I watch him as he lands a somewhat larger, and then a somewhat smaller, salmon. And in the meantime the ducks that we had intended for our supper are flying serenely above us.

"Save me the guts as bait," says Entrel as I begin to cut the salmon up into fillets. "Actually, it's still a bit too early to do any trapping, but we'll give it a try. Maybe Bridschitt wants to bring a souvenir home with her!"

For dinner we have fried salmon fillets. Entrel then fiddles around on his traps while Schnubbel and I take pictures. At dusk we have our supper: Schnubbel made muskrat with dumplings and two little trout for dessert that we had earlier hung in the stovepipe to smoke. When, in far off civilized countries, we are asked if we ate anything other than fish in Canada, and I reply, "Muskrat," I always hear the shocked exclamation: "Oh God! You ate muskrats?" But then again, why not? Except for certain similarities in appearance, the muskrat has as little in common with a rat as a rabbit has. It is an exclusive vegetarian, living in the clean clear waters of Labrador. It certainly isn't the fault of the muskrat that Germany's rivers have become sewers.

And we like the taste of muskrat! Now, folding our hands contentedly over our stomachs, we relax after supper and after a while retire to our bush villa, which is now clean and smelling conspicuously of Christmas because of the newly laid spruce twigs that Schnubbel has scattered on the floor.

After a breakfast of fried trout, bannock and

coffee, we gather up the traps and prepare to leave. To our surprise, we see Entrel put his stove into the canoe. Then we slide the canoes into the water, paddle across Salmon Hole Lake and carry the canoes across the short portage and around the waterfall. There we start to paddle again on Middle Cabin Lake.

It is a windless morning, clear and sunny. As usual, Entrel is paddling along the shore. We follow him to a narrow stream that leads to a small round lake. He paddles directly across the pond to a corner green with grass and reeds, and ties his canoe to some of the stronger reeds. Taking the stove, he goes over to an unprepossessing pile of grass.

"A muskrat's den!" he explained. He cuts off a strong twig from a willow and then begins to plug up the entrances, which are partially above and partially below the water. That is, with one exception. There he presses the stove up against this entrance with his knee so that the inhabitants of the den can't escape out the side, and draws back the little door of the stove. The stove pipe has already been stopped up with a rag. Now we can hear harried movement in the pile of grass, followed by a rattling in the tin stove. Aha! One of them is already in there! Entrel closes the door again, shaking the stove hard in order to stun the muskrat. When the clattering had stopped, he reaches in with his bare hand, pulls out the animal, and hits it over the neck with his stick. Then he throws it into the canoe.

Two more muskrats fall victim to the same fate. Then we continue on our way. Entrel moors the canoe

Entrel Belvin skins a muskrat

next to a large, round stone. There is only scattered earth on top of it and the moss is scanty. Underneath, where the rock falls flat into the water, Entrel constructs a tube with sticks, twigs, and a couple of stones. He lays the head of a salmon inside and places a trap in front of it. He pulls the chain of the trap out sideways, tying it with a piece of wire to a nearby tree. He smears secretion of the beaver which he had carefully collected last fall in a pill bottle.

"To cover the human scent," I explain to Schnub-

A Passion for Wilderness

bel. Entrel closes up the end of the pipe that was facing the water. He builds two or three similar, although smaller, traps for mink at a small stream. Fish is the bait here, too. He blazes the trees where he had tied the traps with his axe so clearly that the markings are visible from the lake.

We paddle further into a small channel and come across a beaver dam. Because of the dam, the water has risen a good half metre and has flooded the lower lying vegetation.

We can see freshly gnawed twigs. That means that the dam has been relatively recently built or is being repaired. We pull the canoes over the dam, paddling further along. The stream there twists through a grassy hollow dotted with autumn yellow larches and evergreens. All the trees near the shore are standing in water and will soon die. In our canoes we slide through the overflooded sparse woods.

To the left of us we see a huge construction, almost of the height of a man and smeared with clay, held upright by the growth along the shore. The beaver lodge! Entrel climbs on top of it, pointing to the spot where a bunch of twigs are half in and half out of the water, and calling, "Watch out!" He begins to jump around on the lodge. We can count four fat beavers trying to escape under the water; Entrel claims that there are five of them — one of which he wants to catch. Fish won't lure the beaver — like the muskrat, it is a pure vegetarian.

Entrel lays the trap in front of the entrance in water about as deep as the breadth of a hand. It is a number four, the biggest one that he has. This time he doesn't tie it to a stick or a tree but to a solid stone. The beaver, when it falls into a trap, will jump back in shock and try to escape into deeper water. But the stone that it is pulling after it will drag it under and the beaver will drown, without getting a chance to free itself by biting off the trapped foot.

Entrel sets a lynx trap on a strong branch of a birch about the height of a man from the ground and a good metre from the trunk. He puts the head of a fish and entrails from a muskrat behind the trap, which was also a number four. "The lynx'll come, smell the goodies, and step into the trap. He'll jump away, but the trap'll hold him tight, and he'll hang there wrigglin' 'til I finish him off. That way he can't bite off his leg and get away on three paws," Entrel explains.

That day Entrel sets about twenty traps — for marten, weasel, otter, mink, and lynx. On our way home, he shoots down the two ducks that he had been promising us for so long. "Now I just gotta set a fox trap," he said. He cuts off a wing from one of the ducks, places it in a haunt, puts one trap directly in front of it and one behind it, and smears the whole thing with beaver pride. Then we go back to Salmon Hole Cabin.

We have a couple of beautiful fall days at Salmon Hole. It goes below freezing at night, but it is warm in the cabin. And during the day, the sun shines from a picture book sky and there is scarcely a breath of wind to rustle the leaves.

We climb up through the woods, dwarfed by towering trees, past the zone of matted, unruly, tough stunted pine and are on top of the plateau, on the free tundra, on a scrubby carpet that stretches as far as the eye can see, a carpet of orange, yellow, grey, green, and dark rust red. The rocky hills surge together like frozen waves, and the lakes glitter hard and brilliant in the bright sun.

It is very calm, an absolute, almost tangible calmness. Occasionally the frozen moss crunches under our feet, the thin ice crust on the puddles crackles. We sit on the highest point leaning back to back, and feeling very content, "Were it not for the fact," Schnubbel said slowly, "that we know that somewhere a poor fox or marten or otter is hanging in a trap, desperate and trying in vain to free itself. These animals have eaten up other, equally poor, things in their lifetimes, that's true, such as mice, muskrats, ducks, moles, squirrels, trout, and salmon. But that is their role in nature. Only man is perverted. Maybe mankind is an accident for nature, a catastrophe that will eventually destroy everything."

Neither can she watch how Entrel grabs the throat of the mink with one hand and squeezes with the other until its heart stops beating, how he delivers a fatal blow with the back of his axe to the otter, marten, and fox who have been tugging at their chains in futile panic, how he finishes off the lynx dangling helplessly from a branch with one quick hard rap with the handle of his axe.

And sometimes an owl will have reached the traps before Entrel, and will have killed and dined upon the trapped animal.

I reply to Schnubbel that you can't reproach

A Passion for Wilderness

Entrel with anything. His father had trapped animals as had his grandfather. For them the trapline is a kind of harvest reaped only with hard work, difficulties, and dangers. The people in this little world which is called St. Augustin don't waste any time thinking about the fate of animals. Entrel is the last link in the chain. The people who are truly responsible for the fate of the animals are those who think that they can cover over the emptiness in their lives with ocelot and mink.

We decide to separate from Entrel and go our own ways. He will later trek back to St. Augustin by the direct route over the small frozen ponds and the frost-crusted tundra. We want to return by a southern route that will take us across Mistaken Pond, a large body of water south of Middle Cabin Lake and still open.

We paddle across Middle Cabin Lake, which runs in a north-south direction for about ten kilometres, with watery arms about five kilometres long stretching out on either side, to the east and the west. Rocks project out of the water like stony islands, the beaches are sandy, generous, and white, the coves are hidden and mysterious, the trout numerous. The origin of the Kecarpoui is a miniature paradise.

We catch only a few fish for breakfast because Entrel had sent packages of meat along with us. I don't dare to point out Schnubbel's inconsistency; she loved the taste of beaver.

Entrel might not be good at spelling his own name, but he sure is good at reading maps. He had pointed to a spot at the west end of the lake where there is a small cabin, albeit without a stove.

The construction is ancient. At night we can see the stars through the roof. The cabin is scarcely one and a half square metres and four feet at its highest point. We straighten out this doghouse, placing layers of spruce twigs on the floor. The scent of spruce soon covers the rotten smell of the mouldering wood. And because it doesn't rain, we are able to have a most comfortable night.

Somewhere in the distance the wolves are howling, their cries carried far in the cold clear night air. "The night song of the coureur de bois," I whisper to Schnubbel in a moment of unpremeditated musing. But she has turned over on her side and is sleeping soundly, obviously preferring her sleep to my poetry. For a moment, as I see the northern lights glimmering in the sky, I think about waking her up. But I don't, saying to myself that we will be seeing them every clear night.

Entrel didn't know anything about a trail between Middle Cabin Lake and Mistaken Pond. The map shows a route about two miles long as the crow flies and without any great differences in altitude. The most important and appearing thing about the route is that four small lakes are to be found along it, so that we will only have to portage half the distance.

"We'll make it there, all right!" I say to Schnubbel. We have had a leisurely breakfast. After our daily trout, Schnubbel extracts raisins and dates from a secret cache and bakes a delicious bannock cake that we eat with hungry appreciation. So by the time we get to the south end of Middle Cabin Lake, it is already noon.

A Passion for Wilderness

And no sign of a trail! At any rate, there is a brook cascading down the steepish sides of the mountains which we can follow — but the woods are too overgrown here to be able to carry a canoe through them. We look around in another bay. No trail, not even one of those old and overgrown Indian and trapper paths that you could go along carrying the canoe without too many difficulties.

Before starting anything, we think it better to have a hearty snack of fried meat. After being fortified both physically and psychologically, I begin to blaze a trail. A good hour later, we have reached the first of the four "puddles." Schnubbel has already made one trip up, carrying our gear.

She is now following me, canoe on my shoulders, with the paddles and fishing rod which I had bundled together. Now we pack everything back into the canoe and paddle the three hundred metres to the other end.

"Should we cross over the hills to the other pond or should we go along the hollow by the stream?" A question that we often ask ourselves in this country. Usually it seems as if it would be easier to pick our way through the matted and stunted vegetation of the hills. But when you do try to wade through the thigh-high confusion of heather and wild rhododendrons tightly interwoven with stunted spruces that conceal the stones and holes, you make very slow progress. And an anger mounts in you against this treacherous thicket, where every step forward seems to be countered by two steps backwards. And after you've experienced getting stuck in the undergrowth with a canoe on your shoulders and one foot in a seemingly bottomless hole, and after falling flat on your face and having the canoe crash down on your shoulders, neck and skull; after all that, you'd prefer to struggle through the densest forest, even if it meant spending a couple more hours clearing out a trail. So then I blaze out the second trail while Schnubbel carries our gear, knapsack, and sleeping bags.

The next pond is long and narrow and lies above the edge of the woods. From the right of its southern point it is only a hundred metres to the third pond, and from that pond, it is twenty metres of relatively open land to the fourth one. We cover this stretch quickly. Now we have about three hundred metres of fairly difficult going along uneven and overgrown land. Half the time I carry the canoe, and half the time I simply drag it behind me.

Then suddenly we catch sight of Mistaken Pond below us, comfortably nestled between dense forest and steep rocky cliffs, where large old birches are still clinging stubbornly to the crumbs of earth. It appears to us that the route ahead of us would be easier to follow than the low land along the shore. The slope here is not neckbreakingly steep, and it is only a few metres to the water.

"We'll simply push forward," I say to Schnubbel. "It's only about five hundred metres to the lake. And downhill all the way!" Things do go okay, but only at the beginning. We manage to get past a four or five metre cliff, but then we get stuck by accident in an old windfall where fallen logs lie in a pick-up-sticks confusion and where tall spindly balsam firs stand crowded close together.

In my valiant attempts to "push forward," I force the canoe so far that it is stuck. I can't budge it forwards or backwards. The firs form a sickly, seemingly impenetrable wall. I try to clear a path but it is incredibly hard work. The young firs are standing so close that I can scarcely swing the axe to get the necessary strength behind my blows. More often than not, the trees spring back insolently towards me. My efforts enter into a race with the oncoming night.

When we finally reach the shore of the lake, it is dark. The sky has clouded over and we can't see anything.

We don't even bother to make a fire, but simply feel our way to a large pine and proceed to make ourselves as comfortable as possible around its trunk.

The Chinese have invented a simple method to force prisoners to speak or to drive them crazy; drops of water splashing at constant and regular intervals on the head of the prisoner (at least that's the way I've read it in novels). And that's what I think about as I feel drops falling on my forehead. More unconsciously than consciously I perceive that it is raining. "Maybe," I think, half asleep, "it will stop when it gets light." I turn away from the dripping and pull the hood of my waterproofed sleeping bag over my head. But it doesn't stop raining.

We break camp and as we clamber soaking wet into the canoe, Schnubbel asks me indignantly when and if we would ever travel to the south, where the sun shone, where it was warm, where you drank iced coffee and ate strawberry shortcake, where you relaxed on a steamer rather than paddling in a canoe, where you could wear a bikini instead of rubber boots and jeans?

Schnubbel rarely talks like that, but when she does, it is somehow at the most unfitting moments. I answer curtly that we had two "steamers" — one with two times one quarter biceps and one with a Four Atlantic, an unassuming and reliable engine. She must have expected this reaction, at any rate, her mood doesn't improve. Especially when the rain turns into snow and the intermittent easterly winds hurl snowflakes the size of silver dollars into our faces.

Our universe is transformed into a whirling, swirling chaos. In no time at all, high steep waves are buckling the lake and sending the first cold liquid greetings over Schnubbel. I can hear a des-pairing and angry "Damn!" whistle past my ear.

"Right on!" I yell back in agreement.

At least we would have no particular difficulty orienting ourselves, I thought, optimist to the end. We simply had to cut the waves at right angles and that would bring us east, to the leeside of the lake, into calmer water. My theory was fine, as far as theories go. In practice, the storm, which the wind and the rain had now become, prevents us from making any real headway, and we are forced to ride the high waves rather than cutting them in order to avoid capsizing. Just to be safe, I alter the course to the southeast. The wind is driving us closer to the flatter, southern shore where there

Elmar moves forward

are better chances to land in an emergency. By now the snow has turned back into rain.

After two hours of hard work, we are on the other shore. It is hopeless to tow the canoe along the brook which is rushing downstream hemmed in by boulders and zigzagged by logs. Fortunately, we do find a trail. I shoulder the canoe and Schnubbel picks up the gear. On empty stomachs we tramp through the dripping woods.

After twenty minutes, drenched with sweat under our oilskins, we are at Little Mistaken Pond, a small lake created by a beaver dam where the storm cannot bother us very much.

Where the lake discharges the brook widens and there is more water. We can either paddle or tow the canoe, although on the last stretch we have to carry everything through the sparse woods.

Finally we reach the north shore of Kecarpoui Lake; between us and the trail which leads down to our cabin is one and a half kilometres of boiling, rough water. We can see white breakers on the other shore leaping high against the steep rocky cape. It is still raining.

"We have to keep moving, otherwise, we'll really start to freeze."

"Do you think it's safe to travel in this storm?"

"It should be, if we allow drifting to the southwest, cross the lake on the leeside of the two islands, and then work up through the bays."

Schnubbel's only comment is a dry, "Let's get it over with, then."

With the bow of the canoe pointing west, we head southwest, cross over to the south shore behind the islands, and then have to fight hard against the storm to make up the kilometres that we had drifted off course to get to the mouth of the Kecarpoui. We do better than I expected.

An hour later, we are sitting in warm woolen underwear at the cozy, sputtering stove, eaves-dropping on the storm which is shooting up waves onto the steep bank under our window. The mugs of hot, sweet coffee warm first our hands and then our chilled spirits. Our Perfect Stove dries the steaming pants, ski jackets, and sweaters, and the fragrance of a Mulligan stew simmering away in one of Entrel's iron pots fills the room.

Two days later a bear visits us for the first time. Schnubbel had baked a cake, but the result was a flop. I don't normally object to flopped cakes, seeing as I'm no sweet-tooth anyway, but this one was flat as a flounder on one side and as plump as a carp on the other. It was also rather burnt, since I hadn't fed our frankensteinian stove right and it had reacted by blazing up into flames. Then again, we could have cut away the burnt parts.

No, what bothers us, and here I must go to Schnubbel's defense, is the fact that the cake tastes of resinous smoke. The tin insulation of the oven is defective. I persuade Schnubbel to donate the cake to the numerous squirrels scampering about the cabin. So with a noticeable lack of ceremony, we dump Schnubbel's creation on top of a stump in the woods.

The next morning it had disappeared and in its stead, left by the grateful creature, was a visiting card of dung — about the size of five squirrels put together. A bear, then! The next morning at dawn there is a rattling noise by our garbage cans at the front of the cabin. I charge out faster than lightning only to see a dark rear end disappearing into the bush. After that we have two nights of peace. I am convinced that my fearless appearance had impressed old Smoky.

A few days later we go cod fishing one last time and spend the night in a fisherman's cabin on a small rocky island. We have totally forgotten about the bear. When we return, Schnubbel goes up to the cabin with a basket full of fish and I moor the Little Onion in our bay. Suddenly I hear a scream of horror! I grab the shotgun, leap onto the shore, slide back into the water, stride forward in water-filled boots and squeak and slop my way to the cabin.

I find Schnubbel dissolved in tears and our cabin dissolved into rampant disorder. It looks as if it had been hit by a bomb. About a quarter of the roof is ripped and sticking through the gaping hole of a broken window is a large tattered piece of rubber from what had been a most presentable mattress which our visitor had apparently wanted to take home for its winter den. The inside of the cabin looks as if it had been struck by two bombs; the stove pipe has been torn down, the table and bench has been turned and clawed topsy turvy, and strewn all about are clumps of moss from the roof, pieces of plastic, dented tin cans and pots, a completely chaotic scene made all the more grotesque by the thin layer of flour that covered everything.

Only our frankensteinian stove, a symbol of

perseverance and survival, has emerged unscathed. It has managed to outwit the monster, having practiced enough on me.

"Would you take a look at that!" sobs Schnubbel. "It even broke the mirror! Oh, that horrible thing!"

"If he comes back tonight, he'll pay for it!" I assure her in a tone of what I hope to be proper grimness and determination. And then we proceed to clean up the place. We fixed up most everything in about two hours. I nailed the beams of the roof back together, covered the gaping hole with a piece of plastic, and spread moss over the whole area. We nailed the legs of the table and bench back on, knocked out the dents in the pots and the stove pipe, closed up the window with a remnant of cloth, and shovelled assorted rubbish out of the door. By the way things looked, it must have been two bears, led by a female bear, maybe? I get everything ready for the night; shotgun, flashlight, and slugs.

We both fall into a deep and dreamless sleep that is not disturbed by any bears. "Cowards!" I say with disdain.

A couple of nights later we are awakened by the rattling of the garbage cans.

"The bears!" I grab the flashlight, rip the door open, switch the flashlight on. And there she stands, the female bear, a scarce three metres away and looking tranquilly into the light. Her eyes are like big, green reflectors.

"The shotgun, Schnubbel, quick! The b-b-bear!" I hiss, stuttering with excitement or cold. I don't have anything on.

A Passion for Wilderness

"The bear! Oh God! Where?"

"The shotgun! Quick!" The bear had still not moved; it is as if she has been transformed into a statue by the light.

"I can't find the shells, darn it!" I shine the light into the back of the cabin. Schnubbel is rummaging a shell out of the munitions pouch and sliding it into the barrel of the gun.

I shine the light outside again — the bear has disappeared. And so we go back to bed again.

Not two hours later we hear a rattling again. This time directly under our window where the leftovers of our dinner are — a pot of empty clams. I grope in the dark for the shotgun, carefully open the door, and switch the flashlight on. There they are again, the big green reflectors, although this time about twenty metres away. A good distance for a shotgun with slugs.

Schnubbel stands trembling beside me, holding the flashlight. I try to breath evenly, aim the barrel in the direction of the green reflectors, and pull the trigger. The reflectors have disappeared, swallowed into the darkness. But don't I see something large, solid and unmoving lying on the shore? I reload the gun, taking two more shells and the flashlight with me, and go to check things out to discover a harmless, albeit large, rock.

From the door of the cabin, I can hear Schnubbel calling, "Come back, please!"

I shine the flashlight around me but can't see anything. At this moment such a shrill scream penetrates the darkness that my heart almost stops pounding. I whirl around to see a dark something turn clumsily about and in greatest panic head back into the woods past the cabin. The beast had cut off my retreat! Fortunately Schnubbel's scream, which I would normally have dismissed as hysterical, succeeded in driving the bear off. And between us, I must add that it was sheer idiocy on my part to start pursuing a possibly wounded bear at night! Trembling and exhausted after our adventure, we crawl back into our beds.

The next morning we find traces of our nocturnal visitor — but neither blood nor fur. Merely her customary, high-piled dungy greeting.

Vaughn   Short

A   CANOEIST'S   PRAYER

Dear Lord, here on this river bank
Before we launch today,
Please, listen for a moment
To what a canoeist has to say.

Now I don't claim to be a saint,
And my soul's not lily white.
Sometimes I yield to temptation.
Sometimes I drink too much at night.

A Passion for Wilderness

Down here I'm not an angel,
Don't even want to talk about the town
With all its woes and pitfalls
And the things that get you down.

So I'm really in no position
To ask for much from You,
But if You could see the way,
Please, try and hear me through.

Life down here's a pleasure
And there's beauty everywhere.
So I'm really not complaining
In my humble little prayer.

The thing I'm trying to get across,
In my stumblin', bumblin' way,
Is a canoeman, he's not really bad,
No matter what they say.

But a canoeist's life's not easy,
Although I'm not trying to alibi.
There's no turning back up the river,
It's no use to even try.

Whatever lies before you —
You've got to see it through.
You can't stop halfway
And back off and start anew.

It's just things aren't as easy
As they look to those outside.

A Passion for Wilderness

It's more than jumping in a boat
And going for a ride.

Now, I'm not too worried
About what's down the way,
'Cause I've done this many times before
When I didn't even pray.

Oh! I don't take it lightly!
I've always got to know,
There's an old lion a roarin'
In the river down below.

But we'll make it through the rapids —
There'll be no problem there.
That's not the reason
For me to say this prayer.

The reason I'm a talkin',
And it's not easy for me to say,
Just, please, don't view us canoeists
In the ordinary way.

I love this world You made us,
And I love the rivers too.
I like the things that are simple,
And I like the work I do.

But could You sort of look the other way
And a few small things forgive?
For it's a little different,
This kind of life I live.

A Passion for Wilderness

I have no neighbors watching
To see what I do each day,
So it's just a little easier
To stray off the narrow way.

Now I have no church to go to.
They just aren't built down here.
But I see Your walls and canyons,
And I feel You very near.

Now, I'm standing here a rattlin',
I've talked for quite a spell.
I still can't seem to get across
What I'm trying to tell.

It's, "Just please try to overlook
Some of the things I do.
I may not be like Your other children,
But I feel very close to You."

Amen.

Part

IOWA   WILDERNESS   SOLO

By

Valerie   Fons   Kruger

VALERIE FONS KRUGER

Valerie Fons Kruger is a long distance canoe
touring and racing enthusiast who has paddled and
portaged over twelve thousand miles in North
America. Her Baja expedition, 2,411 miles of ocean
paddling in a solo canoe, is detailed in her first
book, **Keep It Moving,** published by The Mountaineers Books in 1986. Valerie is listed in

A Passion for Wilderness

Guinness Superlatives for the world record of paddling the 2,348-mile length of the Mississippi River in 23 days and holds the women's title at the World Championship 240-Mile Au Sable Marathon in Michigan. She is one of the few women members of the prestigious Explorers Club, and finds sharing her experiences with others the "blessings of adventure."

Presently Valerie is on a 21,000 mile, two-continent canoe expedition with her husband, Verlen Kruger. In early June, 1986, Valerie and Verlen began paddling from the Arctic to Cape Horn. Traveling the waterways of North and South America and island hopping the Caribbean waters in between, the Kruger team will be observing and documenting the land, peoples and water quality of the western hemisphere, exploring as citizen ambassadors for the State of Michigan.

Valerie Fons Kruger

IOWA WILDERNESS SOLO

Where does the river go? The answer that the map gave was too simple. Ten and one-half inches of blue line squiggles between points marked Des Moines and Keokuk didn't tell me enough.

I studied the Iowa transportation map more closely. Tracing with my finger I followed the Des Moines River as it wandered toward the southeast corner of the state. Two inches from Des Moines the river line widened into a dime-size blue area

A Passion for Wilderness

labeled Red Rock Reservoir, then narrowed again as it cut across country, bisecting county lines and trailing beside highways. Five inches further, a yellow square denoting the town of Ottumwa swallowed the river line. At the opposite edge of the city limits the river line reappeared and meandered southeast five more inches where it knotted into a corkscrew before merging into a long stroke spread to a quarter inch of blue named Mississippi.

The map could not tell the whole story. Directions were clear but the details were clearly missing. I looked two inches southwest of Des Moines, to a small black circled mark named Winterset where I lived. The map did not explain that my farm house was in the middle of a cornfield with no other houses visible all around. My neighborhood was best understood by being there — standing on the wrap-around porch, listening to the birds chatting in the big oak tree that sheltered the house.

The map could only tell me so much. But the possibilities it hinted at were fascinating. Another blue line named Middle River squiggled south of Winterset and ran northeast to connect with the Des Moines river line. The map told me that the Middle River was less than half a mile from my house. I set aside the map, put on my coat and walked out the front door into a crisp September day to find out more.

I was searching for an experience that involved all of my senses. I had a passion for wilderness and I knew that even in the middle of Iowa farm country, wilderness was within my reach. The lure

A Passion for Wilderness

of far off wilderness had always tempted me. But this time the Northwest Territories could wait. Hudson Bay would be there when I was ready. I began to form a plan to explore the wilderness of my own backyard. On this journey I would taste, see, smell, touch and hear the distance between Des Moines and Keokuk while paddling my own canoe.

The old farm collie followed me on my first scouting attempt. We walked down the gravel lane and out to the dirt highway road, then turned down the hill past the cemetery toward the clapboard faded green Williams' place. The dog was deaf but she could feel the vibrations of the pickup trucks that occasionally rumbled down the hard pressed tracks. One truck did go by. Colleen herded me to the far side of the road and I held my breath as the dust blew up in a cloud.

At the bottom of the hill we turned right and kept walking. Within another hundred yards I could hear the river. Colleen quickened her steps, trotting almost at a run. She couldn't hear the river. She could smell it.

The old dog was the first to jump through the barbed wire fence. Her matted coat caught on a point of sharp metal leaving a tuft of hair as she scampered down to the water's edge. I was more careful but just as excited, pushing the brush away and parting the wires to bend my body through. Then we stood on the bank watching the Middle River move. The river was alive, flowing strong and sure underneath the cement bridge, pushing against the mud banks, riffling over the rocks in center stream, gurgling as it shot past. The river seemed to be moving as fast as the pick-up on the road but the river didn't kick up any dust. The water was smooth, flowing between the banks as if it were greased.

I found a big log that made a perfect seat. Colleen ran into the brush chasing rabbits and I leaned back to let the sun shine on my face. Where does the river go? I had to find out.

•   •   •

"I'm going on a canoe trip," I announced as I walked into my brother John's house that evening. His family was sitting down to dinner.

"Where you off to this time?" my brother asked, knowing full well that I had a restless streak.

"Are you going to paddle on the ocean again?" one of his three children asked excitedly.

Before I had a chance to answer, the oldest child began proclaiming exotic destinations.

"Africa!" she blurted out, sure that I was bound for adventure.

"Well," I said with a gleam of excitement, "it's the river, the one down at the bend in the road. I've got to go with it."

The family didn't seem too impressed. To them the river close to home was familiar even though they had never followed it past the next bend where it slid out of sight. They went about taking their places at the table. John motioned for me to join them.

"Are you having dinner before you go?" asked his

wife Marianne as she delivered a bowl of mashed potatoes from the kitchen.

"I guess there's time for that," I said gratefully.

Marianne pulled her chair to the table and handed me the buttered beans. I got quiet for a while, chewing the good food and listening with only half a mind to the family talk. The river was moving even this moment as we all sat together at the oak kitchen table.

When the family conversation died down I pushed aside my plate. Between the serving dishes of spuds, vegetables and pork chops I unfolded the map that had been stuck in my pocket. I shared the route with John's family and the blue lines came alive. My shoes were still wet from tromping along the river bank, and offered proof that the blue lines meant life — a flowing, moving, coursing thoroughfare that I could travel with my canoe.

"Who are you going with?" my brother asked. He was ever practical.

I looked around the table to see if anyone would volunteer. John couldn't leave his job. Marianne was busy with the children. Three little girls age three through nine sat staring back with questioning eyes.

"I'm going alone," I said. There was a moment of silence.

"Well, seeing that it's you, I won't be worried," Marianne decided. "You've got plenty of canoe experience," she said approvingly.

"Not much of my experience is solo," I admitted. "That is one of the reasons why I'm looking forward to going alone. I'm interested in seeing how serious I am about paddling when it's just me in the outdoors."

"Didn't you take a solo trip before?" Marianne prompted.

"My first solo trip wasn't too successful," I explained.

"What happened?" John questioned.

Before I could answer, the youngest child at the table dumped her glass of milk.

"Oh no!" Marianne cried.

I grabbed the map to save it from the flood. Both Marianne and John stood up and attended to the mess. While they were busy mopping up milk from the table cloth and floor I thought back on the panicked scene of my first solo trip. I hadn't planned very well and set off to paddle on Lake Superior from Grand Marais to Duluth in late October. Relying on myself was a challenge that soon overwhelmed me. The water conditions were marginal. Lake Superior was reacting to the change in seasons and acting temperamental. The waves seemed to grow by the minute, aggravated by a steady onshore wind. There was no rhythm to the waves; unlike the even swells of the ocean, Lake Superior water was erratic.

The confusion at the table was soon under control. John sat back down at his place and Marianne, thankful that order was restored, was anxious to return to the conversation.

"What happened?" she asked again.

"When the wind blew up and the lake started to boil it was difficult for me to decide if I should get off the water or if I could continue paddling. Without a partner to talk to, my judgments got a little hazy. I couldn't decide if it was fear or plain good sense telling me to pull ashore. I egged myself on until I was torn between reckless bravado and cowardice. I don't know which won out but I landed in the surf, found a pay phone and dialed Verlen Kruger, a man with sixty thousand miles of paddling experience, to describe the weather conditions and ask his advice."

Everyone at the table laughed at the thought of me standing at a phone booth with paddle in hand requesting long distance instructions.

"Well," Marianne wanted to know, "what did he say?"

"He said that if I had to ask, it was too rough for me." I looked down at the damp table cloth, remembering my dejection. "I set up my tent and camped on the beach at Tofti for three days, waiting for the rollers to stop beating the shore. When they didn't, I packed up and hitched a ride back to my car at Grand Marais." I unfolded the map again and pointed at the Iowa route. "On this trip the route is manageable. I don't want any support system to fall back on except my own experience and motivation. This trip is no pleasure cruise or escape. I'm looking forward to direct confrontation with nature and myself. It will be an adventure but not one beyond my skills."

"You don't have to prove anything," my brother said gently.

"I know," I replied. "I'm going to enjoy every minute of a wilderness experience, even if I do get a little scared."

"Don't take time now to be afraid," John said sensibly. "Wait til you're out there in the dark." He pointed out the window into the blackness, teasing as only a big brother knows how.

His oldest daughter stopped chewing and let her mouth gape open as she looked out the window imagining what might be lurking beyond the security of home.

"I'll bet you make it," Marianne said with enthusiasm. "Have another helping of potatoes. Explorers need plenty of food."

The subject of my canoe trip was pushed aside in the midst of getting the dishes washed and put away and the kids washed and put to bed. But my plan had firmly taken root. That night I lay in bed dreaming with my eyes wide open, staring at the big oak tree outside my bedroom window and seeing the river in my mind. The wind rattled the windows of the old farm house, pressing its force against the glass and shaking the panes in the wooden frames. Just before falling asleep I thought I could hear the river, rushing to join the Mississippi, pressing against the bank as it glided along.

●   ●   ●

An Iowa farm was the last place I thought I would ever be, but it was the perfect place to isolate myself and finish writing a book about my adventures of paddling around the Baja Peninsula on the Pacific Ocean and Sea of Cortez. I was living in

A Passion for Wilderness

Iowa because my brother offered me the encouragement of family and inexpensive rent. An extra bonus was Iowa's location. The state is sandwiched between the two biggest rivers in North America. The Mississippi River borders the east side of the state, and the Missouri flows along the west.

The history of the area is rich with tales of exploration. Joliet and Marquette were the first white men known to have seen the mouth of the Des Moines River. Their journals of 1673 mentioned their visit to the "Indian village on the bank of a river entering the Mississippi from the west." The river is generally believed to be the location of the Des Moines. Joliet's map showed only one river entering the Mississippi between the Missouri and the mouth of the Wisconsin. Although the waterway was not named it was in the position of the Des Moines.

The word "Moingona" was used by explorers and cartographers in designating the Des Moines River. By the beginning of the nineteenth century the word "Des Moines" appeared. In 1810 Zebulon Pike's map of the Mississippi carried the spelling "river de moines" and provided a detailed representation of the river as far upstream as the modern day capital of Des Moines. There were conflicting reports explaining the name Des Moines. One is that Des Moines means the river of the mounds because of the topography of the country along its banks. When the word is spelled "de moyen" the name has been understood to mean "from the middle." This sounded reasonable because the Des Moines River is the principal stream between the Mississippi and

A Passion for Wilderness

Missouri.

The settlement of the Des Moines River valley covered a period of decades. Many of the settlers came from up the river and others reached the river by traveling cross country from other Mississippi River towns. The Des Moines River was a military frontier as the white settlers took over the land from the native Americans. The movement of settlers up the Des Moines valley was soon followed by the need for transportation and supplies. Steamboating developed on the Des Moines and the river was termed navigable. Because of the central position of the river and the advantages of good farm land along the valley, a large majority of the people in Iowa chose Des Moines as the capital.

Wilderness is wide open spaces that afford an opportunity for a person to sense the history and continuity of the land. Away from the neon franchise lights of civilization it is possible to envision the native Americans, explorers and settlers of long ago. When I decided to paddle my canoe 184 miles from Des Moines to Keokuk where the river joins the mighty Mississippi I had no intention of "getting away from it all" or "being where no man (or woman) had ever been." I welcomed the rich heritage of the land's past and the visions of others seeking and seeing the wilderness for themselves.

I had just the right boat for my journey. Outside the farm house, upside down and leaning against the white boat siding was my red Monarch — a one-person canoe designed by Verlen Kruger and made famous on his twenty-eight-thousand-mile Ultimate

A Passion for Wilderness

Windy weather on Red Rock Lake

Canoe Challenge. This boat was designed especially for solo long distance tripping. I grabbed the cockpit and turned the canoe right side up. The stiff 17-foot body fairly bounced. The rudder flopped and squeaked as the boat settled on the grass. I bent to scoop out the leaves that had collected since the last river trip three months before. There was a spider web across the Kevlar seat mount and I could see that the farm cats had climbed inside and made a cozy corner out of the bow. There were fur balls to clean out but besides that the boat needed no persuading — it was ready to float.

I picked up the 50-pound boat and carried it to the driveway. Wiping off the dust of storage I looked up and saw my sister-in-law's wash on the

A Passion for Wilderness

line. Skirts flapped and the arms of my brother's shirts unfurled like banners in the afternoon breeze. The scene didn't make me think of family chores or washing machine advertisements. I didn't wonder at all what brand of detergent had brightened the colors. For me the clothes line was an indicator of the wind. I felt a familiar satisfaction. The wilderness was unknown territory but the feelings of excitement and perspective of an outdoor traveler came back to me easily.

I knew that in the outdoors the conditions were boss. When the wind speaks I listen, when the water moves I respond; when the skies turn grey I am watchful. When traveling in the wilderness my actions are tuned to the natural world. Keeping in mind that I was "at the mercy of the elements" my time schedule would remain flexible. But I still had my goals and a distance to cover. I constructed a time/distance chart for my trip. This chart would serve as a guide for my travels and also provide an itinerary for the folks waiting back home.

TIME / DISTANCE SCHEDULE

Day	From	To	Distance
1	14th Street boat ramp (outside Des Moines)	Red Rock Lake	32 Miles
2	Red Rock Lake	Eddyville	41 Miles
3	Eddyville	Eldon	33 Miles
4	Eldon	Farmington	46 Miles
5	Farmington	Mississippi River	32 Miles

A Passion for Wilderness

By now, I had traded the Iowa transportation map for a topographical chart with a scale of 1:250,000. I plotted my projected progress by evaluating the terrain described on my map, looking for logical break points in the journey and gauging my own experience and endurance. I felt that the schedule gave me a healthy goal. I wouldn't be dawdling along the way.

I looked up a quotation I remembered from the introduction of Alexander Mackenzie's **Voyages from Montreal**; "I do not possess the science of the naturalist and even if the qualifications of that character had been attained by me, its curious spirit would not have been gratified. I could not stop to dig into the earth, over whose surface I was compelled to pass with rapid steps, nor could I turn aside to collect the plants which nature might have scattered along the way, when my thoughts were anxiously employed in making provision for the day that was passing over me."

I wasn't in a big hurry on this trip but I wouldn't be collecting any samples or documenting the conditions of the land. My main purpose was to travel the distance from Des Moines to Keokuk and explore the area where I lived. I was going on a solo trip to care for myself and enjoy the wilderness on my own. I figured this out before I started.

Packing presented no problem. I had done it many times before. My bags were well used and tested. I had a cavernous Duluth pack, a tent and sleeping bag duffel, a waterproof camera bag and numerous stuff sacks. No matter how much experience

A Passion for Wilderness

I had gathered, I always packed too many clothes. This trip was no exception. I assembled two bags of special outdoor garments — polypropylene layers, rain gear, hats and extra socks. My sleeping pad, stove and personal bag made another necessary pile of belongings.

At the grocery store I impulsively added to a well thought out shopping list, and ended up spending $55 on dried pasta, dried soups, fruit, cookies, crackers, cheese, peanut butter, cereal, powdered milk, candy and a host of other items. My food bag now weighed as if it carried provisions for an armada.

On Thursday, September 27, 1984 Marianne drove me, my boat and gear to the 14th street boat ramp in Des Moines. I was feeling some apprehension about taking off alone so when we were caught in morning traffic as we neared the city, I felt relieved. Our slow progress didn't bother me at all. Marianne adjusted the car heater and turned on the radio. I would soon be climbing out of the leather trimmed front seat and putting myself in an environment with no buttons or dials to regulate comfort, and no close friend to encourage me forward.

When we got to the bridge over the river, the traffic all but stopped. For several moments our car sat on the bridge and I had the chance to look out the window at the water moving below. A slight wind ruffled the surface into a glistening bank of ripples. When I saw the brown muddy river running beneath the road and disappearing around a bend about three hundred yards downstream, my apprehen-

A Passion for Wilderness

Valerie starts the solo journey

sions vanished. The river world was calling and I felt the intense excitement of adventure.

Marianne turned off the highway and parked near the sloping concrete grooved launching ramp. I took my boat off the car, arranged my equipment in the canoe, placed the water jug within reach of the seat and positioned the map. Marianne hugged me. Then I pushed off into the current and looked back. She was waving. I took a few strokes at the water and felt my shoulders relax. I didn't wait to see her drive off. She was waiting to see me paddle

A Passion for Wilderness

on.

Around the first bend the brush and trees edged close to the ribbon of river and sheltered the waterway from the town. The highway noises were left behind as if the wall of trees grew in a barrier between civilization and wilderness. There wasn't a lot of time to consider the changes. I was busy steering around tufts of dirt, gravel and grass islands. The river was a wide fluid freeway with obstacles amounting to heavy traffic.

I tried to see bottom but my paddle only stirred the murky water and could not clear a viewing patch in the opaque soup. The river seemed to absorb the grey overcast sky. I knew this was not impossible. Already the river had swallowed mud from fields across the state. The Des Moines is the longest river in Iowa with the widest basin. It drains the largest watershed in Iowa, and carries more silt than any other river in the state, five times more silt than that of the Mississippi just above its junction with the Des Moines and equal to that of the Mississippi at its mouth.

The deck of my red canoe was a welcome splash of color against the surface of dark flowing river. Though I could not see bottom I touched it in the shallow spots. My paddle hit mud on one stroke, then took a full swing of water on the next. The depth of the river fluctuated. Taking soundings with the paddle, I could almost feel the river bottom rolling. At times my paddle hit rocks and slapped underwater branches, clunking against sunken trees. Even the speed of the canoe responded to the depth variance, slowing down in the shallow areas and gaining a hint of speed when the river bottom fell away.

Now that I was traveling with the current it was hard to gauge how fast the river was moving. The current was best observed by watching partially submerged branches and sticks. Anchored in mud, whole branches were tramped by the current, bobbing and quivering as the water rushed past.

The Des Moines wasn't a raging river or a famous river. The water flowed quiet and unassuming — just right for my solo journey. I didn't know how far the wilderness extended to my right or left but the river world seemed to be the center.

Though I had left the comforts of home for a seventeen foot canoe, I didn't step backwards into a primitive world. I was moving forward into adventure. Rather than feeling deprived, I felt more alive. There was nothing desolate about the terrain. The river was rich, full and hospitable. Around each bend were surprises. Turtles, blue herons and deer were startled as I approached. Their world was now mine. I was delighted to find that I did have a place in the wilderness. By paddling my canoe, I had joined the river. Parting the water with my bow I was making a place for me.

I had put in at the city ramp at 8:10 a.m. By 9:10 I had paddled 5 miles to the Highway 46 bridge. Twelve and a half miles further I passed the mouth of the Middle River, emptying into the Des Moines. At 12:51 I passed Hartford and by 1:43 I was paddling under the Runnells Bridge — $20\frac{1}{2}$ miles from the put-in.

A Passion for Wilderness

Keeping my mileage straight was easy. The Iowa Float Trips Guide listed the mileage between landmarks. The pamphlet included a small map of the river and descriptions that evaluated the access points along the route.

All afternoon I concentrated on paddling the river. One bend curved and flowed into another. The scenery blended together but each mile on the river was different. The land accommodated the river by uniquely adjusting to the flow. Cut banks and slopes alternated with brush so thick that the bank was hidden.

Though I was paddling solo I didn't feel alone. The river was urging me forward using a language formed from more than sounds, a language of visual reflections and measurable flow.

Henry Van Dyke said that "a river is the most human and companionable of all inanimate things. It has a life, a character, a voice of its own, and is as full of good fellowship as a sugarmaple is of sap. It can talk in various tones, loud or low, and of many subjects, grave and gay. For real company and friendship, there is nothing outside the animal kingdom that is comparable to a river."

Besides the river's incessant gurgle the birds didn't give up trying to communicate and the trees made swooshing sounds as they rubbed branches above the bank. I had a closeup view of life on the river. Small water bugs hopped across the surface. Logs and interesting debris piled around all the midstream obstructions. The water lifted and swirled around dark rocks and trunks. The movement was the ingredient that made the scene so

A Passion for Wilderness

perfect. Trees moved in the wind, the river moved and I felt movement in me as my arms reached for every stroke.

Minutes turned into hours, and soon half a day was gone. I kept paddling, moving with the flow of the river. I didn't stop to eat but munched while floating. Around two o'clock I decided to beach my canoe and stretch my legs. I hadn't realized how absorbed I had become with the paddling and the movement of the river. When my boat touched the bank, I climbed out without thinking and sank my legs into knee deep mud! I could feel the mud gooshing into my shoes and slathering around my ankles. My reverie was broken. I stumbled toward higher ground, making big holes where each step sank into the goo. I shook my head in disbelief and spent the next half hour scraping with sticks to clean my shoes and pant legs.

I built a log bridge across the mud to get back into my canoe but before getting back into the boat, I dug a cathole. I hadn't seen anyone all morning and there was no one in sight now, but I still looked around to make sure my spot was private. The moment I hunched over the hole, a motor boat came around the bend! I tried to be quick. Re-adjusting my pants, I jumped over the board mud bridge and climbed into my canoe to shove off. The man in the motor boat recognized my distress and veered off without stopping. I returned to paddling on the river but now my mind was a bit unsettled. I lectured myself about staying alert.

By 4:35 p.m. I had arrived at box car bend. It was easy to see how the place got its name. The map showed an old railroad grade that paralleled the river at this spot. A dozen train cars had been derailed and pushed over the bank. Half submerged, the cars protected the corner from erosion and made a playground for fish.

After box car bend I lost track of the bends of the river marked on the map. I didn't know exactly which curve I was on but I knew that Red Rock Lake and Highway 14 were ahead. I continued paddling as evening approached, knowing it was about time to get off the river and make camp.

All day long the paddling had been great. The movement of the river and my canoe was a secure feeling that I had gotten used to. The prospect of setting my tent on the bank made me a little nervous. I paddled harder, not wanting to stop, then realized I had to make camp or face setting up my tent in the dark. I looked for a flat spot above the river. When I saw a likely place I couldn't help but wonder if maybe around the next bend there would be something better.

I finally chose a flat spot on the north side of the river and paddled to shore. I tested the bank with my paddle blade and safely climbed onto dry land. The small clearing was a shelf bank backed by a high hill. The earth in the area was dry and cracked, looking as if high water had covered the ground in the past. I studied the darkening sky and wondered if it would rain. If it did I would be in mud but I decided to accept the risk.

By the time I pulled my boat a distance from the water, put up my tent, hauled my bags into the shelter and crawled inside, it was dark.   I began to relax and realized how tired I was.   Then, I started to worry.   Sitting in the tent all alone I felt vulnerable.

I ate nuts, cheese and crackers for dinner.   I wrote in my journal, then arranged my belongings around my sleeping pad. The night was beginning to sound too quiet.   There was no telling what might wander by or worse, who might be out prowling. Instead of thinking the best thoughts, I imagined the worst. My fears were exaggerated because I had paddled over forty miles and my fatigue nurtured fear.   My heart was pounding but I snuggled deep into my sleeping bag and fell asleep.

In the middle of the night, I woke with a start. There were sounds outside.   A loud slap came from the water side of my camp. Someone was clapping.   I was sitting up now, listening intently.   Slap!   I recognized the sound—a beaver was flapping his tail on the water.   I lay back down then remembered my wooden canoe paddle leaning against my canoe.   My imagination pictured the broad tailed beaver with his furry body and long buck teeth gnawing through the blade.   I had never asked anyone if beavers eat canoe paddles or paddlers, for that matter, but I knew that by morning I would find out.

During the rest of the night I must have awakened twenty times.   There were no windows in the tent to look out, only the tent fabric stretched in a dome around me and no light coming in.   I could almost reach out and touch the fabric but I lay still, not wanting to disturb anything.   The whole outdoors was breathing against the thin walls.

A Passion for Wilderness

•   •   •

I woke up at four a.m. and knew there was no sense trying to go back to sleep. A new day was beginning. I had made it through the night, it hadn't rained and I found my paddle safe, leaning against the canoe just as I had left it.

It was still dark when I finished packing, slid my canoe off the bank and climbed in. As I paddled downstream one lone light twinkled in the distance. The scenery along the banks blurred into silhouette. Clumps of trees became mountains of shadow in the early hour.

Within a few more miles the river opened and spread into a braided delta. I spent quite a while trying to decide which channel to take. The current was imperceptible at first but the light of day got brighter by the moment and I watched for anything that might help to determine the direction of flow. Even the smallest leaf or blade of grass caught on a half-submerged twig could tell me which way the current was moving.

After another long hour of paddling I saw a bridge ahead connecting two hills and spanning the river that had now widened into a backwater lake. The bridge was high above the river and the cars scooted by, probably going to work. My work was cut out for me. Ahead was Red Rock Lake, a portage and over forty miles before my destination for the night — Eddyville.

Red Rock Lake was a wide body of shallow water.

A Passion for Wilderness

I was surprised to find that not only my paddle struck bottom but the entire belly of my canoe scraped through mud. In some areas I had to paddle backwards to escape the shallows. I paddled into channels, hoping for deep water. Huge bluffs of rock bordered the south edge of the lake. I thought for sure there would be deep water areas beneath the cliffs, but I couldn't reach that part of the lake for all the sand bars I was jamming into.

I remembered a lesson I had learned in the Baja Lagoons. In shallow water it is best to watch the birds. Here at Red Rock Lake there were flocks of birds. I watched where they settled on the water. They weren't floating but standing on bottom in only inches of water. I steered away from any areas with sitting birds and found that using my feathered friends as indicators I could navigate the shallows quite well.

By nine o'clock I could see the dam at the southeast end of the lake. The wind was picking up, blowing the water the length of the lake and drawing up white caps. I kept paddling and stared at the dam trying to figure out which side would be best for the portage. With the wind growing stronger, I knew that I should make the right landing choice the first time as I didn't want to paddle along the back of the dam in a heavy cross wind.

I chose to portage on the south side of the dam where I spotted a sloping ravine. The wind was blowing a small size surf onto the beach as I scrambled ashore. After pulling the boat clear of

A Passion for Wilderness

The dam at Red Rock Lake

the water I walked up the high slope, slipping on the rocks as I hiked to the top. Carrying the boat and gear around this man-made mountain looked like it was going to be a bit of work.

At the top of the rise there was an information center and administrative area. There was also a bathroom with hot water where I washed my hands and cleaned up before attempting the carry. One of the rangers in the office gave me a map and two other fellows offered to assist my portage around the dam. The ranger seemed glad to see me and added my name to the list of three other canoers who had portaged the dam in the past two years.

Portaging was short work with two helpers. Within half an hour my boat and gear were deposited on the river side of the dam a safe distance from the dramatic flow of white water and turbulence rushing through the spillway. I thanked the two gentlemen, repacked my boat, climbed in and paddled downstream.

The river was much changed from the day before. Enhanced by the sun sparkling off the water, the river on the southeast side of the dam looked clearer. Given a shove by the forceful spillway, the Des Moines River moved faster on this side. After the forced calm of Red Rock Lake, the river flowed free.

I learned from reading the liner notes on the map that the Red Rock area had been settled by John Bedell in 1843. The population of the village increased in 1847 and 1848. The area prospered until 1851 when a flood washed away the town and sent the few residents to the high ground of the nearby bluffs — the same ones I had seen earlier in the morning.

The brochure explained that Red Rock was situated on a frequented Indian trail and at the border of the United States Territory. It became a place of resort for the Indians and settlers and a famous spot for trading and drinking whiskey. The town rebuilt after the flood and attracted adventurers and desperados. Fights were a frequent occurrence. Though the town was small, by 1877 there had been no less than ten murders. The brochure mentioned that the character of Red Rock changed in the 1960s when the lake and dam were completed. The $88 million used to develop the dam must have had a big influence.

There didn't seem to be any sign of excitement on the day I portaged over the dam. There were a few fishermen angling for keepers, but the desperados were nowhere to be seen. As for the adventurers, I was keeping the spirit alive — me and my red canoe. I was glad that I hadn't known about the history of Red Rock when I had camped the night before. My rambunctious imagination was well fueled without the thoughts of murders, desperados and floods.

The afternoon went by quickly. While I spent my time paddling and watching for sand bars, the number of islands in the river increased. It took a lot of concentration to paddle my weaving course. There were no rapids to make the river dangerous, but a lot of maneuvering was required to steer around the obstructions. I was working with the river, playing every inch of current, looking ahead and anticipating where the channel would deepen. I paddled from one cut bank to another, following the current and going with the flow. There were plenty of ripples to fool me. Many times the bottom whizzed by close underneath my hull. Sometimes the current spread out over the top of a gravel bar and I would quickly draw and paddle to the other side looking for a deeper route. There was always a deep channel. I just had to find it.

Paddling my own canoe was a real satisfying experience. There was no lead boat to follow. I

A Passion for Wilderness

was making the decisions. It wasn't just a test but an exercising of what was in me. My success didn't depend entirely on my experience but the fact I was learning something new about navigating on every mile of the river.

I arrived at Eddyville by sunset and climbed out on the bank at the city park overlook. There was a police station across the street from the landing and I figured this was a safe spot to camp. Putting up my tent drew quite a bit of attention. Two older women were walking on their way to a Friday night bingo game. After hearing my story they invited me to their apartment for a shower, but I knew that camping so close to town was compromise enough with my wilderness river solo. I told them I planned to stay dirty for the next couple of days but thanked them very much.

After putting up my tent I walked into town. Eddyville was a quiet little place, basically a few short streets of stores and houses spread out from the river. One cafe advertised a Friday night fish special. I was hungry and ready to eat my weight so I went inside to sit down and order. When the waitress brought my plate there was a fried catfish staring at me complete with eyes and whiskers sticking out from the corn bread batter.

The townspeople seemed to all know one another and they all knew I was a stranger. My polypropylene clothing was funny looking and they didn't see my car parked outside the restaurant picture window. When they heard I was camped by the river, they shook their heads and warned that the temperature that night was forecast to drop to 28 degrees.

A Passion for Wilderness

I left the catfish on my plate and walked back to camp. With the police station sheltering me I was less scared than the night before. I fell asleep feeling my arms protesting the long paddling day and my feet protesting the cold temperature.

In the middle of the night I woke with a start. There were sirens and people yelling. I could understand from the excited voices that there had been a car accident somewhere on the county roads. I pulled my sleeping bag around my ears and went back to bed. It all sounded familiar and not nearly as frightening as the night before when nothing happened at all.

I paddled out of Eddyville by seven the next morning. Fog blanketed the river. I couldn't see very far ahead and it was difficult to read the sand bars and find the deep channels. It was cold and my fingers began to hurt. I didn't stop for breakfast until the sun burned through the fog and began to warm me. Then I put my paddle across the cockpit and ate breakfast while floating.

The river got deeper and easier to paddle. Within a few miles, a railroad track caught up with the river and crossed it several times, then ran alongside. There were no trains but plenty of clearing for the tracks. I chugged along the river to Ottumwa and approached the second dam on my route. I thought a while about the inconvenience of the barricade and then remembered that the Red Rock Lake brochure had mentioned the history of flooding in the area. The Des Moines regularly flooded its banks. In 1903, eight thousand people had been evacuated from Ottumwa and in 1947 one of the most disastrous floods in the history of Iowa caused more than $30 million damage washing out large sections of the town. It seemed logical to either divert the water or control it with a dam. Right then I wasn't thinking too much about the reasons for the dam, I was trying to figure out how to get around!

There was no trail but I hacked a path up to a road running along the south bank. Getting on top was no problem but the put in was a quarter mile away across a major intersection. The only thing that got me over that portage was the thought that I was headed for Eldon.

The river wasn't cooperating. On the south side of the dam the river had all but dried up. It might have been easier to get out and drag the boat through the shallows but I kept paddling and shoved myself off the bottom whenever I got stuck.

There were more rocks in the stretch after Ottumwa and they scraped the belly of my canoe. I could feel the red coating wearing away as if the rocks were scratching at me. The sun was out and the day was beautiful but I put the scenery out of my mind and concentrated on my task of navigating the river. There were no birds to help me out now but the water was more clear and I could watch the bottom falling from view in places.

"Where are you headed?" a man yelled from the bank.

"Paddling to the Mississippi," I shouted back.

"You'll never make it," the observer replied. "The river's too low. You'll be running out of water for sure."

A Passion for Wilderness

I could almost have agreed with the skeptic but I kept finding a few more yards of deep channel and then a few more. I wasn't giving up and continued to work through the rocky obstacle course.

After passing Eldon at five p.m., the river stopped bending and straightened out past Selma and into Douds. A deep channel floated me for miles. The terrain was rolling now with small bluffs butting against the river and interesting rock outcroppings overhanging the banks.

At 7:30 I stopped paddling just past Douds. There were farms along the river and I pulled up to one and camped in the brush along the bank. I felt silly for not seeking out a more remote spot but I looked at the map, saw the distance I had come and realized that there was no sense pushing further. I was bone tired and overdue for a rest. There were no clouds in the sky so I got the benefit of the last ounce of light from the sunset and I needed it to set up the tent and secure my boat.

I ate dinner inside my shelter, then washed my face with a paper towel and a swig of water from my jug. I bundled up in my sleeping bag and looked at the map with my flashlight. I had come almost forty miles today. All night long I dodged stones and sand bars in my sleep.

The fourth day of my solo journey began in fog. I waited for daylight, hoping the sky would clear but it didn't. By eight a.m., I took down my tent and launched into fog soup, floating and paddling with low visibility. I could only see the bow of my red canoe and a few feet of water ahead. The river obstacles were hidden from view but my hull sought them out!

Besides needing clear skies to skirt the shallows, I was paddling past some of the historic towns of Iowa and wanted a better view. Pittsburg, Keosauqua, Bentonsport, Bonaparte and Farmington were neighboring towns on this stretch of the river with a colorful past.

The last wisps of fog disappeared by 9:30. The sun shone with a bright glare off the water and filtered through the trees along the bank. Miles of undisturbed forest lined the river. Unless I gave close attention to following the bends of the river on my map, I wouldn't have known a town was coming up until the trees abruptly thinned and I could see a house or two, then a bridge.

At 10:37 I was paddling under the bridge at Pittsburg. By 11:20 I had passed Keosauqua. Towns were not my primary interest on this solo journey but I did note that the Iowa Float Trip Guide mentioned that Keosauqua had the oldest county courthouse in the state, and Pearson house located in the same town was a station for the underground railroad during the Civil War.

These facts didn't entice me to stop. The piece of history that interested me the most was the history of the river in steamboat times. Steamboat days on the Des Moines came alive for me as I paddled on. People used to gather on the banks to cheer when the steamboats arrived. I saw people waving from the bridges and banks as I paddled past a steamboat and didn't intend to deliver supplies. I wondered how the steamboats had managed the shallows that were giving me such problems. Upon

A Passion for Wilderness

further research I realized they hadn't. The river was different in those times before the dams; the steamboats relied on heavy rain and traveled on the river only during certain times of the year.

The Des Moines River used to be a highway for the steamboat traffic going up and down. The traffic wanting to cross the river relied on a ferry service. I read that there was one steamboat called the Rope Cutter, so named because the deck hands would cut the ferry ropes stretching across the river and blocking their progress. There were no ferries on the Des Moines now. Instead, there were bridges. The bridges connected to highways far removed from the river world. The river seemed forgotten by all except the occasional fisherman or group of children playing on the banks. The wilderness I was now enjoying had grown up by virtue of inactivity.

I noticed that under every town bridge there was a riffle of water flowing over a bank of stones. These were the remains of the many dams constructed across the river by mill owners. William Petersen wrote in his **Steamboating on the Upper Mississippi** that "It was the practice of steamboatmen to take a run at these makeshift obstructions and force the boat through or over them. Sometimes a boat was hung up on the crest of the dam without being able to run either forward or back." Mr. Petersen went on to tell the story of the indomitable Captain Wilson wrestling with the dam at Keosauqua:

> *The G. H. Wilson stuck several times*
> *in attempting to pass the dam and had to*

fall back and try it again. Getting desperate, eye witnesses relate, the captain ordered the engineer to get up a big pressure of steam, open the throttle valves wide, and shouted his commands so that they could be heard half a mile: "Send her over — or blow her to hell." The boat went over amid the cheers of the spectators. The engineer said afterwards that he rather expected the other alternative.

I felt the same do-or-die attitude as I approached Bonaparte and the only lock and dam still visible on the Des Moines River. The riffles under the bridges upstream were nothing compared to the turbulence at Bonaparte. I had been warned of the rapids in this stretch. The dam had been washed out, and appeared as a treacherous rush of wild water extending the width of the river. I approached the rapids and looked them over. Traveling with a load of gear I was cautious as I didn't want to spill and lose important equipment, so I got out of my canoe and scouted the portage. There was a man on the bank who offered to haul me around but the put-in he suggested was a steep bank that looked more dangerous than the rapids themselves.

I watched the water closely seeing which rocks stuck out from the flow. I chose my path, then got back into my boat, paddled up with a full head of steam, dodging and drawing myself into the route I had decided on. I concentrated and paddled hard, blazing through the rocks at Bonaparte without a scratch. The water was low under the bridge and I skimmed just above the rocks as my canoe continued downstream.

Safely past the Bonaparte rapids I relaxed to view the scenery. The bluffs began to recede as the river widened. The banks got higher as the river flowed closer to the Mississippi. A road followed the river's winding course on the south bank.

The night I camped near Farmington was my best effort at solo tenting. I was getting used to being alone. Instead of being afraid I listened to the river and read a bit of prose by Robert Louis Stevenson: "There's no music like a river's. It plays the same tune over and over again, and yet does not weary of it like fiddlers. It takes the mind out of doors; and though we should be grateful for good houses, there is, after all, no house like God's out-of-doors. And lastly, it quiets a person down like saying their prayers."

The next day the river bluffs withdrew completely as the river plain increased in width. There were only a few towns now and not much access to the river from the highways. The trees towered over the river and landscaped the water as their own branches reflected on the surface. There were a few railroad bridges but the river was spreading out, braiding into large cut bank sand hills. The river was picking up speed again and there were large pools and eddies where the water slowed and sat as if to rest a moment.

I passed the river town of Croton, Iowa, and Athens, Missouri, directly across the river. These towns were the site of the northernmost battle of the Civil War. In 1861 a cannon was strategically placed on the bluffs of the Missouri side and fired across the river into Croton. Cannonballs were still embedded in some of the homes. I didn't stop to investigate but looked carefully at the shape of the river at this particular bend. Over one hundred years before in 1852 the largest steamboat to travel on the Des Moines made it to Croton and Athens. The 485 ton **Jeannie Deans** was 236 feet long with $38\frac{1}{2}$ foot beam and a depth requirement of $5\frac{1}{2}$ feet. I couldn't imagine such a lumbering ship moving up the quiet river that I saw this morning in 1985. A blend of progress and tangled wilderness had changed the river beyond recognition. I paddled on, enjoying the thought of steamboat days gone by.

As I neared the Mississippi I pulled out a small book that contained Father Charlevoix's detailed description of the Des Moines valley in 1721: "On the left side, about fifty leagues above the river of Buffaloes," he wrote, "the river Moingona issues from the midst of an immense meadow, which swarms with buffaloes and other wild beasts, at its entrance into the Mississippi, it is very shallow as well as narrow, nevertheless its course from north to west is said to be two hundred and fifty leagues in length."

By nightfall I reached the Mississippi. The Des Moines River emptied with no fanfare, channeling into the larger stream. There were no buffalo or wild beasts to welcome me. The banks near the river mouth seemed fragile and apt to tumble any

A Passion for Wilderness

moment to join the rivers where they met.

I paddled a few miles upstream on the Mississippi so that I could land at Keokuk. Dodging parked tugs and cutting under cable lines I reached the landing of a city park. There I sat on the bank and watched the Mississippi River flowing by. A tug boat glided downstream, and I watched until it disappeared in the nighttime shadows.

I had a wonderful feeling of satisfaction. I had arrived. Where does the river go? Now I knew. Winding through farm lands, towns and wilderness, the river flows into the Mississippi and now the river flowed in my heart and memory because I had paddled the Des Moines River solo. Where does the river go? Now I could say — to the Mississippi! I had followed it all the way.

Lawrence   Abrams

REMINISCENCE

The sight and sound of rapids
on a lively crystal stream
starts a yearning deep within me,
and I see, as in a dream —

Flashing, dipping wooden paddles
moved by paddler's skillful hands,
as they throw aside the water
to the call of crisp commands.

A Passion for Wilderness

As a boulder mass is looming
"Draw right!" sounds above the roar.
Then the craft moves swiftly over
where the chute's an open door.

Down the rushing chute it passes,
splitting waves along the way;
but it leaves no lasting traces
that will give its path away.

And inside it, carried snugly,
where the water cannot reach,
are the food and gear for camping
and for comfort on the beach.

With a cheerful campfire glowing
like a lamp upon the shore,
and hot soup and bannock cooking
one could ask for nothing more.

Part

BEYOND THE GREAT BEAR

By

Clayton Klein

CLAYTON KLEIN

   Clayton Klein grew up on a farm near Fowlerville, Michigan, and still lives in the house in
which he was born.   Upon completion of work at
Michigan State University, he served as a dairy
technician and operated the family farm for several
years.   In 1951 he founded Klein Fertilizers and

served as its president and general manager until 1984.

Clayton's first book was published in the fall of 1983, launching his writing career. Presently he is working on a historical novel entitled **Challenge the Wilderness,** to be published in the summer of 1987.

An avid hiker and backpacker, he has walked more than a thousand miles every year since 1967. He is an active outdoorsman who, along with his son Darrell, has canoed more than 3500 miles of the rivers in Canada's Northwest Territories. Having spent considerable time canoeing through Indian and Inuit areas of Canada, he also presents travelog programs to various groups dozens of times each year.

BEYOND   THE   GREAT   BEAR

Chapter 1

COLVILLE   LAKE

It was in August of 1984 that our son Darrell
came to me and said, "Dad, how would you like to go
canoeing with me next summer?"

"That would be great," I replied.   "Where would
we go?"

"It doesn't make a lot of difference to me, as
long as it's somewhere in Canada.   Where would you
like to go?"

"Oh boy!" I replied.   Then I cautiously added,

A Passion for Wilderness

"What I'd really like to do is canoe the Anderson River. We could start at Colville Lake. That way we could spend some time with Bern Will Brown. We would be above the Arctic Circle and we could canoe right on down to the Arctic Ocean."

I really expected Darrell to say that he couldn't be away from business or home for such a long time, but without hesitation he responded, "That sounds good to me. Let's plan on it."

"Excellent!" I was overjoyed at the thought! "Maybe we'll finally get to cross the Arctic Circle and actually see the midnight sun." This was being consistent with the past. Each time the two of us had traveled together during our quarter of a century of canoeing, we had gone farther to the northwest each time.

Seven years had frittered away since the two of us had journeyed together into northern Canada. Darrell had, in those years, seen his two daughters, Kristene and Patricia, through high school. He had also advanced to become the President and General Manager of the family fertilizer business.

Plans continued to develop during the autumn. Maps were ordered and the possibility of buying a new lightweight canoe of modern design was discussed. "It would be nice if Debbie could go along with us," Darrell remarked, during one of our chats in December. "What would you think if I ask her?"

"I'd like it," I replied. "But I don't know if she could get away from work for that long."

"Maybe she could get a leave of absence."

A Passion for Wilderness

Darrell's sister, Debbie, had been working for several years in the Department of Food Science and Human Nutrition at Michigan State University. She and I had canoed together during her vacations in Ontario, Manitoba, Saskatchewan, and in 1983 we paddled together in the Dubawnt River system of Northwest Territories.

"If the three of us go," Darrell continued, "we will need a solo canoe for one of us. Maybe you could check around and get us a good deal on a Monarch."

"I could check with Verlen Kruger and also Brad and Bev Gordon at Kazoo Canoe."

"Tell you what I'll do," Darrell added. "If you can get us a good deal, I would pay for half of it."

"I'll see what I can do."

Consequently, Darrell did ask Debbie and "Yes," she would like to go. Brad Gordon of Kazoo Canoe, who handles both Mad River and Wenonah canoe products, gave us a good combination deal on a Monarch and a Wenonah X. Each of these canoes is constructed with durable and lightweight Kevlar material and, at fifty pounds each, "That's a weight that even an old man like me can handle."

It was full speed ahead with the planning. Food and camping supply lists were prepared and, among other things, we corresponded with Bern Will Brown. By March of 1985 we had decided to drive our pickup truck to Inuvik, Northwest Territories and engage a bush pilot to fly us along with our camping equipment the final 220 miles to Colville Lake.

We were uncertain just how we would return from

the mouth of the Anderson River to Inuvik, but we prepared to paddle out across Liverpool Bay and cross the peninsula to the Eskimo settlement of Tuktoyaktuk. From there, if time permitted, we would then move on into the Mackenzie River delta and on upstream to Inuvik.

Our plan called for a departure on the morning of June 28, but a letter from Bern Will Brown dated April 29 caused us to postpone our start by one full week. Here are excerpts from his letter —

> All indications are for a late breakup this year. In fact, I can't remember there ever being this much ice here during the past twenty-three years! On top of that, it has been snowing the past three days, further insulating it from the eventual sun.

> I have booked nine men into the Outpost June 29th and six into the Main Lodge on the same date and am worried that there may not be enough open water to fish or get down twenty-five miles to the Outpost Lodge. We expect to go down there by dogsled the end of May on the ice to open up the place.

Both new canoes finally arrived during the final week of May. We are fortunate to have as a friend the number one canoeist in North America, Verlen Kruger. He is also the designer of the Monarch, one of which he used on his 28,000-mile Ultimate Canoe Challenge. In early June, we took the Monarch to Verlen's home on the banks of the Grand River in Lansing, Michigan. He had offered to help us outfit it for wilderness travel. That day he showed us how to install the spray cover and adjust the seat. He installed several additional layers of Kevlar cloth to the inside ot the deck, strengthening it considerably, and put in several extra shock chord loops.

"I sure would like to be going with you," Verlen said while working away. "I have a complete set of maps for that trip. At one time I had planned to cross Great Bear Lake and portage over into the headwaters of the Anderson and then on down to the Polar Sea."

Verlen would accept no pay for those several hours of work. As we drove away, after thanking him, we were gratefully aware that our Monarch had certainly received 'the master's touch.'

Excitement and anticipation began to build during those final weeks prior to departure. In addition to our usual work, there were the final plans including shopping for and packing food for each day of the journey. The food detail was handled by Darrell as he had agreed to be our chief cook, "providing Dad will prepare the breakfasts and Deb will do the dishes."

There was physical training by each of us. Debbie jogged six miles or more per day, Darrell rode his bike from twelve to thirty miles a day and I continued my usual daily walking and jogging of three to seven miles.

A Passion for Wilderness

Three times per week, we took the canoes to either the Shiawassee River or the Lobdell Lakes for workouts of up to seven hours of steady paddling. We each trained for portaging the canoes and packs.

• • •

We were underway at 3:30 on the morning of Friday, July 5. It was west and north all day. With the box of the pickup truck cap-covered, one of us would usually lounge or sleep on the foam pad alongside the camping gear while the other two kept the vehicle rolling. At suppertime we were in Fargo, North Dakota. Then it was on through Bismark and Minot. Before dawn, we had entered Saskatchewan at North Portal and moved on into Regina for breakfast. Next came Saskatoon, North Battleford and Lloydminster before checking into the Holiday Inn at Edmonton, Alberta. We had rolled two thousand miles in little more than thirty-six hours.

It was on through the great agricultural area around Grand Prairie, across the gorgeous mountains of northern British Columbia and into Whitehorse, Yukon Territory by Monday evening. Securing a room at Regina Inn overlooking the Yukon River, I delivered a case of books to Maxmillian's Gold Rush Emporium which they had ordered about ten days earlier.

The following morning I was not feeling extremely healthy (it must have been jet lag), so we were off to a late start for the drive to Dawson City. Along the way and throughout the Yukon, the roadsides were ablaze with fireweed, the official flower of the

Territory. Interesting stops were made at Lake La Barge, Five Fingers Rapids and Pelly Crossing before arrival in old Dawson City.

By the time we had checked into the Eldorado Hotel and had supper that rainy evening, we were too late to catch the show at either the Palace Grand or Diamond Tooth Gertie's. I was in time, however, to deliver several copies of **One Incredible Journey** to the bookstore and meet its interesting and colorful manager, one Lowry Toombs.

Before calling it a day, we walked the muddy

streets to visit the cabin of poet, Robert Service but were a little late to see him, as he died in Lancieux, France back in 1958. But, it was certainly a pleasure to view the place from where he had written those great poems of Canada's north country and the gold rush.

Wednesday was a most memorable day. It was raining as we drove the twenty-three miles back alongside the Klondike River to the south end of the Dempster Highway. Moving north through the Ogilvie Mountains, we soon broke out into the sunshine. Construction crews were working to improve some of the early built sections of the highway which was first opened in 1979. The Eagle Plains Hotel with its fine restaurant and service station is the only business along the entire 360 miles of the Dempster south of Fort McPherson. Needless to say, everyone traveling the highway stops there. It provided us an enjoyable break.

It was shortly after 2:00 when we arrived at the Arctic Circle, thirty-five miles north of Eagle Plains. This was the first time any of us had been so far north. In 1978 Darrell and I had been within forty-six miles of the 'circle,' while paddling down the Back River and that journey is included in **Cold Summer Wind.** It had taken me more than sixty years to get to the Arctic Circle and I was overjoyed to be there. Jogging back and forth, in an elongated circle, within three minutes, I had crossed the Arctic Circle nine times.

Then a couple of hours later an almost unbelievable thing happened. A new set of steel belted radials had been installed on our vehicle prior to

A Passion for Wilderness

Debbie and Darrell crossing the Mackenzie River

departure.   Stopping on a hilltop in the Rich-
ardson Mountains to stretch our legs, we were
shocked by what we observed.   Neither rear tire
was flat but both were rapidly leaking air.   "Can
you believe that!?"   Darrell sputtered as he
pulled out the jack. "Nearly four thousand miles
without any trouble and now we have two flats at
the same time."

"And, if we hadn't stopped right here," Deb
replied, "both of those new tires would probably
have been ruined."

Fortunately, we were carrying two spares.

Soon we crossed the summit and entered Northwest
Territories.   Then came the Peel and Mackenzie
River crossings on the free ferries and, by nine in
the evening, we rolled into Inuvik.   Finding a room

in that bustling town was something else. All four hotels were solidly booked. Following supper and on the way to the campground to set up our tents, we checked again at the Finto Motor Inn. Lucky us, they had received a cancellation.

As midnight approached, Deb and I drove around for a better look at the settlement while Darrell walked up on a hill to watch and photograph the midnight sun.

Inuvik is a unique settlement. It was built by the Canadian government in the late 1950s and early 60s. It was designed to serve as the main center for administration, communications, education and medical care for Canada's Western Arctic. It is also now used as the terminus for mineral, oil and gas exploration and development in the Mackenzie River delta, the Beaufort Sea and the Arctic Islands.

The name Inuvik is the Eskimo word for 'Place of Man.' It is a modern town and, because of the permafrost, the utilities, including water and heat, are piped through utilidors above the surface of the ground.

Inuvik is situated on high ground along the east shore of the East Channel of the Mackenzie Delta. It was accessible only by river or air until the 460-mile Dempster Highway was opened. Inuvik is now the home to nearly three thousand people, making it the largest settlement above the Arctic Circle in North America.

The Aklak Air people were expecting us. With two Cessna 185s and a canoe bound tightly above the right pontoon of each, we were soon under way to the Hareskin Indian settlement of Colville Lake. It was a good flight and, as we taxied up to the dock, Bern Will Brown stood waiting for us. As I popped the Cessna 185's door open, he said, "You must be Clate."

"That's right," I replied. "And you are Bern."

"Welcome to Colville Lake Lodge!" And, while we were shaking hands, he added, "It's so nice to meet you."

"It certainly is a pleasure," I added. Then Debbie and Darrell were introduced to Bern. Unloading the canoes and gear, we soon made our way up to the Lodge where we met Margaret Brown.

I had corresponded with Bern several times since he first read **Cold Summer Wind,** shortly after it was published in the fall of 1983. So, we already knew a little about each other, but found there was much more to learn. Consequently, most of the balance of July 11 was spent visiting with the Browns in their Lodge and around the settlement.

Bern grew up near Rochester, New York. He always loved the north and, because of the challenge he saw, became in 1948 a Roman Catholic missionary. Then, for the next twenty-two years, he served both Indians and Eskimo at various wide-spread settlements across Canada's northern territories.

In 1962, the then Father Brown was sent to Colville Lake to establish a mission for the Hareskin Indians, who are known by the neighboring tribes as 'The End of the Earth People.' Bern traveled to Colville by canoe with a few supplies and seven sled dogs. Upon arrival, he found about

A Passion for Wilderness

Margaret and Bern Will Brown

twenty-five Indians living nearby, so he pitched his tent and began erecting a mission building from the black spruce trees which grow around the lake.

For the next several years, with the help of the local Indians, he helped build log homes for each family residing in the settlement. His first duty which he diligently pursued was to the Indians and to his church.

In 1971, the Vatican issued a dispensation from celibacy to Father Brown, so that he could marry Margaret. This remarkable Eskimo girl was one of fourteen children and grew up on the Arctic coast east of Paulatuk. Her father was born in Texas and

A Passion for Wilderness

spent his life as a trapper while her mother is of Eskimo stock. As a teenager, she was sent to Inuvik to attend school.

The Bishop flew in to marry Bern and Margaret in the delightful log church, known as 'Our Lady of the Snows' mission, where Bern still carries on as pastor. The beautiful, large mural at the front of the sanctuary depicting 'Our Lady of the Snows' was done by Bern.

In recent years, more log buildings have been built and the settlement is now home to about sixty Indians who still partly live off the land and use both dog teams and snowmobiles to run their trap lines.

"There are six girls canoeing your route," said Bern. "They left here yesterday and you'll probably overtake them within a day or two."

"Is that right!" I replied with surprise. "We expected to be the only ones to do the Anderson this year."

"They're all eighteen year olds except one," Bern continued. "Some of them are most likely still in school. I hope you will stay with them, at least until they get through Falcon Canyon. I'm worried that unless you do, they may not make it. They looked so inexperienced."

"How did they happen to come way up here?" I asked.

"Well, there's this fellow, Mick Smuk from St. Paul, Minnesota. He went down the river in 1981 with two kayaks and a male and female companion. He was a counsellor for a girls' summer camp near Minneapolis. I can't help but worry about them,"

A Passion for Wilderness

Colville Lake Lodge

Bern commented.

To ease his mind a little, I added, "They'll probably make it all right."

Following lunch, Bern showed us around the settlement. There is a store serving the area, known as Kapami Co-op Ltd. We visited the conference building and the fine museum containing both Indian and Eskimo (Inuit) artifacts, many of which we had not seen anywhere before.

Above the museum, Bern took us into his well lighted studio where we enjoyed looking at some of his wonderful oil paintings, of which he produces forty-five to fifty each year. His paintings are in great demand as he is considered to be one of Canada's foremost northern artists. Just as Remington painted the historical West in America in the nineteenth century, today Bern Will Brown is painting historical scenes of Canada's northern frontier. He is putting on canvas the beautiful homeland of the Inuit and Indian, and capturing their old way of life which is so rapidly disappearing. His paintings hang today in museum and government offices in Yellowknife and Ottawa and in many private collections across both the United States and Canada.

Next, as the conversation continued to flow, we walked over to look at some of Margaret's dogs. She and Bern have developed a breed of fine white malemutes, one of which was about to give birth to a litter of puppies. Each malemute had its own house, also constructed of logs.

Then we went into the underground refrigerator room where the temperature remains at 22° Fahrenheit, the year around. To construct it, Bern had dug into the hillside permafrost to a depth of thirty-five feet. Several quarters of caribou and piles of frozen trout and whitefish were being stored inside.

All of the buildings in the settlement including the Lodge's outhouse were constructed from the black spruce trees around the lake. "We just finished varnishing everything last week," he said. "We clean and varnish all of the buildings inside and out, every spring."

"So that's why everything looks so shining clean," I replied.

Margaret prepared a wonderful dinner for us consisting of several of her specialties, including a caribou roast. Everything was delicious. Then, as the visiting continued, Bern brought out a guest autograph book for us to sign. Handing it to Darrell, he said, "I'd like to have you and Debbie sign this one. Clate, I'd like you to sign in another book." He soon brought out his 'Special Guest' autograph book and handed it to me, saying, "This is the one I'd like you to autograph."

Looking at it and seeing who some of his earlier guests had been, I said, "I don't think I rate this one. Are you certain you want my signature in here?"

"I definitely do," he replied. "You are our special guest today, just as those others were in the past."

So, I added my signature below many prominent people, such as Prince Charles of England, former Canadian Prime Minister Pierre Trudeau and Commissioner Stuart M. Hodgson of Northwest Territories.

Later we went over our maps of the Ross and Anderson Rivers. Bern and Margaret took twenty-seven days in 1976 to canoe those 410 miles. He marked on the maps certain things we should watch for such as the rapids, waterfalls, canyon, old buildings, the location of the old Hudson's Bay Company's Fort Anderson and a hillside made up of sea fossils.

Just before 9:00 that evening, we said our goodbyes to the Browns, after expressing our gratitude for all of their hospitality. Walking down to the dock with us, Bern said, "I would like to be going with you." Then, after taking our photos, he added, "Be sure to send me a report of the trip. I'll be waiting to hear from you."

"Will do," I replied. With that, we were underway, paddling west around the tip of the peninsula upon which the settlement and landing strip are located. It had been a perfect day. The surface of the lake was calm as we turned the point of land and headed toward the east shore, with Darrell in the Monarch, and Deb and me in the Wenonah. Fish constantly rippled the surface. Arctic terns, gulls and ducks chattered and squawked in the distance and occasionally came drifting by. Already we were enjoying the 'Spell of the North.' It was a perfect picture.

Clayton Klein

BEYOND THE GREAT BEAR

Chapter 2

THE ROSS RIVER

Two hours later, with aching arms, we found a fine place to set up our first camp, and soon had our tents erected. Darrell and Deb would use his Eureka, and I the old pup tent which the two of us had used while descending the Kazan and Thelon Rivers. Air mattresses were soon inflated, with sleeping bags unrolled inside the tents, and only a few minutes before midnight, we began to relax around a friendly campfire. "The sun still shines,"

A Passion for Wilderness

I commented, "but it's getting pretty low."

"It must be nearing its lowest point for tonight," Darrell replied. "Bern said that it will next drop below the horizon on July 19."

After giving it a little thought, I replied, "That means, here they have about fifty-six days each summer when the sun doesn't set."

"Yes. I guess so. In that case, there must be fifty-six days around Christmas when the sun never appears above the horizon," he replied.

While we sipped on cups of hot chocolate, Deb remarked, "The Browns are certainly nice people."

"Sure are!" Darrell replied.

"Those paintings of Bern's are almost unbelievable," I added. "I don't understand how anyone could ever learn to paint so well."

"Me either!" said Deb. "He certainly is one talented artist. And he's equally good at other things, too. How about all of those log buildings?"

"That is amazing," Darrell replied. "And, I understand the settlement is the only all log cabin village still in use in Northwest Territories. Bern certainly lives an interesting and active life up here."

"I don't understand how any one man can accomplish so much," I added. "He's the missionary to the community and he's a writer. I've read an excellent article he wrote for **The Beaver** about the Hareskin Indians. He's also a trapper, a hunter, a photographer and a dog-musher. Besides that, he's an aircraft pilot and a member of

A Passion for Wilderness

The Explorers Club."

"Certainly one outstanding man, that's for sure," Deb added. "And Margaret is likewise an amazing woman."

Our discussion of the Browns and the day's happenings continued until nearly 1:00 in the morning. Finally, after writing in our journals, we called it a day.

A strong wind picked up out of the northwest within the next couple of hours. Making an early morning scientific sleeping bag analysis of the weather, we could hear a heavy surf crashing onto the sandy shore. When we finally rolled out in mid-forenoon, the temperature stood at 45°. The grey lake was covered with whitecaps. Rain was falling along the opposite side of the lake.

Colville is a body of water which lies at eight hundred feet above sea level. It is twenty-five miles long and fifteen miles in width, with its outlet in the northeast corner. Our plan was to follow the eastern shore to the outlet, but we were wind-bound and would not be able to proceed until there was some change.

A campfire was soon going again for warmth and, following breakfast, we each went for a walk to explore along the shore and back to a small marshy lake. As it turned out, what we should have been doing was to have installed the spray cover on the Wenonah. We had put the cover on the Monarch earlier, so Darrell could get out and dip a kettle of water for coffee and dishes.

Later, with snacks for lunch, we each enjoyed a cup or two of Labrador tea, a hot drink which is easy to prepare. One needs a pot of hot water, into which you drop the new growth from the tips of the Labrador tea plants. Two-thirds of a cup of loosely packed new growth is plenty for a two quart pot of tea. Let it simmer for about five minutes and you have a delicious hot beverage.

By mid-afternoon, the velocity of the wind began to drop and we decided to break camp. Soon a gentle breeze was blowing from the southwest and, as we shoved off, Darrell commented, "We should be able to make it to the outlet before midnight with that nice breeze helping us along."

But that was not to be. Within fifteen minutes after launch, the wind suddenly swung back into the northwest and soon, with increasing velocity, spray from the whitecaps began splashing over us from starboard.

Darrell, in the Monarch, was having fun, riding over and through the waves. The troughs between the crests continued to grow deeper and deeper. At times, he would drop completely out of sight, except for his head, before again riding back up and over the ensuing roller.

Deb and I struggled on for two or three miles as water continued to build up inside the Wenonah. "Darrell," I shouted, "we can't take too much more of this! Do you suppose we will soon come to a break in the shoreline where we can pull in?"

Glancing at the map in its waterproof envelope, held on the deck in front of him with an expansion cord, he called back, "There's no sign of any bays, islands or peninsulas anywhere along here."

"We have to get to shore soon," I yelled.

A Passion for Wilderness

"We'll have to run in on that beach up there."

"O.K.," came the reply. "We're not making much progress anyway, quartering into this gusty wind."

We soon turned downwind, heading for an open beach. "Be prepared to hit the beach running," I called to Deb. "And pull the canoe as far up as you can."

"Ready in the bow!" came the reply.

Three more powerful strokes and a huge wave broke over the stern just before we hit shore, soaking me from the neck down. Jumping into the surf, just as the bow touched bottom, both of us pulled but there was no way to budge the canoe with its load of water. Throwing the paddles ashore, rapidly we grabbed packsacks and equipment, moving them up on the beach. About then, Darrell arrived and within a couple of minutes, the worst was over but all hands were soaked.

Quickly Darrell moved up into the trees to find a place out of the wind. Shortly he had a fire going as Deb and I rounded up more dry fuel. Soon the tents were up and we all put on dry clothing in an attempt to keep warm.

A little later, glancing at the thermometer, the mercury stood at 42° and the camp fire was our constant companion that evening as we reorganized and began to dry our wet gear.

Wind velocity dropped so we were up and out of camp before 8:00 the following morning. It was good to be moving north again. This time, however, spray covers were all in place, where they would remain. We had decided to each have a turn in the Monarch, and this was my day.

A Passion for Wilderness

It was a fine day to be on the lake. Pushing along about one hundred yards off shore, I noticed a large spruce stump that had been sawed off about twelve feet above the ground. Several green branches remained on the stump below the cut.

"Look at that tall stump over there," I called, pointing to the right.

"Wow!" said Deb. "A tall Hareskin must have cut that one!"

"Bern must have cut that tree in the winter while standing on top of a snow bank," Darrell replied.

"Certainly looks like he did," I added. "The northeast wind could easily build up a ten foot snowbank where it drifts over that steep slope, just behind."

Around 1:30 in the afternoon, we thought we saw an Indian encampment but as shore was about a half mile to starboard, we continued on. We could also distinguish three upturned canoes. An hour later, while taking a leg stretcher, after rounding a point, the six girls from Minnesota showed up. It was their camp we had passed. We exchanged 'hello's!' with them from two or three hundred feet away. Pulling on their pea green ponchos just as rain began to fall, they continued on toward the outlet. We did likewise, trailing along behind. They were paddling with power and within a few minutes had disappeared around an island.

Before 5:00 we arrived at the vacant outpost camp of Colville Lake Lodge. It was time for another shore break. Stepping up on the dock, we were promptly attacked by three arctic terns

A Passion for Wilderness

Those birds were certainly unhappy to see us, scolding all the while and diving, time after time. They struck our heads with force enough to knock our hats off. Their attack continued all the while we remained near the dock. "There is no question," said Darrell, "these birds have a nest or little ones nearby."

On a hill, just behind Bern and Margaret's fine log cabin outpost camp, a United States flag flew from the top of the tall flag pole. We puzzled over that all evening, wondering why a U. S. flag was flying there. It was one more special treat for us provided by Bern Will Brown.

With more bumps on our heads by the terns, we soon moved on, leaving Colville Lake. Suddenly we were in a fast flowing stream and, within a mile, were shooting our first white water. The Ross River was a delightful change. It appeared to be alive with fish. Grayling were surfacing at every ripple. Ducks and solitary sandpipers were now scolding as we moved through their territory. Bonaparte gulls were feeding on the small fry. In all, there were about three miles of excellent canoeing before entering Ketaniatue Lake. There the rain really began to fall.

We had been looking for a campsite but could find nothing. Finally, I sighted a hill along the northwest shore. Deciding to check it out, I scooted across the lake and found an old Indian camp near the hilltop and we soon settled in for some rest as the steady rain continued to fall.

The weather kept us in camp until mid-afternoon the next day. Two downpours hit while we paddled the remaining twelve miles of Ketaniatue. (The name comes from the Hareskin translation meaning 'the narrows lake'.) Paddling through the narrows near mid-lake, a bald eagle and a pair of whistling swans were observed.

With the inclement weather continuing, we again set up camp at the extreme east end of Ketaniatue, as we were not anxious to battle a rapids in the rain. Our map showed that, in the next two and one-half miles, the Ross drops twenty-three feet before flowing into Lugententue (frozen fish lake), giving us an indication of the strength of those rapids. Back in 1963, a party of three in two kayaks met with an accident there, when one of the crafts broke a rib and ripped its skin.

With great anticipation next morning, we entered the river and cautiously were sucked into the fast water. Much to our surprise, we sped around bend after bend, with Darrell leading the way in the Monarch. The river water level was high and all conditions were perfect including the scenery as a brown bear scurried up over the right river bank. Then on a gravel bar at a sharp bend to the right, a big tan wolf stood looking at us. We were so busy on the paddles that it was impossible to shoot a picture without crashing into the gravel bar. Then swinging back to the left, a white wolf ran up the riverbank and looked back at us. In less than ten minutes, we had descended the rapids and entered Lugententue.

Rounding a peninsula after entering the lake, more whistling swans appeared. Solitary sandpipers were nesting on every point and island, as we moved across the lake.

Below Lugententue it was another twenty miles of the Ross, much of which is a swift stream, alive with wildlife. There were more bald eagles, terns and gulls feeding on the fish. An otter put on a show for us and at each riffle families of ducks appeared as the mother often tried her broken wing trick, attempting to lure us away from the ducklings. Common loons wimpered to one another in between their prolonged dives beneath the surface of the water.

Camping time found us on a point of land near the outlet of an unnamed lake where the river turns south for a couple of miles. There is where we learned from experience, that it is unwise to camp in a territory claimed by a solitary sandpiper. The bird remained within forty feet of us, continuing its shrill *weet-weet-weet-weet* all night long.

Heading south next morning, we anticipated three sets of rapids before the river once more swings to the northwest. A six-foot drop in elevation was shown on our 1:50,000 scale map. Once more no rapids appeared and, after six miles of paddling, we entered another unnamed lake, sixteen miles in length. Swinging west out of that lake around a large area of low muskeg, we finally came to those three sets of rapids. The map makers had misplaced them by about twenty-two miles. Furthermore, Sokatue Lake is shown on the Niwelin Lake map as being three feet higher in elevation than is the sixteen-mile-long, unnamed lake upstream, above those rapids.

A Passion for Wilderness

Camp just above Sokotue Lake

Just before entering Sokatue Lake, we again encamped near the foot of an esker along the left side of the river. Following supper, it was a two-mile walk along the esker and from up there the scene was magnificent. Looking to the northwest across Sokatue, we could see the old and deserted Indian settlement of Soka and the river channel winding its way on west into Niwelin Lake.

Back in camp a weasel scurried along the riverbank, and returned a few minutes later with head held high, carrying a brown lemming in its mouth. Common loons were even more vocal than normal. "Those birds must be trying to tell us

167

something. If I understand them correctly," I said, "we can expect a rough and windy day tomorrow."

"That's the way it sounds," Deb replied.

A strong wind from the northwest flapped and rattled the tents throughout the night and a blowing snowstorm was in progress as we rolled out next morning. The temperature stood at 32°. Right after breakfast, it was back into the sacks for protection from the cold. The windchill factor was hovering between zero and five above. By lunch time in mid-afternoon, the mercury had risen to 34° and the snow showers had moved elsewhere. It was impossible to keep warm by the roaring campfire, so we were soon once more inside our sleeping bags with our clothes on.

Around 5:00 as the wind continued, we heard an aircraft. Sticking our heads out of the tent flaps, we discovered a Cessna 185 circling around. Before we could get out of the tents, it had splashed down in the river in front of camp. Nosing in toward the bank, the plane's door opened and a man called out, "Are you the Klein party?"

"Yes," I answered, hoping it was not some bad news from home.

"Would you come down here?" the man continued. "There's someone on the radio who wants to talk with you."

Sliding down the steep twenty-foot sandbank to the river, I shook hands with Reggie Pfeifer. He had been sent in by Bern to make sure we were all O.K. I chatted with Bern for a few minutes on the radio. He also asked about the progress of the six girls. I replied, "We think they are somewhere ahead of us. They passed us near the outlet of Colville Lake and we haven't seen anything of them since." Thanking Bern for checking on us, Reggie then snapped off the radio.

There were two passengers in the plane, a father and son, Eric and Stuart Bodtker of Midway, British Columbia. The pilot and owner of the Cessna was Reggie Pfeifer from Victoria, B. C. The three came up the bank to meet Deb and Darrell, who by that time had another fire blazing. Trying to keep warm, we visited and sipped hot coffee. The three were on holiday to do some fishing. Their report was 'lots of lunkers,' wherever they had tried. They were soon ready to leave in an attempt to locate the six girls, before returning to their fishing camp on some unknown lake.

The temperature had risen to 40 degrees as we took a few snacks including a handful of gorp and crawled back into the tents as the wind howled on. It had been our first 'zero' day of progress.

Early Thursday morning wind velocity was more reasonable and came out of the west. With a good start, we crossed Sokatue and slid down the three miles of river into Niwelin Lake. By then we were facing another rising wind. Digging ahead to the west, eventually we turned north keeping just offshore, riding parallel to the waves. Frequently water rolled across the spray covers. Arriving at the narrows, we could find no place to safely take a much needed shore break, so we struggled on, finally completing the two-mile crossing to the west shore.

A Passion for Wilderness

It was Deb's day in the Monarch. We were all pretty well beat but it was so good to have some protection from the shore that we continued on to Niwelin's outlet. There, for the first time, Darrell strung up his fishing rod to secure a fish for supper. Hooking a laker on the first cast, we put it on the stringer. Within ten minutes, he had caught two more and Deb one. That's where we called a halt to the fishing. Those trout were of uniform size, each weighing in between five and six pounds. Certainly all the fish we could possibly use in the next few days.

The time was 7:15. It had been a long and difficult day paddling into the wind. We were not only tired, but hungry and ready to find a campsite. The area around the outlet of Niwelin is low and marshy. We decided to set up camp at the first opportunity and have our fish fry. "Surely," said Darrell, "we'll find a spot down near the falls."

"That would be cool. Whoops! I didn't mean that. I'm cold enough right now," Deb replied. "But it would be great to camp near those falls."

We kept moving along, and within three minutes could hear the roar of the waterfall ahead. As we approached, we watched closely for either a campsite or some sign of a trail leading around the falls. There was nothing, not even a blaze on a tree. The river narrowed and sped between rock walls, disappearing from view. Our map showed that the Ross swings to the right a short distance below the falls, so at the last possible moment we put ashore to starboard.

A Passion for Wilderness

Pulling the canoes up into the willows, we each shouldered a pack. Carrying something in each hand and in single file, we started up over a knoll. Trees and brush were extremely thick. No trail could be found, but the line of least resistance led us away from the river as the roar of the falls faded in the distance. The far side of the knoll turned out to be a sheer rock bluff with a drop of about 60 feet. By going still farther from the river, we managed to work our way to the foot of the cliff. There we crossed a brushy ravine and climbed up over another ridge of rocks as we tried to get back to the river. Finally it came into view in the distance.

There was no portage trail. At the start, Darrell had been leading the way with me close behind, while Deb brought up the rear. Now, however, I found myself bringing up the rear and even having difficulty keeping my two kids in sight. I was beat! Finally we arrived at the river and dropped our loads.

"We made a mistake," said Darrell as he bent down to dip a cup full of water from the river. "The trail has to be on the other side." Deb and I also enjoyed a cold drink from the cup as we caught our breaths, and Darrell continued. "It's impossible to bring the canoes down through all of that tangle of brush and over those bluffs. Let's pile our gear here where it will show from across the river, then go back to the canoes, cross the river and look for a trail over there."

"Sounds like our best bet," I replied.

Retracing our footsteps back to the canoes, we

A Passion for Wilderness

soon nosed out into the current. By paddling with power upstream, we were able to ferry across the river and work our way into the willows hanging out from the left bank. Soon, Darrell was scouting for the trail along the edge of the hill. "Maybe this is it," he called. "I don't see a trail but here's some old axe marks on a stump."

Unloading the remaining gear, we pulled the canoes out of the water and started over what turned out to be the ancient and seldom used trail. It was rough going! Again the trail led us well away from the river, and even though we were on high ground, the terrain was a wet, spongy muskeg everywhere. We sank halfway to our knees with nearly every step. In reality it was not a trail, but eventually we managed to pick our way through the forest and back to the river's edge at a place where we could see our packs piled on the opposite side of the river.

Returning to pick up the empty canoes, the stringer of trout and the remaining gear, we tried to find a shorter route by following the high rocky ledge near the river. It proved to be impossible as a tangle of trees, deadfalls and brush prevented us from even getting close to the edge of the cliff. Much to our disappointment we did not manage to get a look at those falls.

There was no suitable camp site anywhere in the vicinity. While Darrell and Deb took the Wenonah across the river to pick up the gear, I loaded the Monarch. Finally at twenty minutes after ten, we shoved off down river, desperately needing a camp site and some supper.

A Passion for Wilderness

We descended another three to four miles of fast flowing river and entered the grassy, weedy bay at the south of Gassend lake. Still we found no place to camp. Low brushy tundra was all we could see. It was in desperation that we finally climbed up on a boggy bank of peat moss a few feet above the lake and set up the tents.

Cleaning the four trout, three of which were boiled for future meals, took extra time. At midnight we were eating supper under heavily overcast skies. The temperature had risen to 48°, bringing out the insects in full force.

With our camp in that muskeg bog, and no trees for protection from the wind, little did we know what we were in for. Rain set in before morning. The downpour continued until 3:00 in the afternoon. We had a quick breakfast of coffee, an orange and a cup of oatmeal. That was it for the day as rain soon returned and the strong northwest wind whipped on. The temperature had been 38° in the morning, but continued to fall as the day wore on. The only place to keep warm and dry was inside the sleeping bags.

Saturday morning, July 20, I rolled out well rested at 5:15 thinking we might possibly pick up and move out of our miserable bog, but I stepped into winter. There was more than an inch of wet snow covering everything and more windblown snow was coming at us. The temperature stood at 31°, so it was back into the sack once more.

Shortly after 9:00 the storm began to subside. We were out for our first substantial meal since Thursday evening's fish dinner. Wind velocity

A Passion for Wilderness

began to taper off and we soon broke camp to paddle the six miles north to the outlet of Gassend Lake. While doing so, we crossed the 68th parallel. There are several fine beaches in the vicinity of the outlet which would have made excellent campsites.

Re-entering the river, we were again in picturesque country. The Ross is certainly a beautiful, wild, free flowing river. It was rapids after rapids around every bend. A pair of peregrine falcons were nesting in some cliffs. We enjoyed and photographed a mother loon with a baby on her back and another white tundra wolf. There were more swans, ducks, terns and eagles. We were able to canoe right on down into the Anderson River by 5:00 in the afternoon and an hour later found a good campsite in a clump of trees. Rain showers continued off and on throughout the day but it seemed much warmer in those trees.

In all, we had taken nine days to descend the 148 miles of the Ross River. In that distance, there was only one portage required and we had dropped 360 feet nearer to sea level.

Clayton   Klein

BEYOND   THE   GREAT   BEAR

Chapter 3

THE   ANDERSON   RIVER

The Anderson more than doubles in size below its confluence with the Ross. Now we were on a sizeable river. With the rain still falling, we slept in on Sunday morning. By noon the mercury stood at 36°. With breakfast out of the way, we headed on even though intermittent showers persisted.

An intersecting limestone ledge soon appeared bringing us to Sulfur Rapids, where, after looking

it over, we decided to make a short portage on the
left. It may have been possible to shoot this one
or line it down but we wanted to 'play it safe.'

Several other drops occur within the next few
miles. Stopping above each to look them over, each
time we were able to shoot through successfully.
We relied heavily on Darrell, a proven expert at
reading a river. He led the way in the Monarch. We
would watch for his signal as to whether a rapids
looked shootable, "so follow me," or "we'd better
stop and look this one over." He always requested
that either Deb or I come along to help him make
the decision.

"Rain keeps getting on my glasses," he said,
"and it impairs my vision. I tried it with my
glasses off, but I can't see very well that way
either."

"It's difficult on such a dark, rainy day," I
replied. "Sure hope it clears up soon. The
thought of entering Falcon Canyon in this poor
visibility really worries me." Neither did we
relish the thought of being caught in the canyon
and not being able to find a campsite.

Moving on, we soon arrived at the final bend
above the canyon. There we decided to camp. It
had rained all afternoon and, with the 36° to 40°
temperature, we were cold, wet and miserable.

"Maybe," I said as we unloaded the canoes,
"we'll have a sunny day tomorrow."

"Let's hope so," Deb replied. "We need more
light than this if we're going to get good pictures
of this stupendous scenery."

"It's impossible to properly read the rapids in

such poor light," Darrell added.

A roaring campfire and a good supper dispelled the gloom. The rain stopped falling and we were soon drying our wet pants, boots and socks near the fire. This was becoming an almost daily ritual. Each evening around the blaze, we would drive stakes and turn wet boots upside down over the stakes. Then it was a matter of turning the boots from side to side to keep them from burning while the heat dried them out. Socks and gloves steamed as they also dried near the fire. Sleeping equipment was carried inside plastic liners in the packs and was only aired when conditions were favorable.

While holding a pair of socks to dry near the blaze, Darrell said, "Those girls must be miles ahead of us by now. I'm wondering if we'll ever catch them." Nine days had passed since they disappeared ahead of us in Colville Lake. We had found not a trace of them since.

"Don't know," I replied. "We may never catch them."

"Maybe we passed them in one of those big lakes on the Ross."

Next morning, under heavily overcast skies and 36° of temperature, we entered Falcon Canyon. The Anderson drops 32 feet within four miles as it swirls down the canyon. Continuing our regular procedure of walking ahead to scout each drop before proceeding, we moved forward. Only one time did we choose to make a short portage over a rocky ledge. The canyon continually bends one way or the other with a rapids around every curve.

A Passion for Wilderness

Falcon Canyon

Sheer cliffs drop to the water's edge and the scenery was indeed 'stupendous.' Peregrine falcons nesting on high ledges along the rock walls circled overhead, uttering their alarming call.

At 1:30, shooting down some fast water where the canyon bends to the left, we came upon three upturned canoes on the rocky shore. Swinging around in the eddy below, we put ashore. There were the six young ladies. One named Maude Patnode, the 25-year-old group leader, had just rolled out. She soon told us that a girl named Kim Benson had nearly drowned in the fast water there on Saturday evening. They had been lining their canoes down the rapids which we had just shot, and Kim on the stern rope was swept off her feet into the frigid torrent. They had fished her out of the eddy below and set up camp right there. Rapidly they put her into some dry clothing and sleeping bag, but by then the cold water had taken its toll. She went into hypothermic shock. "We worked over her and did body to body warming in the sleeping bag. Eventually we got her warmed up." Maude continued, "But we had to lay over another day."

"How is she now?" I asked.

"She's all right again and we're soon going to break camp."

By then, Kris Stone and Karen Pick appeared. Deb broke out a package of Oreo cookies and passed them around and, as we chatted, Jennifer Cowger joined the group. Speaking to Maude, I asked, "Do you happen to know a fellow from St. Paul by the name of Mick Smuk?"

She nodded, "Yes."

At that, the other young ladies giggled and a couple of them simultaneously replied, "Yes. She knows him real well!" Then more giggles and grins.

Quickly changing the subject, Maude asked, "Did Reggie Pfeifer spend very much time with you last Wednesday?"

"No. Maybe about a half hour," I replied. "It was just too cold to stand out in that wind any longer. Where did he find you?"

"We were weathered in along the east shore of Niwelin Lake. They stayed with us for several hours."

"We were beginning to wonder if they would ever leave," Karen added.

A Passion for Wilderness

Darrell leads the way through the rapids

Just as we were about to head on, Kim and Tara Fahey appeared just in time to get the last of the cookies. Kim did have a very close call. Everyone was happy that she was once more ready to travel. The young ladies planned to be canoeing until August 15 and wanted to paddle and pack all the way back into Inuvik.

Later we learned the five young women canoeing with Maude were all from Minnesota except Jennifer Cowger of Urbana, Illinois. The other girls were Kim Benson of Moundsville, Tara Fahey of Mendota Heights, Karen Pick of Falcon Heights and Kris Stone of Minneapolis. Their trip, known as the Widjiwagan Voyageurs Expedition, is the culmination of "Y" camping and only five women are invited to participate each year. They are selected for the trip based on their previous camping experiences.

Their trip ended in Sitidji Lake east of Inuvik on August 17 because the connecting creek was completely dried up.   They were flown the last forty miles, according to Karen Pick, "by some friendly people who operate Antler Aviation." These young women are to be congratulated for their skill, persistence and determination.   They hung in there when the going was far from easy. They have already achieved more than most people do in an entire lifetime.   They are true explorers of the north.

Now, back to our journey.   We shoved off and soon broke out of the canyon, but still had plenty of interesting river, with several riffles and rapids to negotiate.   There was a short portage just before the river makes its major turn to the west.

Then, hearing a plane, we looked up and it was Reggie Pfeifer heading directly at us.   Skimming past only 30 or 40 feet above our heads, he continued on south where the six young ladies would certainly be in view.

Three miles to the west,   we camped above a high bank on the left.   It had been a good day   on the river even though overcast, cold and windy. While drying boots and socks, Darrell reported, "We progressed twenty-two miles, and have descended another 145 feet nearer to sea level since morning."

Sometime around midnight, peeking out of the tents, we saw three canoes with the young women moving down the river.

Miraculously, next morning the sun was shining in a picture book sky. It would be a great day for canoeing. Around noon we quietly passed the tent camp, with the three upturned canoes but no sign of life. When we were well down river, Deb turned and, speaking with a grin, said, "The girls will probably think we are still behind them."

"They certainly do like to sleep in," I replied.

In early afternoon it had warmed up to 47°. Three hours later we arrived at the Limestone Steps which are a series of rapids and a waterfall as the river swings first to the right and then to the left. Here, mosquitoes and black flies gave us a real workout. They must have been especially hungry as they attacked relentlessly. Spraying with 'Off,' we moved the packs and canoes across nearly a mile-and-a-quarter of tundra to a backwater below the falls. This was the longest portage along the way and two-and-a-half hours later, we were able to shove off downriver once more. Then came still more shootable rapids and, to close out the day's exciting run, we enjoyed chasing a moulting swan downriver for several miles. The bird kept up a continuing "squawk" at nearly every stroke of our paddles, but never once attempted to go ashore.

Wednesday, July 24 dawned bright and clear. In the first hour we lined down to and portaged Flatrock Rapids where the river drops over another limestone ledge. Then it was on and on with high hills on either side.

Lunchtime found us enjoying gorgeous scenery

A Passion for Wilderness

Debbie at head of Limestone Steps

at a place known as the Limestone Towers where a nesting pair of peregrine falcons entertained us. Later passing a gravel bar, we startled a bull caribou with huge antlers.   Jumping to his feet, he splashed to shore through shallow water.

Bern Will Brown had told us to watch for a fossil bluff on the right.   We took a leg stretcher at the place he had marked on our maps.   It was most impressive.   The entire bluff more than a hundred feet in height and at least a quarter mile long is gradually eroding into the river.   The entire hill is one gigantic pile of sea fossils which were once at the bottom of a tropical sea.   For the next thirty minutes, we entertained ourselves, searching for small pieces to carry home with us. Looking closely, we found the bluff to be made up of several varieties of coral, clam shells and numerous other varieties all fossilized and held in place by permafrost. For our collection, we scratched out a number of complete tiny clams, petrified in their shells.

Several miles downstream we set up camp on a flat rock ledge as another storm headed our way. The place was about five miles upstream of Juniper Rapids. Huge eroded gravelly hillsides towered above on both sides adding to the solitude.

Rain set in shortly after we crawled into the sacks and continued until breakfast time. Popping out, we quickly broke camp as everything was soaking wet and getting wetter on the flat rock ledge. The rain persisted as we moved down to Juniper Rapids. Darrell looked it over and reported, "We can shoot it but will have to thread the needle, hitting it in precisely the right spot, just to the right of the big rock."

He led the way in the Monarch and we followed only about eighty feet behind. He disappeared over the first drop, then shot along the edge of a couple of subsequent standing waves. Deb and I were already committed. There was no turning back in the rushing surge. Could we hit the same spot? Oh! But we tried! Sliding to the right of the big rock, I realized the bow was slightly too far to the left. "Draw right!" I yelled. Shooting over the drop, we were unable to bring the bow back to the precise heading, and crash! The Wenonah shuddered and slid, scraping over the lower ledge and right into the center of a huge standing wave. The spray cover was what saved the day for us as we floundered through the standing waves and scraped over another rock. We had survived.

The rain refused to let up and we were unable to find a place to set up a shelter. Moving on, the three of us were soaking wet, cold and hungry. Finally, in early afternoon, we could take no more. Climbing a steep bank, we hacked out a little spot between two black spruces and put up a tarp for shelter. Soon, in front of our makeshift lean-to, Darrell had a fire going. For the next couple of hours, we hugged that fire while standing under the edge of the tarp, trying to warm ourselves, dry wet clothing and take on a little food. Even though I had worn my rain suit the entire time, my jacket and shirt were dripping wet when I took them off.

A couple of hours later, we were up to moving on in hopes of finding a decent camping place, even though lighter showers now prevailed. On downstream, wolves howled in the distance. Later four of them watched from a hillside as we passed below.

The skies once more began to clear as we set up camp on another huge gravel bar. Drying our wet things required several hours as the welcome fire consumed piles of fuel. Following a big supper, Darrell baked a loaf of corn meal bread. We even devoured half of that, along with butter, while it was still hot.

Lounging around the fire, we discussed our situation. Our original plan was to paddle into Tuktoyaktuk after crossing Liverpool Bay. Two weeks had passed since leaving Colville Lake and it was still another 160 miles to Krekovick Landing at the mouth of the Anderson.

"As far as I'm concerned," Darrell said, "I would just as soon terminate this trip when we get to the Canadian Wildlife Service Cabin at Krekovick Landing, if there's anyone around."

"Sounds good to me," I replied.

"Me too," Deb responded. "I will have had plenty of canoeing by then. Somewhere it has to be summer. I'm anxious to get there and warm up these cold feet of mine."

"That will save us about a hundred miles. It would probably take another week, if we continue on to Tuk."

"If the Ranger isn't at the station when we get to Krekovick," Darrell continued, "we can paddle on out to the Dew Line station at Nicholson Point. That's only another twenty-two miles or so — a day's travel if the weather is good."

Friday was another very fine day. "Maybe we're finally going to have a streak of good weather," Darrell said, as he rolled the tent.

"Could be," I replied. "We're certainly due for a break."

"That'll bring out the insects," Deb added, "but I prefer insects to what we were having yesterday at this time."

Maintaining a steady pace, by noon we were passing the confluence with the Carnwath River, one of the Anderson's major tributaries. The hills along this section of the river reach up to six hundred feet in many places.

Small groups of caribou grazed and trotted along

the shores. Whistling swans again swam ahead leading us downriver. Red-throated and Arctic loons entertained us, flying along and splashing down in the water in the distance.

Basking in the sun as we paddled along was truly enjoyable. Suddenly the John Denver tune, 'Sunshine on My Shoulders', came to mind. Little by little we recalled the words. Soon, with canoes in close proximity, we were singing —

'Sunshine on my shoulders makes me happy
Sunshine in my eyes can make me cry
Sunshine on the water looks to lovely
Sunshine almost always makes me high.'

Camping time found us setting up near the padlocked Canadian Water Resources shack, to enjoy another period of rest and relaxation. It had been a 70° day and the only time during the entire journey when it warmed to more than 58°. We had progressed another thirty-eight miles.

More rain was falling as we headed out next morning and continued until early afternoon. The high point of the day came when we located the ruins of old Fort Anderson atop a fifty foot gravel bank on the east side of the river. The site is marked by a wedge-shaped clearing which extends about three hundred feet back from the river. The entrance to the fort, still traceable on the ground, is about forty feet from the present eroded riverbank, with only a few decaying timbers visible. The outline of the picket palisades still shows at each of the four corners. The perimeter of the old trading post was 125 feet across the front and about 115 feet along its sides.

Fort Anderson was built during the summer of 1861 by the Hudson's Bay Company, under the direction of Roderick MacFarlane, who was then manager of the Company's post in Fort Good Hope. From here, the Company served the Hareskins from the south and the Eskimos from the north until, following the death of sixty-four sled dogs in 1864 due to distemper and the death of many Eskimo hunters due to a major outbreak of scarlet fever in 1865, the fort was closed. Small black spruce trees and grass interspersed with fireweed now grow where Fort Anderson once stood.

An hour after leaving the historic site, the rain let up and a strong northwest wind soon picked up to gale force. With the river flowing toward the driving wind, we had our work cut out for us. Within an hour, further progress became impossible. We were blown off the river on an island where we were forced to wait out the cold wind. Huddling around our fire, we watched a grey wolf trot along the shoreline.

A few ruins of trappers' cabins still stand near the river, one of which came into view the following morning as we moved on. The wind had died while we slept so we were out early in 36° temperature. Seeing an old cabin reminded me, Bern Will Brown had told us, "At one time about forty-five years ago, there were about twenty white men trapping along the Anderson. The last to leave was Tom Lessard who moved to Aklavik in 1955. George Clark opened a trading post near the

A Passion for Wilderness

Carnwath in the mid-1960's, with Billy Cockney in charge to serve the native marten trappers working out of Inuvik. The death of one of Billy's children, plus difficulty in supplying the post, soon closed it."

Before noon, we crossed the 69th parallel, the first time we had been this far north. Several groups of caribou were again seen moving along, most of which swam across the river. By pushing along until 8:00 in the evening, we set up camp at Windy Bend.

Then came more rain and it was noon next day by the time we completed Windy Bend. There, as our old nemesis, the cold north wind, whipped up the river with thirty mile per hour gusts, we realized that Windy Bend was indeed well named.

Caribou were becoming more and more plentiful. On our earlier journeys, we had paddled through the Beverly and Bathurst herds of barren land caribou. Now, however, we were in the territory of the Bluenose herd. Nearly every time we came upon a group moving along the shore, they would look us over, then run ahead and attempt to swim across the river. Consequently, we learned that by paddling with power toward a group, we could often move right in amongst them. Many groups were small while others contained more than a hundred animals.

At times, as they crossed the river, we would zero in on a single bull or a small group and chase them ashore. At times, we could maneuver in close enough to slap them on the rump with a paddle. It was good fun! Had we been hunting, it

A Passion for Wilderness

Caribou bulls crossing the river

would have been 'duck soup' or, in this case, 'caribou soup.' It was easy to see how, before firearms, the native peoples could paddle their kayaks right up to these animals and spear them as they swam the rivers.

The barren hills along the lower Anderson range up to six and seven hundred feet above the river. At both Windy and Husky Bends, those hills are brilliantly colored, with slopes of various colors ranging from reds to yellow to white and even lavender.

In the afternoon more groups of moulting swans paddled downriver ahead of us. At times, if we moved too close, there would be a great flapping of wings combined with splashing water as these great white birds attempted to run along the surface. Seldom would they gain more than a hundred yards on our canoes, before once more settling back into the water. We were traveling through the major nesting area in North America of those magnificent birds.

As we scooted past the end of an island, a large barren ground grizzly wandered along the shore and up into the bushes.

Evening found us trying to find a campsite in Husky Bend. Finally, we set up beside a little stream flowing out of the high and colorful hills on the right. Dipping a kettle of water from the stream for cooking, I tasted it. The water was very strongly acid, impossible for either cooking or drinking. "This stream must flow out of a sulfur pit," I told Darrell, offering him a taste. "But be careful! Don't swallow any!"

He took a slight sip. "Wow! It is sour!" Spitting and throwing the dilute sulfuric acid out, Darrell took the kettle and headed for the big river for some fresh water we could use.

With the cold north wind blowing in off the Arctic Ocean, we had a problem keeping warm, even while huddling near the fire. With no insect problem and a real nip in the air, we went for a long walk up and across those picturesque hills before crawling into the sacks.

Fog had settled in and the thermometer showed 32° when we broke camp. Heading west out of colorful Husky Bend, the fog began to lift, revealing a clear blue sky. "It's thirty-six miles to Krekovick Landing," said Darrell, "and there's a chance we might make it before setting up camp again."

"Let's give it our best shot," I replied. "Possibly there's an aircraft in there right now."

"With our luck, it will probably be flying away just before we arrive," Deb added.

The three of us were anxious to get back to civilization. It seemed that our passion for wilderness had been fully satisfied for at least a few weeks.

Caribou herds were almost everywhere along the way. Some groups contained up to a hundred head and more. Most were bulls, yearlings and two-year-olds. No cows or calves were detected. The mature females and calves still hadn't returned from the calving grounds. Many of the bulls carried huge racks of antlers. They appeared to be darker in color, and somewhat larger animals than those Darrell and I had seen in the Beverly and Bathurst herds, during our descents of the Thelon and Back Rivers. Group after group would look us over, then run ahead and invariably swim across the river. They were a joy to watch.

A stiff breeze from the north picked up before noon and continued throughout the day, impeding our progress. About twenty miles short of the ocean, we discovered we were paddling in tidal waters. First, there was no river current moving our way, then we were pushing against an incoming tide. Our work was cut out for us, and especially so if we were to reach the CWS cabin that day.

With aching arms and bottoms, we stopped for a speedy supper as huge caribou antlers appeared above the dwarf vegetation. Then it was on towards the river mouth, as it widens out into the delta. Piles of driftwood lined the shores. Hanging in

We make it to Arctic Ocean

there persistently, we finally arrived at Krekovick Landing and had our first look at the Arctic
Ocean at about a half hour before midnight. We had
completed the descent of the Ross and Anderson
Rivers in nineteen days.

Pulling the canoes ashore over the pebbly
beach, we headed up the steps to the white CWS
cabin. A heavy board was propped against the
entrance, a solid wooden door with rows of spikes
protruding about three inches. Other spikes with
points extended were around the windows, the edge
of the roof and corners of the bear proof cabin.

We had our answer. There was no one around so

we soon found a level place down near the shore, erected the tents, and built a cheerful fire from the piles of driftwood. It was hot chocolate time. Then at 1:00 in the morning, we called it a day.

Darrell was out early. He decided to have a look around and inside the CWS cabin. In a little while he reported that he had found a two-way battery powered radio inside. He had snapped it on and apparently it was in working order. With that news, I was soon up there to check it out. We had no idea what the radio was tuned to but could hear someone talking to an aircraft flying over Victoria Island. When a lull in the conversation occurred, I held down the mike switch and had a go at it. "This is Krekovick Landing. Do you read?" Then, after repeating it again, a man's voice replied.

"Go ahead Krekovick Landing."

"There are three of us in the Klein party. We request that you contact Aklak Air in Inuvik, and ask them to dispatch an aircraft here to fly us back to their base. Over."

"Is this an emergency? Over."

"Negative."

"Are you short of food? Over."

"Negative. We have canoed down the Anderson River and need transportation to Inuvik."

"I'll see what we can do," the voice replied.

"Thank you very much. Over and out." With that, I snapped off the radio.

Good news! We enjoyed a big breakfast, leisurely washed and packed the cook kit and everything else except the tents. We would leave those up until the dew dried off or until we heard an aircraft approaching.

Walking back up to the cabin to look around, we found a log book on the table. The latest entry was dated July 24, seven days earlier and signed by Sam Berry of the Canadian Wildlife Service. The note read, "Upon completion of the Grizzly survey, we estimate the bears in this area have destroyed at least ten thousand swan eggs this spring."

Just after eleven, I decided to use the radio again to learn whether or not the man had been able to get the message through to Aklak Air. This time a different person was at the controls. When I asked the question, he responded, "Where is Krekovick Landing?"

"At the mouth of the Anderson River," I replied.

"Oh! So that's where it is. I'll put your request through right away."

Having more time to kill, I walked along the pebbled tidal flats for about a mile to the north. Moving along, I realized we were at the end of our journey and more than likely this was the farthest north that I would ever get. In a prayerful mood, I thanked God for dozens of things including His seeing us safely to the shores of the Arctic Ocean, and for my two wonderful canoeing companions. Returning to camp, Deb and Darrell were relaxing near the fire.

A half hour later, with Deb standing not more than twenty feet from the sea, we watched two caribou bulls trotting our way close to the shore. Those animals kept on coming and passed between

A Passion for Wilderness

Deb and the ocean without ever noticing us.

Finally, around 3:00 in the afternoon, we heard an aircraft approaching. Sure enough, it was a Cessna 185 from Aklak Air. We tied the Monarch just above the left pontoon, loaded our packs and were soon flying toward Inuvik. The pilot would return during the evening for the Wenonah. We asked him what radio base we had communicated with, to which he replied, "Arctic Shelf Exploration in Tuktoyaktuk. They were quite upset that you were using their frequency."

Hot showers in the Finto Motor Inn were most welcome as we watched the dirt, built up during three weeks in camp, go down the drain. Then early next morning, we began the long drive back to Michigan.

Debbie   Klein

CROSS-COUNTRY

COMPANIONS

Cross-country skis are my wintertime friends
They take me to places unknown
Over field and creek and into deep woods
Where I can be free and just roam.

A snowy white carpet is laid all around
Giving nature a silent solitude
Everything is hushed and still
I wonder if I should intrude.

A Passion for Wilderness

The cold crisp air is invigorating
As I push off on each rhythmical stride
It envelops me in winter's refreshing embrace
Lifting the spirit and clearing the mind.

For a moment I lose this calm feeling
And know skiing as an exciting sport
It's good exercise for the body
And gives cause to play and cavort!

There's an element of excitement, even fear
As I sweep down a hill, round a bend
Will I conquer the slope like an Olympian
Or land on my bottom again?

Once back on level ground I can relax
All is peaceful as far as eye can see
The only sounds are my skis as they glide
And the call of the small chickadee.

Snow settles gently from the sky to earth
It partly obscures the sunlight
Creating a scene of a magic wonderland
Of twinkling stars and glistening delight.

An unending trail of parallel tracks
Leads into a stand of dense evergreens
Cottony snow has been caught, lining each branch
One of winter's joys to be seen.

Though all is silent I am not alone
To watch for wildlife signs is a habit

A Passion for Wilderness

Hidden eyes watch as I ski along
There are tracks of the deer, the mouse and the
rabbit.

One wild companion I just can't overlook
Suddenly there's a bright flash of red
It's the lovely cardinal come to grace the day
Then away on the wing he has fled.

Tall oaks stand dormant against the gray sky
Will the warmth of the spring ever come?
Yes, there's the promise of rebirth and new life
Keep your eye on the tree's tiny bud.

The winter season is a remarkable one
And though harsh, I'm convinced it's plain to see
That to truly appreciate its beautiful side
Just slip on those cross-country skis!

Part **4**

NAHANNI ADVENTURE

By

Theodor 'Ted' Mellenthin

THEODOR 'TED' MELLENTHIN

Theodor 'Ted' Mellenthin usually spends his holidays canoeing wild rivers in northern Canada with friends from the Bow Waters Canoe Club. He is an expert canoeist, conquering such rivers as the Coppermine, the MacMillan and the Nahanni. In 1985, he made the first solo trip in history down the 650-mile Back River, into the Arctic Ocean.

He was born in Hamburg, Germany, in 1937. During World War II, he and his sister, a year younger, pretty much had to fend for themselves as they didn't have a father. They dodged bombs and ate whatever they could find. Ted ended up in a hospital in 1944 suffering from malnutrition.

He says, "We waved white handkerchiefs at the Russians as they came in as occupational forces with their tanks. In late 1945 we fled across the border to the west in open railway cars, hungry and cold. Finally, in a small town between Hamburg and Hanover, I went to school from 1947 until 1953. My dream didn't end there. Anxious to leave home, I worked on a farm for a year. They worked me from four in the morning 'til ten at night with very little decent food. Later I worked as a bellhop, a construction worker, and in the coal mines. At last I had enough, and emigrated to Canada, wherever that was."

Eventually Ted settled in Calgary, Alberta, and now lives in a fine home he built himself. For the past twenty-three years he has worked for a Calgary trucking company.

Ted says, "When I can challenge the powerful water of a rapids, I feel as if I am challenging life itself, and I probably am. I even enjoy being by myself out there sometimes, away from people. I hear things normally uncommon, and my thoughts fly far away. There is just nothing better than being close to nature and floating with our earth in space."

He adds, "Canoeing is my life. I compare the

rivers with the blood veins of the human body, and the oceans as the heart of it all. Without the rivers and oceans, nothing would survive. When I kneel in my canoe I feel as if I am in the cradle of it all. I am so happy when I feel and hear wind and rain, cold and warmth. I am so grateful that I am alive."

Theodor 'Ted' Mellenthin

NAHANNI ADVENTURE

Over the years, I had heard many things about the beautiful and challenging South Nahanni River, with its hot springs, deep canyons, waterfalls, wildlife and mysterious stories.

In December of 1983, while trying to decide on a summer canoe trip, the name Nahanni came up again and I made the decision that this would be the river. I began collecting information from a variety of sources, Travel Arctic in Yellowknife,

A Passion for Wilderness

Parks Canada at Nahanni Butte, Simpson Air, and, of prime importance, topographical maps. Any trips of this nature should have a minimum of three canoes and, due to the vast expanse of water, I wanted six people for muscle power. This was my only goal, but I soon found that it was hard to get people to commit themselves so far ahead, but the numbers were important in order to keep costs down. I had made some rough estimates of $500, to fly in, from Fort Simpson to the Moose Ponds for each person, plus another $200 each in costs for the round trip from Calgary to Fort Simpson. If we didn't have six people, this figure would increase.

No matter how hard I tried, the number remained at three. Then, just one week before our departure date, three more decided they would like to go. I was thankful for the extra bodies, but this created a new problem, no time for screening and assessing their skill levels. Tossing caution to the wind and after considerable discussion, this is how we would team up. Mike Wood of Calgary would paddle with Sylvia Grondin of Quebec. Gordon Harris would canoe with George Jelinek of Czechoslovakia, and my partner would be John de la Mare.

We left Calgary for Fort Simpson early on Friday the 13th of July, 1984. As things turned out, it was a good omen. Our transportation for the drive to Fort Simpson was my Ford LTD wagon loaded with four people, one canoe and some of the gear and Mike Wood's one-half-ton jeep with two canoes, two people and the bulk of the gear. The

A Passion for Wilderness

1100-mile trip took us $22\frac{1}{2}$ hours, including brief
stops at the 60th parallel, beautiful Lady Evelyn
Falls and Whittaker Falls, plus a one-hour delay
at a road construction site. Finally, after
crossing the Liard River on the free ferry near
the confluence with the mighty MacKenzie River,
we arrived in Fort Simpson. The time was 5:00
P.M., Saturday, the 14th.

Everyone needed to stretch their legs and get
away from my German cassettes which I had played
repeatedly throughout the journey. We made our
way to Simpson Air to find out if we could fly
earlier than scheduled. But the unusual wet
weather had created a backlog and we had to wait
our turn. The wet weather had also caused more
bad news for us, in that the twin otter on wheels
could not land us on the gravel bar beside the
Moose Ponds, as the ground was too wet and
swampy, causing the plane to possibly skid out of
control. The alternative was a smaller plane with
floats and, due to its size, two trips would be
needed and that nearly doubled the cost. The best
laid plans of mice and men had struck again. I was,
of course, outraged, and indicated that I had been
given unreliable information, but my heart was set
on landing at the Moose Ponds as this is the
highest point at which one may start the trip. We
haggled, settling on an additional $100 per person
over our original cost. We passed the time from
Saturday until Monday morning at the Fort Simpson
campground, trying to shelter ourselves from the
almost constant rain, and fighting off the mosquitos that were as big as sparrows.

A Passion for Wilderness

The Pilatius Porter turbo prop

Monday morning, we awoke at 6:00 A.M. and went immediately to our next mode of transportation, a Pilatius Porter turbo prop float plane. We loaded our gear and assisted the pilot and owner of Simpson Air, Ted Grant, at tying the canoes to the floats. Then, it was a short wait for the fog to lift and by 7:30 we were airborne.

One last look at Fort Simpson and the mighty MacKenzie River, with a glimpse at Little Doctor Lake, and we were in the first mountain range still climbing until we reached 6,000 feet. How beautiful, simple and clean everything looked from the air.

Ted Grant, our pilot, said we might see some dall sheep in the mountains and, as if by magic, they appeared. Shortly the Nahanni River came into view with its beautiful and inspiring Virginia Falls, twice as high as Niagara. Then it was Glacier Lake and the giant mountains called the unclimbables. We landed on Glacier Lake to take on fuel. Once there, the pilot climbed on top of the plane and asked us to hand him some gasoline in a bucket from the drums he had stashed there. It felt strange, almost as if we were in some kind of adventure movie.

Not long and we were off again, looking down on the Nahanni. After what seemed the longest time, I checked with the pilot to determine if that was indeed the Nahanni River below us. He answered, "Yes." It was still another sixty miles to our drop-off point. I kept my mouth shut, but thought to myself that it could be sixty miles of walking, from the looks of things. Up in the air, all I could see of the river was a white streak with boulders everywhere. From a canoeing point of view, it was hard to believe we would have to try to maneuver around so many boulders. After $3\frac{1}{2}$ hours of flying, we finally landed at the Moose Ponds. I felt reluctant to leave the comfort of the warm plane for the wet muskeg and bone-chilling rain. Not wanting to show my feelings to the rest of the group, I took charge of the unloading which didn't take very long. Then the plane took off to pick up the second group who were at a gravel bar not far from where we had refueled.

This group consisted of three people and one canoe plus extra fuel for Simpson Air's fuel cache. They were pressed into the labor of unloading the extra fuel.   But this is how we kept our second flight costs down.

While waiting for the second group,   I took a walk down the lake shore in search of a more suitable campsite.   Not wanting to spend the night on wet muskeg,   I couldn't even follow the lake shore as it became overgrown and of course very wet.

About to retrace my steps to our landing site, I noticed a big tree which seemed to be moving.   I followed it a short distance to a clearing and, as it turned, I had a great view of a huge bull moose. Very appropriate, as I was at the Moose Ponds.   I arrived back at the landing site two and one-half hours after leaving to find the whole crew there and the plane gone.   At last,   we were truly alone.

A group decision was made to paddle to the outlet of the lake to find the start of the Nahanni River and maybe find a gravel bar to spend the night on. Good fortune was with us and we   had accomplished the above by 5:00 P.M.,   including setting up camp and having supper under our shelter of canoes and my trusty 9 x 12 tarp, an item we found to be invaluable.   It was still raining and cold but a buzz of excitement was with us as we hiked to a hill not far away to watch a moose.

Returning to camp, we met George, our Czechoslovakian group member who had only recently joined the expedition. We had picked him up in Edmonton, Alberta. That first evening, he had an adventure all by himself. Our lean-to with a small fire had almost succumbed to flames as George hung his wet pants on the cross brace made

George Jelinek and Gordon Harris

from a paddle to dry. Both the pants and paddle tipped into the fire and were burned. Fortunately, the tarp was saved. George was an unusual character. Having no pants, he wore his rain pants for the rest of the trip. He also brought along only dehydrated food which consisted of an over abundance of Chinese noodles. After the first few days, he got sick and tired of those to the point that he could never complete a full meal. This lack of good nutrients left him weak at times and the work was left up to his partner. At one point, while negotiating a long rapid, George fell out of the canoe while trying to retrieve his dropped paddle.

A Passion for Wilderness

Being agile, George managed to jump back in the canoe before Gordon in the bow even suspected he was alone. On another occasion, George decided to use his body as an anchor while slowing the canoe through a long rapid. He was out and in again as if it was the normal thing to do. I've never tried this unique style of canoeing myself but on film it certainly looks impressive. It's doubtful that George will be able to teach his style in Canada as he returned to his home country in the fall of 1984.

Day two, we awoke to more cold and wet. Nearby Mount Wilson had new snow on it. We were underway around 10 A.M. The river wound itself around through the muskeg for about ten miles. The banks were impenetrable with brush, and occasional beaver dams could be seen. Finally, we left the valley of the Moose Ponds. The mountains narrowed in on the river which made the flow of the river much faster and the rapids more numerous and difficult. We were to learn that the river would be like this for the next sixty miles, the very reason we wanted to start at the Moose Ponds.

Our first major rapid, which we scouted thoroughly first, was a steep gradient with a rock garden and small ledges. The river makes a right hand turn around a large boulder then drops through some offset chutes. Due to the excitement, I pushed off before my bow man, John de la Mare, and the camera man, Mike Wood, were ready. We made the run successfully but later I was to get a lecture from my partner on this and working as a team in the future.

A Passion for Wilderness

The weather improved and we camped on a large island where firewood was plentiful. Our spirits were high as we went for a three hour hike. The only wildlife we saw was a porcupine who ran for safety up a tree. However, the tree was only six feet high. Talking around the campfire that evening, we didn't turn in until midnight.

Day three gave us nothing but whitewater rapids. One particular set of rapids was very long and complicated so we did a good bit of scouting, covering up to a quarter mile at a time. The river had increased in width and an island gave us a choice of two channels with rapids on each side. We decided the best channel was the rapid to the left of the island, which carried approximately half the river's water. At the exit end of the island, the water flow tipped to the right to join the other channel. When a river tips to one side like that, it exposes a lot of boulders and one has to try to turn with the water. This can be difficult at times.

Leading on this stretch, my canoe negotiated safely but each of the other canoes flipped over and we had to scramble to make some rescues. After the joining of the two channels, a huge turbulent wave is created which runs straight into a rock wall. Two canoes made it safely on this one but Mike and Sylvia tipped a second time and there was a great danger of them and their canoe getting pinned against the rock wall. It took considerable time for them to show below and, as Mike explained that evening around the campfire, "They were caught in a strong eddy." He was

A Passion for Wilderness

Sylvia Grondin and Mike Woods

thankful he was paddling his sixteen-foot Rocky Mountain Cruiser canoe, which is easier to handle full of water than a seventeen or eighteen footer.

The next big rapid is named Eye of the Needle and, as one might guess, it takes some expert maneuvering to thread your canoe through that maze of rocks. The main section begins as you round a right hand turn in the river where a huge boulder obstructs the chute. Complicated and precise maneuvering is required, including back paddling and side slipping to line up with the chute. Then a really strong bow draw and stern pry is required in order to wiggle your way through the narrow opening.

This stretch is where a girl on a trip the year earlier lost her life. We later learned that she struck her head on the large boulder, knocking her unconscious. No rescue personnel were deployed below and she drowned.

John and I, in our seventeen foot fiberglass canoe, ran this stretch with no problem, as did Mike and Sylvia in the sixteen foot rocky, but Gordon and George lined their seventeen foot aluminum Grumman around, as they felt they didn't have the maneuverability in the aluminum canoe that we had in our fiberglass models.

The spectacular rapid on this stretch was a right hand turn where most of the water runs into a truck-sized boulder and then bounces off to the right going over a considerable drop. After scouting, we decided we would all run this stretch. Our rescues set up and positioned, we would run it one canoe at a time. We back ferried as close to the right hand shore as the rocks would allow, then after straightening out and setting our position, we shot down and over the ledge. Due to our spray covers, we all managed this stretch. Without them, we would have filled with water. Many times the alternative to running these stretches would have been a number of tedious portages due to the terrain.

From this point on to the confluence of the Little Nahanni, the water was very fast but without the good rapids that we had enjoyed for the past sixty miles. We were all a little disappointed that this stretch was over, but relieved that we had challenged the whitewater of the Upper Nahanni and won.

The Little Nahanni from Tungsten is an alternate access point. It can be reached by car, thus saving one the air fare. This route, however, makes for a really long car shuttle around through Yukon Territory. Here we met two Frenchmen with an unusual canoe consisting of an aluminum frame covered with polyester; it seemed to be full of patches from bow to stern. They told us they had come over from France for this trip and they were running out of food and also patches for the canoe. They had a third partner who had gone back to Tungsten to charter an aircraft to fly him to the Moore Cabin, where they were to meet. The Moore Cabin being only fifteen miles down stream and with their assuredness that they would be all right, we paddled on, leaving them alone as they wished.

After about an hour of paddling, we heard a motor boat. Recovering from the initial shock, came feelings of disgust that such a monstrous noisy machine should be allowed in there to shatter the tranquillity. Eventually, it came into sight. It was a rubber raft with a large outboard motor mounted on the back. When it came alongside, the woman who was driving asked if we had seen the Frenchmen. We said, "Yes, but how did you know about them?" She replied that she and her companions were staying at the Moore Cabin to do some filming and had been contacted by short wave radio to check on the Frenchmen.

Arriving at the Moore Cabin, we noticed several more motorized rafts, three women and five men.

A Passion for Wilderness

They were from Germany and Czechoslovakia and were sponsored by a German television station to film the Nahanni Wilderness. We also met Norman Kuus, a fellow from Ontario, who had come into Island Lake from Tungsten via the Little Nahanni with his canoe a year earlier. He took a liking to the place and decided to live there in one of the abandoned cabins.

It was getting late but we were determined to visit the Moore Hot Springs and have a good soak. Getting directions from the people staying at the Moore Cabin, and assuring them we would return the next day, we set off. The Hot Springs are about a mile downstream from the cabin. We found them with no problem and, as it was our sixth day, we all felt in need of a good hot bath. The water, however, was so hot it scorched our skins. When we got out, the mosquitos may have been related to the ones in Fort Simpson because they were as big. They must have thought our white skin was lunch as they attacked relentlessly. We spent an hour at the Hot Springs, then paddled 300 yards upstream to an island which looked like a good campsite, to spend the night. We quickly set up our lean-to just before a heavy rain storm hit which lasted about twenty minutes.

The next morning, as we promised, we packed out and paddled the mile upstream to visit the people at the Moore Cabin and Norman Kuus at Island Lake. Norman told us an amazing story. It seems that when he first arrived there, he was almost killed by a grizzly. The bear was raiding Norman's food tent. Norman tried to chase the bear away and it

A Passion for Wilderness

attacked.   Norman was injured and the bear took off.   Of course, Norman had to tend to his own injuries and recuperate by himself without help from anyone, as no one knew he was there.   He considered himself lucky, and has taken precautions that it doesn't happen again.   According to Norman, the reason he lives in this solitude is to straighten out his mind and to practice yoga.

He made us what he calls mountain soup.   The ingredients seemed to be anything he had on hand, but the taste was excellent.   It was getting late and we had to say farewell to Norman and his unusual lifestyle.   Walking back the mile to the Nahanni, many thoughts went through my head;   to each his own.

The next two days, the river was fast and we floated a lot and enjoyed soaking up the sun unbothered by mosquitos.   Arriving at Glacier Creek, we talked to someone sitting at a picnic table.   He was a member of a two-canoe group and the others had gone on an overnight hike to Glacier Lake and would be back soon.   After swapping a few stories and ideas, we went on down to Rabbit Kettle Lake which is the beginning of the Nahanni National Park.   This area was declared a world heritage site by UNESCO in 1978.   Since we didn't want to carry our gear the two kilometers to the lake, we camped across the river on a sand bar.   Then, after registering with the park warden, we signed up for a tour to the Tufa Mounds the following day.

We had traveled 120 miles from the Moose Ponds to Rabbit Kettle Lake.   The next 186 miles would be

A Passion for Wilderness

through the world-famous Nahanni National Park. Our first morning in the park, we paddled across the Nahanni River from our campsite on the Gravel Bar to visit Rabbit Kettle Lake. The hike to the Rabbit Kettle Hot Springs took most of the day but it is well worth the effort.

Arriving back at the river, we decided to pack up our gear and canoe a few miles to a new campsite. The river was fairly fast until the day before Virginia Falls. There it seemed to come to a halt and even begin to flow upstream. We saw a beautiful bald eagle perched in a tree. It remained there for the longest time. When we finally got in camera range, it took off.

Late in the evening and dead tired, we reached Virginia Falls. The cataract is 90 meters high, which is twice the height of Niagara Falls. Its voice can be heard for many miles.

We planned a one-day stay in order to hike Sunblood Mountain. George, however, decided to hike in the opposite direction alone to a lesser known waterfall. The hike up Sunblood Mountain was strenuous, and by far the longest, highest hike that I had ever done. But I was bound and determined to make it to the top.

John had a small problem on the way up and couldn't make it all the way, so Mike, who had lost his wallet, stayed with him. Later, they decided to make their way back down the trail searching for Mike's wallet containing $500. Fortunately, they found it (the lucky devil).

We were above the tree line, and had a spectacular view for miles in all directions. We were

A Passion for Wilderness

Virginia Falls

at such an elevation that Virginia Falls looked almost the same as we had seen it on the way up aboard the plane.

At the summit, we wrote our three names and the date, which we placed in a jar, in a five foot stone cairn. While looking at the notes, we discovered they were dated as far back as 1976, a total of eight years. Maybe in the next eight years, I could return. The hike up took us four hours and the journey back down three. So, we were very tired when we returned to the river.

Something had happened in our absence. Some animal (no other word will suffice) had stolen

A Passion for Wilderness

Sylvia's life jacket. So, one of us had to ferry across the river without a life jacket. You can imagine our tense moments as this was just above Virginia Falls.

With the continuing bad luck, I slept fitfully throughout the night. Being the leader and responsible for the people on the trip, I was most concerned about George, who had gone off on his own and not returned. He finally arrived around four in the morning, and surprised me from behind as I was checking his tent for the tenth time. The story he gave was that he got a little disoriented and had to use the river shoreline to find his way back to camp. This meant passing Virginia Falls in the dark and, with the shoreline very slippery, we could have lost him forever. Needless to say, I gave him a good talking to about traveling in numbers and the cost involved if a search party had become necessary.

The next day, we portaged around Virginia Falls on the right and were so close we got soaked with the spray. Back on the river again, our first bit of excitement below the falls was Five Mile Canyon, the first of four such canyons. The ride was nice with roller coaster type five-foot standing waves and yellow looking cliffs along either side. The Nahanni is of great value to geologists as it is antecedent, meaning the river was there before the mountains. As the mountains were pushed upward to 3,000 feet, the river stayed at its original level. So, what we now see above the river was once below the earth to a depth of 3,000 feet.

A Passion for Wilderness

Mike, Ted, Gordon, Sylvia, and John

Our next exciting stretch was Hell's Gate or Figure Eight Rapids. Hell's Gate had already claimed the lives of three Swedes in one canoe. So, we were really apprehensive. The river has a fair rise here and runs straight into a cliff which creates strong eddies on both left and right before taking off to the left. We figured we should run this along the left eddy line as there was a danger of getting pinned against the cliff on the right. After some tense moments, we all managed to pass it okay and camped at Wrigley

A Passion for Wilderness

Creek for the night.

Next day, we paddled past the Flat River and through the third canyon, which was really beautiful. Weather conditions didn't look good so we set up camp early at a place known as Pulpit Rock. It was a good thing we did, as we witnessed the heaviest rainstorm that any of us had ever seen. The river rose a foot within an hour and churned up so much debris that the water remained muddy for many days. We watched from our safe refuge on the shore as tree after tree moved down river.

The next morning, we climbed Pulpit Rock, a mere 300 feet, which didn't take us long but the view was spectacular. Then packing up, we were on the river by noon. The group had a lazy afternoon just drifting and soaking up the sun.

In what is known as the second canyon, we stopped at Headless Creek to search around looking for the skulls of the legendary MacLeod Brothers. That night, we camped at Deadman Valley, a designated campsite, and spent the whole of the next day looking across the Alluvian Fan of Prairie Creek watching for bears and sheep at the salt lick.

We decided to help the Parks Department, and built new steps up the banks to the campsite. George, our lone wanderer, took off on what we estimated was a three-day hike to Tlogotsho Plateau. We told him we would be breaking camp the next morning. He must have really rushed, as he made it back just as we were leaving.

These designated campsites like the one in Deadman Valley are usually occupied by more than one group, so it's a good time to socialize and swap stories. Located at Deadman Valley Campsite is an old forestry cabin with a registration book. It is interesting to look through and read the comments about the park. We also saw a bear with two cubs close by our campsite so we took all necessary precautions.

Next day, we canoed down the river a stretch and spent half a day hiking Dry Canyon Creek, no water, just huge boulders to climb around and very steep canyon walls. Back on the river, a section known as George's Riffle created some excitement, as the river flows around an island and creates big waves just below.

Next, we entered the first canyon and, in my opinion, this is by far the most spectacular. There are caves in the cliffs that you are forbidden to enter, so we just passed by without stopping. Lafferty's Riffle has big standing waves and we played here before arriving at Kraus Hot Springs where we were to camp for the night. Once again, the silence was shattered by the sound of motors. There were jet river boats tearing around, one of which was beached on the gravel bar with a broken drive shaft. Even though this boat was silenced, its crew managed to keep us awake most of the night with their singing and drinking.

We found two hot springs, one near the river and the other inland half a kilometer. The trail to them both was well worn as countless feet had obviously experienced their pleasures long before we came along.

It was at this place that I had an experience

A Passion for Wilderness

that will stay with me forever. While the rest of
the group were sleeping, I took a walk to stretch
my legs. Less than a quarter of a kilometer away,
I found a log about three feet above the ground
which I sat on and watched some busy beavers at a
pond feeding and swimming around. Sitting for a
while very quietly, the bushes about 50 feet away
started shaking. It seemed like a herd of ele-
phants was coming through the bush. Not wanting
to attract attention to myself, I remained perfectly still as this continued for almost an hour.
Then, something started moving towards me. It
entered the clearing in front of me and I discovered it was a grizzly, heading directly towards
me. I was a sitting duck but could not move, as
to do so, I thought, would be foolish. The bear
came to no more than 8 feet from me and stopped.
Then, he lifted his head and sniffed at me. Thank
God, he wandered off, while I tried to recover
from my mild heart attack. It didn't take me
long to get back to camp and invite myself over to
the jet boaters who were still there. We sang
songs with them until dawn.

The next day, we left the park and moved on to
Nahanni Butte. The trip that day seemed endless.
But, we finally arrived at the Indian settlement
of Nahanni Butte. We camped at the edge of the
village and bought some souvenirs. The one store
in the settlement was almost empty of groceries as
the plane bringing in the goods was not due for a
few more days as they only have one plane each
month. The settlement had no wells. They took
their water directly out of the river, which at

A Passion for Wilderness

this point was still silty. Power was supplied by a plant built two years earlier. The houses constructed of logs had no running water and wood stoves were used for heating and cooking. The only vehicles at the settlement were a tractor and flatdeck trailer used to haul supplies from the plane.

The following day, we visited the warden's station to close our travel plan, then paddled on down into the Liard River. The next 115 miles were completed in two days. We visited author Dick Turner on the Blackstone River. His books, **Nahanni** and **Wings of the North,** make good reading. Mr. Turner advised us of the rapids on the Liard named the Beaver Dams. He suggested that we stay along the right side of the river as this was the safest passage. The rapids have claimed several lives. It was here we also saw our last bear of the trip and, fortunately, it was not as close as had been my earlier hair-raising encounter.

We arrived at Fort Simpson at 7:00 P.M. on Friday, and spent another night at the campsite we used when we were waiting for the plane. Then, it was the new Liard Highway back to Calgary where we arrived Sunday noon.

This was a trip I will never forget, and I am sure I will go back again some day.

E . Pauline Johnson

IN THE SHADOWS

I am sailing to the leeward,
Where the current runs to seaward
    Soft and slow,
Where the sleeping river grasses
Brush my paddle as it passes
    To and fro.

On the shore the heat is shaking
All the golden sands awaking
    In the cove;
And the quaint sandpiper, winging
O'er the shallows, ceases singing
    When I move.

A Passion for Wilderness

On the water's idle pillow
Sleeps the overhanging willow,
    Green and cool;
Where the rushes lift their burnished
Oval heads from out the tarnished
    Emerald pool.

Where the very silence slumbers,
Water lilies grow in numbers,
    Pure and pale;
All the morning they have rested,
Amber crowned, and pearly crested,
    Fair and frail.

I can scarce discern the meeting
Of the shore and stream retreating,
    So remote;
For the laggard river, dozing,
Only wakes from its reposing
    Where I float.

Where the river mists are rising,
All the foliage baptizing
    With their spray;
There the sun gleams far and faintly,
With a shadow soft and saintly,
    In its ray.

A Passion for Wilderness

And the perfume of some burning
Far-off brushwood, ever turning
   To exhale
All its smoky fragrance dying,
In the arms of evening lying,
   Where I sail.

My canoe is growing lazy,
In the atmosphere so hazy,
   While I dream;
Half in slumber I am guiding,
Eastward indistinctly gliding
   Down the stream.

THE SPIRIT OF MONUMENT MOUNTAIN

CANOEING THE JACK

EXPLORING VERMONT'S NORTHEAST KINGDOM

SOLO

By

Richard E. Winslow III

RICHARD E. WINSLOW III

Richard Elliott Winslow III was born in Boston, Massachusetts in 1934 and now lives in Rye, New Hampshire. The son of a career naval officer, Dick is currently employed as a writer and historian for the Portsmouth Marine Society and as a librarian at the Portsmouth Public Library.

Educated at Union College, the University of New Hampshire, Penn State, and the University of Maryland, Dick also attended a University of Wyoming summer geological field trip course. During 1957-1959 he served in the United States Army. Upon discharge he has also worked as a geologist, teacher, and camp counselor.

Dick has enjoyed the outdoors all his life, and has climbed mountains in New England, the Rockies and Cascades. During a 1971 summer-long trip to Canada and Alaska, he hiked the Trail of '98 over Chilkoot Pass. In recent years he has gone whitewater canoeing and rafting in the East. His next goal is to canoe Quebec's Moisie River.

Winslow has written books and articles on the American Civil War, local Portsmouth history, and canoeing. Other interests include reading accounts of exploration and expeditions and visiting libraries, museums, mining camps, and battlefields.

Richard E. Winslow III

THE SPIRIT OF
MONUMENT MOUNTAIN

Monument Mountain is both rock and spirit. Straddling the Stockbridge — Great Barrington boundary in the Berkshires in western Massachusetts, its summit ridge falls away with great cliffs.

According to legend, an Indian maiden jumped to her death off a high crag on the mountain. At the base, members of her tribe piled up rocks as a monument. Some say the maiden is buried under

A Passion for Wilderness

these rocks. As each passing Indian added another stone to the pile, the monument gradually grew higher.

In the 1820s, William Cullen Bryant published the poem, "Monument Mountain," immortalizing the legend. On an overcast August 5, 1850, Nathaniel Hawthorne and Herman Melville met for the first time in Stockbridge and climbed the mountain with Oliver Wendell Holmes and others. Caught in a thunderstorm, the climbing party found shelter under a crag. There one hiker read the poem.

Monument Mountain is one of those spiritual high places in America where minds mingle with the winds. Thoreau climbed Monadnock, Wachusett, and Katahdin, so today his disciples make a pilgrimage to hike up the same slopes and breathe the same air, just as many climb Desolation Peak in Washington's Cascades because Jack Kerouac spent a summer at the fire tower there.

Great significance attaches to spirits abiding in the mountains. In the high country in the West — the San Juans, the Wasatch, and the Sierra Nevada — tommy knockers, the ghosts of dead miners killed on the job, hammer away forever in the shafts and tunnels. Living miners hear them. At Independence Rock, Wyoming, pioneers stopped, climbed the butte for a lookout, and carved their names in the cliff face. Becoming a traditional rest place on the Oregon Trail, members of wagon parties buried their dead, those carried away by disease and exhaustion during the long trek, at the base of Independence Rock. The spirits of those who never made it to trail's end are likewise part of America's Westward Movement. The ghosts of Custer and his men stir on the rattlesnake-infested hills above the Little Big Horn River, Montana.

Approaching the Berkshires early in the morning in April, 1984, I saw the hills shrouded in spring showers. Mist spiraled up from the valleys like smoke from Indian campfires. The newly formed pure air was invigorating. Its freshness awakened me.

As I stood in the field below Monument Mountain, I felt its spirit pull me toward it. I was committed to make the climb.

As noon approached, the day became increasingly hot and muggy. Stirred up by recent rains, mosquitoes buzzed around me. I skirted mud puddles as I entered the woods on the Indian Monument Trail. The wide path was a onetime carriage road. Dead leaves from the previous autumn were matted down, and pressed into the earth by countless footsteps. I could smell the dark of dankness from the dead trunks and branches. Buds sprouted from the twigs of live maples and birches.

From the dirt road trail I bushwhacked to the Indian monument, a tent-shaped pile of rocks. The lichen blanketing the rocks shone light yellow where the sun's rays shot through the forest canopy.

Bushwhacking back to the established trail, I soon found it quickly narrowed to a rude path, maintained by the boots of hikers. The path made a sharp turn for its final steep climb. I was happily oblivious of time, but I knew there were many hours of daylight ahead. I met no one.

The summit ridge of Monument Mountain was white

Crag on Monument Mountain

quartzite, a quarter mile long, dipping and rising like feathers in a war bonnet. Squaw Peak, the name given to the highest point on this ridge, rose 700 feet above the valley floor.

Pitch and stunted scrub took root in soil pockets. Over on the east face, I spotted the Devil's Pulpit, a free-standing pinnacle that resembled a chiseled arrowhead without final shaping. No vegetation grew on it.

I rested a long time atop Squaw Peak, eating lunch and watching. To the east and north were roads, a sawmill, a gravel pit, and the village of Stockbridge on a bend of the Housatonic River. Only a wide stream here, its water shone like ripe blueberries. To the south were orchards, plowed fields, and meadows near farmhouses, with stone walls and rows of trees marking property lines. Westward to the horizon, the ridges of the Taconic Range rolled like waves, creating four separate undulations. Spruce trees filled the valley troughs, maples and beeches dominated the ridges, and the trunks of white birches with their clusters of crooked branches showed distinct profiles on the hillsides. I inhaled the air of this majestic land.

Breezes swept over Monument Mountain, dispersing the mosquitoes and blowing through the clouds to open up blue sky patches.

In the distance a hawk soared on great wings, riding the wind current. The bird seemed suspended in flight, so effortlessly did he hover over the valley. I felt my own spirit break loose to glide with him in freedom. Soon my mind was floating over the earth.

Perhaps these dreamy illusions were caused by the hot sun, reddening my face and making me drowsy. Perhaps it was laziness. I thought about never coming down. I would stay up here forever. My feet had fallen asleep on the rock perch. My relaxation was complete.

There remained a feeling of familiarity with this mountain, one like hundreds of other wild places I had seen and climbed. But contentment has its limitations: the hawk would eventually drop to earth; the mountain had become an unhappy place for the Indian maiden; Hawthorne and Melville began a friendship there, but it was too highly charged to last; and I too would need realistically to bring this elation to a close.

At last I kicked my boots against the rock and felt the prickly fuzziness drain away from my feet. When I stood up, I felt a shock of reality and awakened to head down. I wanted to return to the outskirts of Stockbridge to hike into the Ice Glen, a cold ravine preserving snow in its shadowy recesses throughout the summer. There were other things to do besides sit here.

Other climbers had scaled more remote and technically more challenging mountains on this same day, but I doubt few derived a fraction of the satisfaction that I had found here. The place galvanizes the mind as if by electricity from a passing storm. The spirit of Monument Mountain broods high over the valley.

Richard E. Winslow III

CANOEING THE JACK

Chapter 1

THE BAKER LAKE BUNCH

Day One / Saturday, May 11, 1985
Baker Lake

As our van rattled over the wooden bridge of a logging road, I caught my first glimpse of the St. John River. Marty, the driver of the van and the director of Sunrise County Canoe Expeditions, turned left immediately to enter the Baker Lake campsite. We passengers in the van cheered, glad to see the end of the all-day drive, the last 135 miles of it over rough dirt roads. Just a few miles back, St. Francis Lake was still frozen over.

Our group arrived in two vehicles, ready to begin a week-long canoe trip down the St. John River from Baker Lake the next morning. I jumped out of the van and walked stiffly around the site. Baker Lake, just a week since ice-out, shimmered blue against the conifer forest. There were no buds on the few hardwood trees near the shore of this unspoiled Maine wilderness lake.

Appearing on a map as a small blue smudge surrounded by a large white space, Baker Lake is located in the northern Maine woods in Somerset County about fifteen miles east of the Quebec border. Except for logging roads and bridges and an occasional warden's cabin, we would be abandoning civilization for a week. No one lives permanently along this stretch of the north-flowing St. John, where only canoeists venture as they paddle through in season. This watery country, left essentially unchanged since the white man came to New England, is a tangle of rivers, lakes, swamps, forest, and hills. We were the only party at Baker Lake campsite and at this last hour of daylight, we doubted any others would arrive.

In the early evening chill we unracked the canoes, carried the wanigans, food boxes, to the fireplace, and pitched our tents. Following a beef Stroganoff supper, we rinsed our tin plates and utensils in the lake.

I took a twilight stroll back to the bridge

A Passion for Wilderness

about a quarter-mile from the campsite and watched the St. John course through its gravel and boulder channel. The music of its gurgling was haunting. This last wilderness river of the American Northeast flows about 300 miles in a wide horseshoe route before joining the Atlantic Ocean. For the next week our party would run a 110-mile stretch of the most spectacular and challenging section of the St. John, from Baker Lake north into Aroostook County to the grand finale at Big Rapids. Our take-out would be at a campsite on a bluff just beyond the rapids. This place is at the end of a dirt road a few miles upstream and west of the tiny river settlement of Dickey, Maine, located in a sparsely populated area just south of the New Brunswick border.

In the Rocky Mountain West many backpackers rave about hiking the Bob, the nickname for the Bob Marshall Wilderness Area in western Montana. Californians exult about running the Stan, otherwise known as the Stanislaus River which washes down rafts, canoes, and kayaks as well as gold dust, flakes and nuggets into the channels, gravel bars, and boulders of the Mother Lode country. But Maine has its own whitewater bonanza. Here in the East, I was convinced that canoeing the Jack, my expression for the St. John, would provide just as much fun and excitement.

The St. John has sufficient water for a run only during the spring runoff; by mid-June the water level is way down, making it scratchy for canoe bottoms. The black flies arrive in all their biting fury by the last week in May. Nature has fortuitously granted a two-week reprieve during May to guarantee adequate water without flies. Only about a thousand people a year run the St. John, compared to the forty thousand who migrate down the nearby Allagash, with its much longer season and more numerous access points for re-supply and emergency take-out. When I canoed the Allagash a decade earlier, I kept hearing that the St. John was the river the Allagash guides headed for during their time off. I had frittered away ten good years before traveling the short distance between the two rivers to arrive at the Baker Lake outlet bridge. Many top Maine guides, past and present, have never run the St. John, being tied down with operating hunting and fishing camps or running a favorite river nearby. It is always next year for them, the next spring that never comes.

A special biological grace should grant canoeists lifespans of five hundred years, with an option to extend, for running all the rivers in North America. With perfect health, guide service, an unbreakable lightweight canoe, and unlimited financial support, a canoeist could theoretically begin running the rivers as a teenager and keep doing it for an average lifespan of 75 years. Even if he did nothing but canoe, however, he could never run all the rivers. Someone else would have to explore all the caves, another climb the mountains, a third fish all the lakes, and they still would not finish. It is a humbling thought.

I ambled back past our tent village to the night campfire. Marty, with his magnificent handlebar mustache, caught my eye as I approached.

A Passion for Wilderness

He was holding forth with one of his canoeing tales, leaning into it as he had with so many paddle strokes on the river. Years of paddling had given him a massive chest with a voice to match. Marty had just started a story about the Moisie River in the Quebec wilderness where he leads a ten-day trip each fall.

"We had to catch the train coming down from Schefferville. The last ten miles of the Moisie are unrunnable. The tracks parallel the river down to the St. Lawrence, down to the town of Sept-Îles. Otherwise we would have had to wait a week for another train to come by.

"I clambered up out of the gorge and waved to stop the train. We had fourteen canoes to load in the freight car. The baggage master was in a hurry and became very impatient. A rowdy group rides that train from Schefferville: Indians, miners, and sportsmen.

" 'Just a couple more canoes,' I told him, as the canoeists rushed to climb up the bank. Some of the canoes weren't even in sight and were still around the bend when I stopped the train. I pleaded and pleaded, the group kept huffing and dragging their boats, and I finally got all my canoes aboard.

"The baggage clerk wanted $100 a canoe. Heck, that would be $1,400 for fourteen canoes. I really couldn't pay that. I got to the station at Sept-Îles and waited in line to pay my bill. The office of the baggage master was closed. A hunter in back of me happened to mention that I ought to pay by the load. When I got to the ticket window, I told the clerk on duty that my baggage took half a car. He figured up a bill for $130, the standard rate for half a baggage car from Schefferville. My canoes were aboard for just ten miles. I paid and walked away."

We all laughed at Marty's tale of the North as he took a drag from his cigar. He was ready to launch into another story. I wished I had energy to listen to more, but I was drained from the long day and all the excitement in preparing for the expedition. No matter how often I changed my position around the fire, the smoke caught under the kitchen fly kept drifting into my eyes. I walked away and crawled into my goose-down sleeping bag. Sleep came immediately.

Day Two / Sunday, May 12, 1985
Baker Lake to Turner Bogan

Dawn brought sun and wind, a blustery blow that sent waves crashing against the shoreline. For breakfast we ate scrambled eggs, bacon, and English muffins. Marty and a few others made bacon sandwiches with the muffins.

"No one is going to dump on this trip, only you," he said jokingly to someone. "If you don't dump the first two days, you should make the rest of the trip all right."

Marty and the other driver begin packing their personal gear to return to their Cathance Lake basecamp. They opened the hoods of their vans and adjusted their engines, thoroughly loosened by the bumpy drive the day before. The other driver revved his engine time and again as it kept sputtering and dying. Finally it started and hummed. We shook hands with the drivers and watched them clatter over the bridge. They were gone. Now it was Tom's trip.

Tom was the head guide of the outfit and our leader for this trip. A 34-year-old outdoorsman, he had traveled up and down both American continents — hitchhiking, canoeing, climbing, doing and seeing everything. Tom had already canoed the Allagash thirteen times and the St. John six times.

Tom and a companion were the first to canoe the Korok River in Labrador. "It was oatmeal for breakfast, granola for lunch, and pemmican stew for supper for fifty-five days," he said, "interspersed with spruce partridge and trout."

Tom canoed and traveled through Labrador, absorbing the culture of the Eskimo and the Cree Indians and collecting archaeological artifacts for the Smithsonian Institution. During winters he led trips on a remote stretch of the Rio Grande. The summer before he had run the Snake River in the Yukon, a virgin river that had never before been run. Two centuries ago, Tom would have been a riverman in the same mold as a mountain man in the West. He was tall and bearded and smoked a pipe. He seemed more fully at home on a river than he would be in civilization.

But experience and ability aside, the trait that everyone soon recognized in Tom was his helpful and accommodating manner. He had the perfect

A Passion for Wilderness

temperament for a guide — a patient and unperturbed outlook. Everyone with him felt safe.

Mark, a junior at the University of Maine at Orono, was the assistant guide. He was learning the rivers and worked well with everyone. He was the first one up in the morning and the last to go to bed at night. Of French-Canadian extraction, he lived in Old Town, the home of great canoes and great guides ever since Thoreau's time. He must have been a descendant of a voyageur, for he seemed to have inherited the knack of running rivers.

Our complete party consisted of the two registered Maine guides and nine "sports," a mixed lot from various backgrounds. Differences aside, we all possessed one common ambition: to canoe the St. John. All other considerations meant little. I was a writer and librarian, at 50 the oldest of the group. Don, my tentmate and canoe partner, was a Nova Scotian businessman in his forties. The rest were in their thirties and twenties. Jim worked as a chimney sweep. Wearing his $175 wet suit, Steve was a lawyer from New York City who enjoyed scuba diving. Walt was a pilot and navigator in the American merchant marine; his wife, Sharon, served as a registered nurse and health officer in Boston. Eric was a Harvard graduate student, pursuing a double doctorate in medicine. Denise worked out of San Diego as a venture capitalist businesswoman. Interested in cross-country skiing, bicycling, and hiking, Tamara was a legal secretary in Boston and had taken a Canadian river trip a year earlier.

Oh, yes — there was also a twelfth member, Sags.

A Passion for Wilderness

He was Tom's bowman, but he never paddled a stroke. Able to eat anything and sleep anywhere, Sags ended the trip in the best physical shape of all of us. Sags was Tom's mixed-breed dog, named for Saglek Bay, Labrador. From his happy, alert face, it was easy to see that he anticipated the trip more than anyone else.

Tom and Mark conducted a dry demonstration of canoemanship. It was too windy at lakeside to hear much of what they said, so we hauled a canoe back into the woods. Nodding to Walt, Tom said, "I feel ridiculous explaining to you what a bow and a stern are." But our class went well and we all learned something. Tom continued with demonstrations:

"Use a drive and glide stroke that you can maintain all day with comfort. A push stroke will quickly tire you out. Kneeling on the canoe floor will provide fifty percent more power and stability. In rapids, paddle. Without a grip in the water, the river takes over. The blank stare with the hands on the gunwales is no good. The air brace is worthless.

"If you get into problems, slip into an eddy pool, the calm water in back of a rock. Watch out for strainers, also called sweepers, the fallen tree trunks down in the water; they are the most dangerous and unpredictable things.

"There is a ton of force per loaded canoe going downstream. Between a dumped canoe and a rock, a person is sandwich material. If you dump, work your way to the upstream side and ride the water on your back with your legs extended high. My best advice in two words is, 'Lean downstream.' Leaning backward will lower the gunwales and allow the water to pour in."

Mark explained the canoe signals. An upraised paddle meant "Go ahead." A paddle held sideways signified "Stop!" A paddle waved left or right conveyed "Turn."

For the first few days, there would be no major rapids, so we had time to master the basic skills before running Big Rapids on the last day.

Some paired off to canoe tandem while others elected to paddle solo. Don and I took the yellow canoe **Sunbright.** Tom selected sleek black **Icebreaker** as a solo canoe. Our river flotilla consisted of four tandem canoes (**Sunbright, Lone Star, Kitty,** and **Aircraft Finish**) and three solo (**Icebreaker, Huevos,** and **Rodeo**), for a total of seven boats.

At the shore the wind blew incessantly, so we conducted a wet run with unloaded canoes in a cove near the bridge. Otherwise, on a calm day the group would have unlimited room on the expanse of Baker Lake. We bumped and jostled in these close quarters, since most of us had not paddled in some time.

Tom supervised the loading of the canoes, bow heavy, and used a single piece of cord to secure all the camp and personal gear. If a canoe dumped, every piece of cargo would remain tied in the boat instead of floating away free in a heavy current. "We teach people," Tom said, "to fly to the moon but not to tie correct knots. Executives earning $150,000 a year who can't tie a knot or load a canoe come on these trips."

Don and I looked around before shoving off.

"I could spend a few days here at Baker," I said, "fishing and exploring."

"So could I," Don said. "It's such a beautiful place."

Sags hopped into his special spot in **Icebreaker** as Tom swung back and turned downstream. Mark and Tamara in **Aircraft Finish** would bring up the rear. We were finally off for a week on the river, Don in the stern and I in the bow. The breeze blew against my face as we started to move.

We guided our canoe through the bridge pilings and left civilization behind. The river was quite narrow here, about two road-widths across, a tiny water trail through the Maine woods. The St. John was flowing at a rate of four miles per hour; theoretically, we could get to Big Rapids without paddling a stroke. There were no hills or ridges bordering the river in the initial stages of the trip, so it was impossible to see beyond the trees over the gunwales in this flat country. As the river swung right and left to create rips, Don and I soon developed a coordinated rhythm in our paddling to maintain an efficient and easy pace. An hour-and-a-half paddle went quickly.

Tom signaled that it was time to pull over for lunch. We went "bushing" to pick out an undeveloped place along the river to beach our canoes. There was no food until Jim landed with the lunch box, which he was assigned to carry. We improvised a table by pushing together two boxes and then gathered around to prepare sandwiches from

A Passion for Wilderness

The St. John River in northern Maine

piles of ham, roast beef, chicken, lettuce, and tomato. Our lunches comprised these fresh foods for the first few midday stops. Once that was gone, we relied on tuna fish, jam, and peanut butter for our lunch breaks.

We always needed these lunch stops — if only to stretch and walk around. Paddling developed our arms, wrists, and shoulders, but our legs had no exercise. Perhaps canoe designers should consider installing a bicycle wheel to remedy this oversight. Each time we landed, I hobbled stiffly until exercise sent blood to my cramped limbs.

As we resumed our journey, both Tom and Walt propped their fly rods against the stern gunwales and trolled for trout. Fishermen to the last, they trolled daily for the rest of the trip. A fish fry is supposedly a standard bill of fare on every Maine canoe trip, but the entire catch for our trip was a single kipper that Tom landed. It was not big enough to eat, but at least it provided a few laughs.

At midafternoon we approached the Turner Bogan campsite sign. along with a few others, I clambered up the high banks and scouted the area. Tom conducted his own reconnaissance. "We're staying," he said. Every afternoon thereafter, we awaited those magic words, the signal to tie up and unload. We formed a chain to haul the boxes and gear up the bank. Don and I pitched our tent on the pine-needled forest floor. As he rested quietly on his sleeping bag, watching the river flowing from the open tent flap, white froth and sticks floated silently by. "It's hypnotizing," he

A Passion for Wilderness

said.

On a little hike through brush I checked out the bogan, an area of flat water back around the point. A beaver dam, old and rotting, had cut the bogan in two.

For supper we enjoyed baked halibut, potatoes, and carrots. "We hooked them back at Baker Lake at a secret fishing hole," Tom and Mark assured us. Another pair of diners soon joined us. Sitting on our makeshift seats at the campsite table — tree stumps and flat rocks — we had eaten maybe half of our meal when two Canada jays flitted excitedly overhead in the tree branches. "Camp robbers," I said. "They've found us." With each dive they dropped lower and lower. "They'll eat out of your hand if you let them," Tom said. We threw out scraps and leftovers as they swooped down to snatch them and fly away.

Everyone went about various early-evening activities. Mark and Tamara gave the tinware a soap scrubbing and hot rinse. Tom fished from his canoe. Jim and Steve practiced solo canoeing techniques in the bogan. Several of us bushwhacked up to the beaver dam. As the log-and-branch bridge quivered under my weight, I decided not to cross. No one else dared attempt it.

At the campfire Tom spoke about canoes and guiding. We sports wondered why we found sand in our tents. Tom smiled:

"That's special Rio Grande sand from our last trip before taking this one out. I scouted the Rio Grande with a doctor friend and we liked it. I decided it would be a nice commercial trip in the spring, something for college kids on spring break. We left from downtown Presidio, Texas, to enter the Lower Canyon of the Rio Grande. It was 100-degree heat in hot sun. This last time a writer on assignment from **Sports Afield** came along and is writing up the trip. I ran the week-long trip twice with a day layover.

"Our outfit will make money on the St. John trip, but there is a long period of slack time between the Rio Grande trip and the opening of the Maine season. And the overhead and upkeep of the Cat Base (Cathance Lake basecamp) goes on just the same.

"The time used to be that all the guides did was to take the sports down the river. Now you've got to know every bird, every tree, and be an expert on natural science.

"I give slide lectures around cities in the winter to promote our trips. Marty has a Christmas tree business in New Jersey during the winter, and he actually makes more from that than all the canoe trips combined."

When I returned to the tent, Don was awake. He had felt ill during the day and ate very little for supper, which he lost shortly thereafter. Now he was feeling better.

I was tired and turned in, but I slept poorly. Why I should even think about it I did not know, but I had a premonition that I would dump tomorrow.

CANOEING THE JACK

Chapter 2

HUNG UP WITH THE RAIN FALLING DOWN

Day Three / Monday, May 13, 1985
Turner Bogan to Doucie Brook

Every morning began the same way.   From inside my tent I could hear the noises of woodchopping and coughing.   Sometimes I heard the staccato of a woodpecker, drilling against a tree trunk.   I liked the sound of nature's alarm clock.

253

A Passion for Wilderness

Outside, it was warm, and I removed my jacket. We finished breakfast, delicious French toast, struck our tents, and broke camp. Don and I switched positions; I was now paddling stern.

Each morning I felt exhilarated as we back-paddled away from the bank, leaving behind the old campsite, swinging into the current, and paddling forward. Ahead was a new day on the river. A breeze wafted over the water and rilled fresh air into my face.

The river kept winding. Tributaries joined the St. John. Often I heard a distant roar ahead, believing rips or rapids would come into view. Then a stream would tumble out of the woods and discharge into the St. John with a loud roar. In less than a minute, the sound would drift away. All these spring freshets would dry up in a month.

"It's a beautiful river," Tom enthused as our canoe approached his. "It's a guide's trip." He was happy. Often during the week someone would say half to himself or to the group, "The silence is wonderful" or "The river is so majestic." As we glided ahead, the river took on a mystical quality that gripped us more with every passing day.

But the river had its moods, changing quickly, and so did the weather. The skies became gray, then charcoal, then black. Huge drops pelted us as we hastened to pull slickers from the tops of our duffels or dry bags. Intense bursts redoubled and drenched us.

Tom led us toward shore for lunch. Somehow, in that tangle of fallen trees, we poked through and managed to land on ledges. Gingerly maintaining

A Passion for Wilderness

our footing on the slippery surface, we dragged the canoes forward and tied them to live trunks. We knocked down and tossed aside a few dead snags to clear out an area in the duff. We left one log to serve as a makeshift table for sandwich materials. I snapped off a stout twig to make a satisfactory jam spreader. For dessert we cut slices from a pineapple.

Following lunch, we resumed our paddle in the cold rain. The sky was so dark that we had difficulty spotting submerged rocks. I recalled that some canoeists had an eye painted on the blade of their paddle to search for them, an extra eye to assist their vision. I was not that well prepared. The river swung back and forth with rips coursing around exposed above-surface "dry" rocks and boiling over the menacing ones below the water's line. This stretch required careful paddling. Denise and Eric hit a rock, were hung up momentarily, and then plunged over, free. "We almost bought it," Denise said later.

Another branch of the St. John joined the main river from the left. Tom yelled back to us to eddy out to await the rest of the canoes from around the last bend. He pulled close to the bank. A second later, he called to me, "Watch out for that rock." At the last second, I saw a submerged boulder and swung the canoe toward the middle of the river to avoid it. I had faced this situation a dozen times that day, but this time the canoe bottom caught the rock. We were hung up. The canoe seemed suspended in air. The current swung the canoe halfway around.

A Passion for Wilderness

Don and I quickly knelt and pried with our paddles. We swung off the rock and dropped free. "We're off," I yelled. I was jubilant. Suddenly the canoe took a crazy lurch upstream, and in a split second I perceived the whole awful thing. The canoe pitched right on a tilt. The upstream gunwale was too low. With the full power of the river behind it, water poured into the canoe.

We dumped in the frigid water. The paddles left our hands, shot forward, and were instantly swept downstream. My hat went. It was hopeless to think that we could retrieve any lost items. Don and I held onto the canoe as we kicked our feet and used our free arms to guide it to shore.

The cold seemed relatively easy to take; the humiliation was worse. Tom waded out from shore, grabbed our painter, and pulled the swamped canoe to the sand bank. He cut the rope to free our bags.

"I feel like a damned fool," I said.

"Don't worry about it," Tom said. "I wrecked seven canoes and dumped fifty times when I was learning. At least you have the consolation of having the cleanest canoe floor."

Jim joined us to tip the water out of the canoe. "I looked back," he said, "and saw that you had freed the canoe. A second later I saw a yellow bottom."

At Tom's urging we opened our bags to check the condition of our sleeping bags. Don's was dry. Mine seemed dry. Don and I immediately rubbed down with towels and changed into dry clothes. Tom stayed with us as Mark led the rest of the party downstream with instructions to stop at Doucie Brook. Reaching down into **Icebreaker,** Tom supplied us with two wooden paddles he had stashed away for just such an emergency. I used my new paddle for the rest of the trip. Some time later, Mark and Tamara recovered our lost paddles beached on a point. The hat was never found. I used a wool cap for the rest of the trip.

Don and I started out again in our dry clothes on the wet seats. We swung easily through the pilings of a bridge.

The fun of that day's paddle ended with that dump. The horizon dipped down to meet the river with heavy rain. The drops were cold. Along the shore, the forest looked very black and indistinct. The rain soon created a puddle of water on the canoe floor, and it swished back and forth as we shifted our weight.

I spotted our group at the Doucie Brook campsite and guided the canoe to the gravel bank, since I wanted to scout out the site. Our other option was a site two miles downstream. I jammed my wooden paddle between the canoe floor and one of the thwarts. Don stepped out and held the bow as I prepared to disembark.

I tripped on a thwart and pitched heavily into the shallow water. Breaking my fall with my hands, I stood up, soaked from the waist down. My friends gasped. "I'm OK," I said.

Tom reconnoitered the area, found seven level tentsites and made the quick decision to remain. Don and I pitched our tent but put nothing inside. We wanted the wet canvas to air out and dry. We draped our wet clothes on the rafters of a half-collapsed abandoned shack. I looked in my duffel bag for my third and last change of clothing. So-called waterproof bags, I discovered, represented more advertising than reality. My wool shirt was a little damp but warm.

Tom and Mark kindled a fire. Someone had thoughtfully left a bundle of birch bark under the campsite table. Full of resin, the bark burned brightly in the rain.

As supper was cooking, three canoes came into view. Tom walked to shore. "There's a beautiful campsite on the right about two miles downstream," he told the people in the lead canoe. The party kept on paddling in the rain.

"You've got to negotiate for the campsites," Tom said. The other group had a legal right to land and set up at Doucie Brook, but we were occupying every available tentsite, and additional campers would have created very crowded conditions.

In the steady rain, logs and nailed-together boards of a pier swirled by. The river was taking everything it could find.

Our supper was baked chicken, potato, and corn on the cob. We all ate heartily after our long day. After washing the dishes, we placed and propped our socks, boots, and clothing on the fireplace rocks. We even built a second drying fire in another fireplace near my tent. To hasten the process, some of our group waved shirts and pants just above the flames. Clouds of vapor rose from the steaming clothes.

A Passion for Wilderness

Feeling chilled, I crawled into my sleeping bag, essentially dry except for a few moist spots near the bottom. My body heat soon dried the damp places.

The group gathered around the fire outside my tent, and I could hear the usual campfire stories. Earlier in the day I had urged Tom to talk about his pioneering river trip on Canada's Snake River the previous summer for a wealthy client who wanted to try something new. Sandy, the client, quickly became a legend in the Yukon with his wild spending habits. He even bought whole motels to house his family for one evening, ousting the guests already checked in for the night. To maintain daily contact with New York investors and businessmen, Sandy brought a powerful radio transmitter and receiver to beam calls from his campsites to the outside world. Local Yukon radio hams were totally cut off when Sandy sent out his calls, jamming their lines.

The day before Sandy and his family were scheduled to finish the trip, he suddenly decided to summon a bush pilot to leave the wilderness. Marty and Tom tried to explain that the party simply had to paddle another eighty easy miles to a prearranged landing site. There Sandy and his family could meet their bush pilot with his plane and be whisked away. But Sandy was adamant. Tom said:

"The pilot risked his life getting in there, just a wide stretch on the river. The pontoon plane landed on the water and loaded up. Wind blew the plane close to a cliff, so the pilot

A Passion for Wilderness

could not take off. Marty and I got into our
canoes and tried to push the plane out into the
middle of the river. We pushed and pushed, awk-
ward and dangerous as it was, to satisfy Sandy's
demands. Finally the plane took off, couldn't
gain altitude, and landed immediately a short
distance down the river.

"We paddled down. This time we had to leave
the canoes and wade out into the river, finally up
to our necks, standing on tiptoe in the cold
water. After awhile it was freezing. We tried
with all our strength to push the plane away from
the cliff. The exhaust from the chugging engines
kept kicking up the water and we couldn't hear
each other speak. The fumes started to become
suffocating.

"Suddenly I sensed a rushing of wind with a
strange feeling of floating in air with the water
whizzing below me. The plane had taken off, while
we were hanging on. Marty dropped almost immediately into the water. I couldn't, as my sleeve
had got caught on the pontoon. I was momentarily
dragged, the sleeve tore off, and I dropped on the
bank. The others watched from the first landing
site and thought I was gone, dead. I was scraped
and bleeding but otherwise OK. It was the closest
call I have ever had in my life.

"Sandy keeps calling me at Cat Base to do another trip. Marty has had enough with such an
impossible arrogant person and wants to turn him
down no matter what the proposition is. But I
told Sandy my services are available for $500 a
day."

A Passion for Wilderness

I knew that neither Tom nor anyone else could top that story. I hunched down in my bag and fell asleep.

Day Four / Tuesday, May 14, 1985
Doucie Brook to Burntland Brook

During the night, drizzle became heavy rain, lightning, and thunder. My air mattress deflated and I woke up, lying stiff on the hard tent floor. I breathed a squishy dampness. I stepped outside in the mud and puddles to retrieve a hand pump.

As dawn broke, the whole camp laid in for another hour, knowing we were in no hurry to get underway on the river. I swallowed hard, trying to shake a sore throat, and pulled on my driest clothes and went to the camp fire.

"Are we moving today?" I asked Tom.

"Oh, yes, after a little breakfast."

"I heard your story. You ought to charge Sandy $1,000 a day."

Mark had just come back from the river, where he checked a measuring stick.

"The river," Mark said, "rose eight inches during the night."

Eventually the rain became an acceptable drizzle. As my friends gathered around the fire for breakfast, I felt upbeat.

"Someday I'm coming back," I said, "to dig that rock out of the river and place it as a memento in my front yard."

A Passion for Wilderness

During breakfast the gray shroud pulled apart to show blue patches. Jim suggested that perhaps we had gotten rid of the bad weather once and for all and would enjoy sunny skies for the rest of the trip.

As we settled into a leisurely pace, we bailed rainwater out of the canoes and dried clothes and boots over every rock and branch near the fire. It was impossible to dry out everything. I stuffed my duffel bag, arranging the clothes in a kind of progression from soppy to dry. "It's natural to be damp on a trip," Tom said reassuringly.

Across the river, the spruce forest was blighted and dying at the treetops in a sickly yellow fuzz. Spruce budworm had attacked the trees.

At last we were paddling on the river, slickers and all. Every day, no matter how chilly it was, that first hour of paddling warmed me up. Soon the sun shot through a break in the clouds. We all felt much warmer. Before long the skies cleared.

The St. John kept widening and gaining power as it picked up more water from tributaries. An osprey circled, then skimmed close to the water, its wing tips flapping just above the surface. Often we drew close to a pair of ducks, always a male and a female. They spotted us and darted away in flight, with the male in the lead.

The river cut deeply through the old glacial gravels and swept around to the right. Many giant boulders, undercut and exposed, were hanging on the steep thirty- to forty-foot banks, ready to

A Passion for Wilderness

crash down into the river with the coming of the next ice breakup or even a heavy rain. Snow lurked in dark shadow in ravines, sometimes as patches and occasionally in long ridges. Trees were scattered about in a wild tangle on the top of the bank, with individual logs and branches strewn down the slopes, defying gravity until the next avalanche. For the moment, everything was quietly in place. As we canoed by, we avoided the rock- and tree-strewn banks.

Our canoes shot through the waves in this fast stretch. Canoeing was anticipating the next bend in the river. Canoeing was hearing your heart thump wildly as you bounced through the waves. Canoeing was a long journey from the highland ponds downriver through white- and flatwater to the sea.

We eddied left to the Ledge Rapids campsite for our lunch stop. I dug my boots into the gravel and climbed up to the lip of the bank. From there, the St. John appeared in a great panoramic sweep, with whitewater awaiting us after lunch. Jim arrived with his lunch box, and we ate our sandwiches at a site that we all considered the most splendid place for a hunting and fishing camp in the State of Maine.

"I've waited ten years," I told Steve, "to go on this trip."

"A buddy told me about this trip nine years ago," Steve said, "and urged me to go. Now I'm doing it and my friend is still waiting."

"When you return to the outside," I said, "there will be only two or three people you can talk

A Passion for Wilderness

to who will understand why you went."

After lunch, some lay in the sun and fell half-asleep, like boys and girls at the beach. The whole trip had taken on the pattern of sleeping, eating, paddling, pitching tents, and telling stories. It was a canoe party.

I hiked along a scouting trail through blowdown and swale and worked my way down to the river. There were two dry rocks about fifteen feet off-shore. Boils and high water stretched out along the submerged ledge. I thought the river could be run either of two ways, shooting between the two dry rocks or ferrying out in the middle of the river to avoid them entirely. A couple of others joined me to look over the situation.

Tom and Mark read the river and decided the close-in approach through the two rocks would be the best. They pointed and gestured like army generals planning a battle with appropriate strategy and tactics.

We would run the rapids singly. Mark and Tamara went first, shot through the inverted V at the rocks, and eddied around the boulder closest to shore. Mark cocked his arm to aim a throw bag if one was needed.

"Hold it! Hold it!" he yelled as each canoe approached. We all caught that V and held it. Don and I paddled hard through the thrashing waves. The blade of my paddle hit one wave at the wrong angle and slapped a sheet of water in my face. Once through and the danger past, we looked upon Ledge Rapids as an easy run.

As we relaxed during a long stretch of flat-

A Passion for Wilderness

water, that afternoon felt like midsummer in the hot sun. I wore a heavy wool cap for sun protection and kept it on despite the heat. We saw no one during a languid half-paddling passage down the river. We had the place to ourselves, the uncontested rulers of this watery empire. Tom and Walt trolled for trout.

Eric and Denise approached our canoe. Eric asked Don and me to pose for a photograph. "Do you want a straight shot or a dump shot?" I asked. Eric was satisfied with a traditional picture of an upright canoe. I could wait until Big Black Rapids before risking an action shot.

We quickly woke up from this daydream as we approached the pilings of Moody Bridge. Encountering no problems, we passed under, only to see whitewater ahead. Rocky Rapids, however, presented no rocks, just standing waves that we ran easily. The hard work on the river was over for the day; all I had to do was to keep the canoe aligned in the current.

To avoid setting up a dark camp Tom always tried to arrive at every campsite in daylight. On personal trips with a buddy, he would occasionally catch a tail wind and push on for maximum mileage. Such ideal conditions might not return, so he would paddle well into the night for a fifty-mile day.

"One party," Tom said, "canoed the St. John from Baker Lake through Big Rapids in twenty-four hours in a speed stunt. A buddy of mine cross country skied the same route in the dead of winter. It took him two weeks."

On this afternoon, Tom looked forward to

A Passion for Wilderness

reaching Burntland Brook campsite, one of his favorites on the river. He also wanted his party to dry out their clothing.

"There it is," Tom said. "See that stand of poplar trees?" Burntland Brook had, as its name suggested, burned, but after a forest fire, the poplar, a cousin to the birch, is the first tree to re-forest itself. I looked ahead and spotted the gray trunks, pencil-thin in the distance.

We drew close. There were no canoes on the bank and no signs of activity. The site was ours. We landed and unloaded. Within minutes, the place became a tent city. With the sun still high, everyone spread out damp clothes and boots, hundreds of items, in every place open to sun — on the ground, in branches, over logs, canoe thwarts, and even the Burntland Brook sign itself. It became Laundryville, USA.

I suddenly realized that the sun had sapped my strength and I was very tired. I drank water and crawled into my sleeping bag for an hour's sleep. After my nap, I walked down to the campfire. As supper was being prepared, Tom urged us to gather up our clothes. With such a clear sky and the sun's rays fast climbing from the ground to the treetops, a heavy dew would soon form to saturate our garments. A frost was even possible by morning. Nature had washed and dried my clothes free of charge. Picking up took but a minute. I hurried the chore as everyone was gathering around the campfire. I investigated.

A massage before supper? Why not? Who would have believed that in the wilderness I could en-

A Passion for Wilderness

joy the luxury of a professional massage to loosen up my neck and shoulders. Sharon's nursing experience made her a master of the massage, and several of us soon lost our stiffness from the day's paddle.

Supper was pork chops, fried potatoes, green beans, and bran biscuits. Mark prepared a special dessert, peach cobbler, baking it from fires below and above the pan. I shall forever associate each campsite on the trip with a particular meal. I often wondered why explorers, mountaineers, and voyageurs faithfully recorded in their journals such information in great detail; now I understood.

As we washed and rinsed our plates and cups at water's edge, a distant point of woods upstream shone brightly in the last burst of the day's sun. I lingered to view it, a changeless scene a thousand years ago, now, and, I hope, a thousand years hence.

At the campfire, Walt described his merchant marine service at Diego Garcia, an island in the Indian Ocean. He always wore his Diego Garcia Yacht Club cap, explaining that the sport was about the only available recreation on that little-known base in which the United States Navy has invested a billion or more dollars.

"The coral reef is fifty-two miles long and a half mile wide in the form of a horseshoe," Walt said. "The highest point of land is about twelve feet above sea level where the Officers Club is. They don't have a golf course on the island, since any errant shot would land in the ocean."   Walt was returning to sea a few weeks after the canoe trip.

Tom spoke of the rivers of northern Quebec, the Moisie, the Churchill, and the fjord rivers of Labrador.

"I wonder how much will soon be left," Tom said.   "Quebec is damming many rivers for hydroelectric power.   They are creating manmade lakes the size of the Commonwealth of Massachusetts. Crews of men go into the bush, and, working from both ends and flying in supplies and equipment, they can build a 500-mile road quickly.

"The Cree Indian had his own culture for thousands of years.   Now alcohol has taken its toll.   The tribe used to go on annual quail hunts in the fall along the rivers.   With the dammed-up rivers and the creation of huge lakes, that is gone now.

"And how can they oppose the destruction of their land?   They can't.   The natives have no power.   The political power in Quebec is in the southern part, from Montreal to Quebec City.

"With the price of oil, the cry now is for alternate sources of power.   And as the Canadian government and the province of Quebec see the untapped hydroelectric power in the North, they sense unlimited potential."

Don leaned forward.   "What's going on now," he said,   "is just a mockup of what's going to happen."

"The Moisie, the river we do," Tom said, "cuts through a huge gorge.   From the point of view of the power companies, the Moisie would be a perfect river to convert into a hydro-producer. Who knows how long it will be left the way it is?"

It had been a glorious day, but on that sad thought, I excused myself for a night's sleep.

Day Five / Wednesday, May 15, 1985
Burntland Brook to Simmons Farm

I awoke after midnight. As I sensed light through the side of the tent, I zipped open the tent flap and stepped outside. In my bare feet, I felt my way down to the river. The air was cold and crisp. The Northern Lights pulsated across the sky, a thick stream of stars creating an awesome spectacle.

In the morning I put on several layers of clothes, knowing I would peel them off one by one by early afternoon and then reverse the process as the day became night. The sky remained crystal clear.

Mark cut up several apples to prepare apple pancakes. For starters we chewed and sucked on oranges and grapefruit.

"My objective for today," Tom said, "is the Seven Islands campsite." Most St. John trips scheduled one night or a layover day there.

As we were finishing breakfast, someone spotted a solitary canoe, and we all turned to look. Soon we watched five canoes pass, hugging the far side of the river. The canoes swung around the next bend, their red hulls shining in the sun.

Don and I switched canoes with Walt and Sharon.

A Passion for Wilderness

We exchanged **Sunbright** for **Lone Star,** a green canoe that felt tippy and unstable. But the canoe had been lucky and upright for Walt and Sharon, so we hoped we would continue **Lone Star**'s streak. We backpaddled and then leaned forward into that mighty river.

The first hour went quickly. My upper body warmed up and when we stopped for lunch I was ready to shed my windbreaker. Again and again we sensed the severity of the last break-up, with boulders stuck precariously in the muck of the steep banks. Fans of dark brown earth reached the water's edge, indicating that recent mud slides had tumbled into the river. Ridges of snow hid in the shadows.

We skirted an abandoned towerlike concrete piling at Nine-Mile Bridge. The bridge had collapsed and would never be repaired. In back of tall grass on shore, the roofs of several cabins sagged.

Soon we heard a sound, the approach of a motorboat. Its rattle-trap putt-putt noise destroyed the illusion of the wilderness that we had sought in coming here. The boys in the boat waved and seemed amiable enough. "That noise," Jim said, "represents an obscenity and an insult to this place."

Later on, jet planes from Loring Air Force Base, in Limestone, Maine, shattered the sky and the sound barrier with an earsplitting sound. First I heard the noise, and then twisted to catch a glimpse. Even then, the planes went so fast that I occasionally missed spotting them. The

A Passion for Wilderness

A pole in the hand is worth two in the river

jets regularly used the St. John Valley as a designated zone for aerial maneuvers in mock combat. Whether or not they considered us as simulated moving targets as they screamed by, I don't know, but it seemed so.

Tom pulled **Icebreaker** over to the shady bank as Sags jumped out. We looked forward to lunch and a stretch of the legs. Again we were bushing, as there was no authorized site — just a huge snowbank and fallen trees. At this point in our trip, our lunch meats, fresh tomatoes, and lettuce were gone. We now relied on canned tunafish, peanut butter, and jam for our sandwich spreads.

After lunch, Tom conducted a poling demonstration. With effortless assurance, he stood up in the canoe, placing his pole to move forward or shifting his weight and repositioning the pole to move backward. Tom never wasted an ounce of energy or made a false move — whether poling, running rapids, or fanning fire with a pot lid.

"There's a place," Tom said, "the size of a quarter where this pole should go. The idea is to find it. But watch when you are swinging the pole. Don't whack your bowman in the head. Sags ducks his head when he sees the shadow of the pole over his head."

Those paddling solo accepted the challenge. Sternmen in tandem canoes declined, if for no other reason than to avoid decapitating their partners. We resumed our journey.

Later that afternoon, Tom pointed to the sky. "A great blue heron," he said. The bird, with its tremendous wingspan, surveyed the world during its high, circling flight above our heads. Then it silently disappeared over the tops of some dead trees.

A motorboat approached and the boatman cut his engine. Tom paddled over as we wondered what was happening. Tom told us later that it was the area game warden. They were old friends and were having a social chat, catching up on the river news. A Maine game warden is an important person; he has more legal authority than any other law officer in the state. He can perform marriages, has the power of search or arrest, and is the supreme law of the land, above and beyond the mere regulation of the game codes.

By mid-afternoon we were nearing our day's objective of Seven Islands campsite. We were tired and ready to land; the hot sun had beat down all day. The river had long ago cut through the alluvial plain to create these islands, where for many years loggers had maintained a supply and farming settlement. This village had long since been abandoned, but it remained a popular campsite. First we saw the stubble of brown fields and then five red canoes at the campsite landing. The site, unfortunately, was occupied. Two or three members of the other party left the shelter area and walked to the edge of the bank. Their red, fleshy faces were grim and hostile-looking. Tom pulled in close, exchanged greetings with their spokes-man, and then swung downstream.

We had no choice except to push on. In about a half hour, we approached a logging road bridge where workmen were repairing the extensive damage caused by the breakup, an annual spring job. An electric generator reverberated loudly. We had little interest in camping at Priestly campsite, on a shoulder beside the bridge. That place was noisier than rush-hour traffic.

About twenty minutes later and around bends, we braced for the beginning of Priestly Rapids. Without ample water, these rapids represent trouble. During high-water periods such as we were enjoying, the rapids were supposed to be easy, just standing waves with some bounce.

A Passion for Wilderness

We plowed straight ahead. At the critical moment in the midst of the rapids, I stopped paddling abruptly. Sweat had dripped down my forehead to wash the suntan lotion into my eyes. The smarting pain was overwhelming. My eyes filled with tears and I couldn't see. I shouted to Don about my situation and he managed to keep the canoe aimed straight. I frantically rubbed my eyes and doused them with scooped-up handfuls of river water. Finally, I regained my eyesight and composure. I had run Priestly Rapids half-blind and then and there decided to try a different brand of lotion.

Our objective now was Simmons Farm campsite. As we viewed the site from upriver, we recognized the same situation we had encountered at Seven Islands. Canoes were beached at the landing.

Tom in the lead signaled us to slow down. At that moment, the party at Simmons Farm was gathering at its canoes.

"Turn around and head upstream," Tom said.

Tired as we were, we slaved away upstream, battled the current, stalled, and killed time. Then we turned around. The other party had left!

Tom decided to check out a backup campsite on an island opposite the Simmons Farm site. We didn't wait for the "We're staying" ritual. We beached and unloaded. Impressed with a magnificent spruce near the water's edge, Tom decided to remain. Earlier canoeing parties had chopped off its lower limbs for firewood. The day's run had covered twenty-two miles.

The island once was part of Simmons Farm, with

level fields, so there was no difficulty in finding tentsites. The island could have accommodated a hundred tents or more. I chose a secluded site behind a second-growth pine grove and turned in for an hour's sleep.

Without the usual campsite table and cooking shelter, two overturned canoes served as tables. Tom and Mark called us over for a supper of spaghetti, Italian sausage, salad, and red wine. The hamburger for the meat sauce was the last of the fresh meat and fish that had been preserved over dry ice. For the rest of the trip, we would be eating out of cans.

The spaghetti was heavy in my stomach as I hiked around the island. Others also decided to walk off their meal. Some went immediately to bed, having had far too much sun.

I followed a sunken path, watching the St. John roll down against the backdrop of forest and the setting sun. The treetops appeared to be engulfed in a band of orange flame. "The Spell of the North," they call it, and I knew now what this phrase meant.

On the far side of the island, Walt and Sharon motioned to me to stop and remain quiet. They pointed to a beaver that had not yet noticed us. Once it did, it was gone in a second.

Back at the campfire I lingered a few minutes, pointing out the Big Dipper and the North Star in the twilight sky. The position of the North Star and the direction of the St. John were perfectly aligned to guide us the next morning.

CANOEING THE JACK

Chapter 3

THE DRY ROCK NOBODY SAW

Day Six / Thursday, May 16, 1985
Simmons Farm to Seminary Brook

In the middle of the night I walked outside. Again aurora borealis lit up the sky so brilliantly I could have walked around the island again without a misstep.

Morning broke warm and sultry. I noticed Sharon sleeping on the ground near the canoe-serving tables. She had been ill during the night. Walt was also feeling bad. The bug that Don had picked up a few days before was still traveling as a hidden and unwanted companion.

For breakfast our guides served fried Spam, hot cereal, and fruit. I passed up the Spam, remembering the old G.I. Joe definition of Spam as "ham that flunked its physical." We leisurely broke camp. Sharon and Walt regained enough strength to travel.

At the river Mark took note of the weather. "Yesterday we had a headwind," Mark said. "Now it's a tailwind, and the wind is blowing in a new weather system toward Big Black Rapids. We'll have rain before the day is out." A billowing gray cloud mass was spreading downriver to invade the blue sky in the distance.

Mark used his measuring stick to check the water level. "The water's dropped during the night," he said. "It rises and then drops just as fast."

The morning paddle was delightful as the river swung through the forest, looping back and forth to pick up speed. Basford Rips presented no problems. Tom approached a bend and waved us left. He eddied out and we followed, the water thrashing about our canoes. Ahead I heard the continuous roar of water. Ashore, we followed a game trail and picked through a tangle to scout the river ahead.

Big Black Rapids rolled down for a mile ahead, an elemental, primitive, powerful force. The river churned left against a wall, and the right

Tom scouts approach to Big Black Rapids

side was strewn with rocks. A rock tongue ledge extended from the cliff, with a dry boulder sticking up to the right. The best route, we all agreed, was to follow the olive-colored water out from the cliff and then swing right to avoid the boulder.

"Reading this river is fifty percent of running it," Tom said. "Once you are committed, there is little you can do to alter your course. How the water is reacting on the surface represents an X-ray of what is going on down below.

"We'll stay to the inside of that wall; if you allow the current to pull you outside, you'll hit and never make the turn. Let's make that ledge the first leg of the run and eddy out there."

There was no portage trail that I could see. Unless we were prepared to make a wretched bushwhack portage through the blowdown, we were committed to making the run. We did not have a precise route ahead, just a general direction through what we thought was there.

Tom pushed off and shot down the rapids as we watched. It was so fast, so quick. His canoe made a few bounces, maneuvered away from the wall, a final flurry through whitewater, and then a distant figure raised his paddle in triumph. He eddied out and stood on the point. He could do nothing more for us; now it was our job to follow.

Two canoes preceded Don and me. We braced our knees against the gunwales. My heart was pounding, and a cold sweat pricked through my flesh. I had not been more physically alert on the entire trip.

We were off. We paddled through the first easy obstacles and headed into the main current. Stroke, pull, dig, lift, forward, stroke. We accelerated madly. We were going fast.

We plunged off a ledge into a hole. Wham. Water poured over the gunwales into the bow. Another hole. Wham. More water. With each ledge drop, we picked up more water and more weight.

Then I saw Tom frantically signaling us to swing to the right. We did the best we could, with water attacking the canoe. In a second I glimpsed what none of us had seen from our scout-

A Passion for Wilderness

ing perch; there was a **second** dry rock out from the point.   We angled over diagonally to avoid it. Standing waves sloshed into the canoe. We couldn't maneuver.   With one final wave, the canoe swamped and rolled over, throwing us free. We hung onto the sides and kicked our legs to aim the canoe toward the point.   Tom rescued us again and pulled **Lone Star** ashore.   Others helped us haul the canoe into a channel.

The rest of the canoes took on water, but made the run without dumping. When the canoes were beached on the rock ledge, everyone bailed diligently for a few minutes. If all the boats had run Big Black Rapids in its entirety through to flatwater, more of them undoubtedly would have dumped. This halfway point afforded a haven, a place to begin again with bailed-out canoes.

Don and I shook off the water and the incident as best we could. Fortunately, the air temperature was warm, so we were not chilled. I ravenously devoured tuna fish and peanut butter and jam sandwiches.

"What happened, Tom?" I asked. "Could you analyze the accident?"

"Well, everyone made the same move and mistake. We all hugged the wall too closely,   which threw off the timing and position in swinging around to avoid the last rock.   None of us at the scouting saw that second rock; it was totally unexpected."

We were all listening to Tom's explanation. Sags was eating our handouts.

"I used to teach rock climbing once," Tom continued. "In canoeing if you dump, you can swim and live. There is a second chance. In rock climbing if you fall, you fly without a parachute."

Lunch over, the second half of Big Black Rapids awaited us. A gigantic V pointed to right center. Then the whole surface resembled a charge of wild horses with white manes flying in the wind, a solid line of standing waves and boils with white crowns. At this point, the plan was to aim slightly left and hit the waves head-on. In the distance was the final line, calm water. I wished we had run the second set before lunch.

Tom went first. As I watched, he seemed to be a drunken jockey riding a bucking horse, up and down, up and down. His run went extremely fast and he eddied out to a rock point on the left.

Don and I paddled down and met the V at precisely the right point. We paddled hard and aimed the canoe through the center of the standing waves. If we had inadvertently swung broadside, it would have been all over. A single missed stroke or a sudden shift of weight at the wrong time would have dumped us. We ran through and eddied over to the safety of the pool.

Don and I joined Tom and the others to watch the last canoes come down. Mark and Tamara in **Aircraft Finish** went last and selected a different route. They hugged the left wall quite closely and bounced violently on their rollercoaster ride. I thought their route choice was a little risky, but they made a magnificent run.

"Running a set of rapids successfully," Tom said, "doesn't mean you have it made. There is the Omo River in Ethiopia, with plenty of rapids. After eddying out in one section of the river, some canoeists have been killed by hippos in the eddy pool."

The dangerous work of the canoeing day was over. Only bears, not hippos, could possibly get us on the St. John. We shoved off for an easy paddle to the Big Black campsite, named for the river of the same name. Located on a bluff at the confluence of the Big Black River and the St. John, the site would provide both a spring for drinking water and a vista. Overhead, the gray skies darkened quickly. Soon there was drizzle, then rain.

We approached the campsite and spotted five red canoes pulled up on the bank. Our rivals had taken the best site. They were watching us.

"We take the next one," Tom said, not even bothering to make inquiries. We were river nomads in search of a patch of solid ground for the night. I glanced up the valley of Big Black River, flowing down from the northwest, just one of the many inviting places I wished I could have explored.

The skies lightened and the rain stopped. The next campsite was three or four miles downstream. Little brooks, their banks overflowing from the rains, swept down to join the St. John. Tom let Sags jump onto land for some exercise. We watched the dog running along the shoreline, and jumping over the swollen brooks to keep pace with the canoes. He was faster.

Around a bend, we approached Seminary Brook campsite. The St. John was probably a half mile

A Passion for Wilderness

across in this section, the widest on the trip. Having picked up so many tributaries since Baker Lake, the St. John was now a major river.

We beached and carried our gear up the steep slope. The grass and earth on the plain above were covered with puddles. Most of the group selected tentsites near the shelter and fireplace. Tom's site was on a knoll above Seminary Brook itself.

Don and I decided to pitch our tent on a grassy flat beside the deadend of a logging road. Walt and Sharon pitched their tent on the roadbed itself, with no trucks expected during the night. I called our little settlement Seminary Brook suburbia. Don and I again let our tent dry out and spread our damp clothes on some saplings. I turned in for a nap.

"It's raining," Don yelled a half hour later from outside the tent. "Let's get our clothes inside." The words were more effective than blowing reveille. As we hurried to gather our clothes, I battled both raindrops and mosquitoes; the shower had stirred them into a biting mood.

The shower lessened. Tamara and I took a short hike on the logging road, dotted with deer scat every half dozen strides. Spanning Seminary Brook was a dilapidated bridge missing many of its boards; I doubted a logging truck could pass over it safely.

As we walked back to the cooking fire, the rain began again. "We're lucky," Tom said. "The sooner it begins to rain, the sooner it's going to stop." A fog shroud lay in the river and the bank beyond

A Passion for Wilderness

Supper in rain at Seminary Brook Shelter

was gray and indistinct.

I glanced at some of the names, hometowns, dates, and messages penciled, inked, and carved on the beams of the shelter. Many mentioned the weather, one noting that it was a beautiful day, another complaining of rain. "It stinks," one graffiti message declared.

Tom and Mark maintained an excellent cooking fire, despite the rain. Earlier Mark had discovered that there was little firewood in the immediate campsite area, so he paddled across the

A Passion for Wilderness

river to collect a canoe-load of logs to saw and chop. Mark stirred up chili in a huge black pot over the coals. Tom kept fanning the fire, which held its own against the rain.

For supper we had chili, salad, and corn-bread. Tamara and I ate little. My stomach felt tight and uncomfortable. I hoped the sneaky St. John bug would not strike me, so I was taking no chances.

All of us were feeling emotionally low as evening approached. It was not the rain, the mosquitoes, sunburn, stomachaches, or the trip itself. We were all physically tired but spiri-tually elated with our life on the river. Soon the trip would be over. "This week has just flown by," someone said. In two days we would be leaving the river, and in three days the group would split up to return to homes and jobs. But none of us were anxious to go home. Nostalgia was flooding over me already.

As I washed my plate and cup in Seminary Brook, the rushing water roared down in a continuous cascade. The whitewater looked like snow. Several logs and sticks were jammed against the rocks upstream and held there by the sheer force of the current. I would hear Seminary Brook from my tent during the night.

I said goodnight to my friends and jumped across puddles on the way back to my tent. Once zipped inside, I heard a mosquito buzzing in the dark-ness. I slapped repeatedly and the buzzing stopped. Then, to make the tent mosquito-proof for the night, I stuffed a wool shirt against the

Rain shroud over St. John valley

little hole where the two zipper ends of the tent door met.

Day Seven / Friday, May 17, 1985
Seminary Brook to Fox Brook

After midnight I made my usual reconnaissance outside. Automatically, I looked skyward; the rain was over, and a few stars even shone dully amid the clouds. I looked forward to a good day.

At daybreak, Don crawled out of the tent. "It's raining again," he said. I lay there, knowing there was no special hurry to break camp. Everyone would be sleeping in. We all could sense the mood and momentum of the trip. We had but a short run to Fox Brook, our next proposed campsite, without major rapids.

Finally I rose. The river level was high from the rain. The whole valley was covered with a layer of mist.

"I feel better, Tom," I said. No mosquitoes had bitten me during the night. The tired, burned feeling I experienced the previous day was gone. My forehead was cool and I was hungry for breakfast.

"That's good," Tom said. "At least no one is dying."

Shortly thereafter, I learned that Mark had become ill during the night with the mysterious bug. I wondered who would be next. But Mark had recovered quickly, and he stirred up a breakfast of scrambled eggs and mushrooms.

As we finished breakfast, I spotted one red canoe upstream, appearing ghostlike out of the mist, then another, and another, until there were five. They probably would run Big Rapids today and leave the territory. We were planning to reach the Fox Brook campsite, where a truck would meet us by evening. Then, on the following and last day, we would run Big Rapids in empty canoes to the Walker Brook take-out.

Every day, inevitably, there was talk and anticipation of Big Rapids. What was it like? What should we expect? I knew the rapids were not to be taken lightly; it was not an old guide's tale to keep the sports amused around an evening campfire. Many loggers and canoeists had drowned there over the years. Apparently the loss of life during the present age of recreational canoeing was invariably caused by ignorance and stupidity: the use of alcohol, lack of a life preserver, overloaded canoes, foolhardy runs during exceptionally high water, and so forth. With our training and leadership, no one feared catastrophe, but the anticipated excitement of finally facing those rapids hung over us like the mist.

We dallied that morning, packing up and breaking camp. As the mist burned off under the sun, we pushed off.

Our morning paddle took us through magnificent country. After five days on the river, I felt at home on the St. John, with my exhilaration increasing at each bend. Our party easily ran Long Rapids, Castonia Rapids, and Schoolhouse Rapids. At Schoolhouse, the banks were so straight it looked as though someone had made a giant cut with a cleaver, exposing first loam, then soil, clay, gravel, pebbles, and finally rocks. The recent rains made the earth fresh and cool.

We spotted a campsite area but weren't close enough to read the sign. Tamara and Mark paddled in and she jumped out. "Ouellette Farm," she shouted to us. We pushed on for Fox Brook, a couple of miles downstream.

Tom went on ahead, as securing this campsite for the night was critical for our pickup. And in the distance, there they were, those five red canoes. Tom stopped, climbed the bank, and disappeared from view. A few minutes later, Don and I landed to check on our status. A couple of the men stared at me hostilely. "Seen enough?" one of them asked. They looked like a Hell's Angels gang with canoes. Don and I moved back.

Tom, as usual, saved the day. "Let's go downstream about fifty yards," he said. "There's a backup site there."

We paddled down and found the site unoccupied. Kicking into the soil to secure our footing, we hauled the boxes and gear up the steep slope. The site was too small to accommodate our tents, but that was not our immediate concern. It was lunchtime, our last lunch on the river. We made and ate our sandwiches.

Following a tip from Tom, I walked a short distance to the logging road and down to Fox Brook. I found the makings of a campsite that was once the front yard of a now-abandoned log cabin. Its roof sagged heavily after a great many winters. With the camp axe and saw and five minutes of work, I brushed out saplings and deadwood to create the best tentsite in the area. Don and I pitched our tent to face the St. John, with Fox Brook cascading down on the left. Their confluence created Fox Brook Rapids.

The afternoon was free. Eric practiced poling, a cakewalk on water for him. Mark let me examine the construction of his dome tent. Some lay at the bank under trees in reverie to watch the water flow by. Others turned in for a nap. Drowsy, I soon found myself back at my tent, listening to the music of the water as it lulled me to sleep.

A Passion for Wilderness

Canoeing, eating, and sleeping suited me fine.

Tom and Mark prepared an excellent supper — ham in molasses sauce, pineapple, mashed potato, corn, and chocolate mint cake.

Several times Sags barked excitedly and ran out to the dirt road. After a number of false alarms, the dog heard the noises he was anticipating. A van with an empty canoe trailer rolled into the parking area off the road. We ran up to greet Charlie, the driver, anxious to hear about the outside world, of which we had heard nothing for a whole week.

"I barely made it here," Charlie said. "I took the most logical dirt road, and, not knowing the area, was about to go back and try another. The dirt roads are terrible and almost washed out."

"We've saved supper for you, Charlie," Tom said and waved him to the table.

"The black flies have already arrived at Cathance Lake and are moving north," Charlie said. "They'll be here soon, but we'll be getting out before they arrive. I heard the extended weather forecast on the radio as I was passing through Presque Isle. It's for heavy rain, starting tomorrow."

Charlie was a Mainer from Down East, about thirty years old. He worked as a forester for one of the major timber companies. Summers he drove canoe parties in and out of the woods, and winters he resumed his forestry duties. He would sleep in the van for the night.

Tom and Charlie decided to drive to the village of Allagash, about ten miles east, on a beer and soft drink run. We detached the trailer and they left.

I headed out for an evening walk on the dirt road, with Sags running ahead and scouting the side trails. As I skirted puddles and blowdown on the road, Sags just crawled under the branches to achieve the same purpose. I climbed a long hill and spotted the Ouellette Farm campsite with the steep cutbank across the river. The bank was in shade, while the budless treetops glowed in the last sunlight.

Returning to Fox Brook campsite, I waited for Tom and Charlie. They were late because Allagash turned out to be a dry town, so they drove a dozen extra miles to St. Francis, a wet town. Mark baked a pan of brownies for a snack.

At the campfire, Tom spoke again of running rivers. If anyone asked him a casual question on any aspect of canoeing, guiding, travel, or, as we found out, almost anything else, he always answered directly and often added pertinent observations from his experiences. We listened as Tom spoke:

"When I was in high school, a bunch of kids and I would canoe by a rock wall close enough to strike and light a match gripped with two fingers as I swept by with my paddle. I hugged the wall closely, and if the match lit, the others knew I was successful."

He drew again on his pipe and spoke of the great rivers of North and South America that he had done, wanted to do, or had heard about: the Tatshenshini, the Bío Bío, the Back, and the

A Passion for Wilderness

Moisie.

"In the North you have to be a genius of logistics to run a trip. Three Texans want to do the Back River in Canada's Northwest Territories. The air transportation charges alone would be $10,000. Sometimes it's cheaper at the end of a trip up there to sell the canoe for whatever you can get for it. It would cost more to air-freight it out."

I asked about Quebec's Moisie River, which his firm ran every autumn, the only commercial outfitter to do so. I kept dreaming about running the Moisie.

"The Moisie," Tom said, "has schoolbus-sized boulders. At one place, we run between two such rocks, each with its own waterfall streaming down the side. We invite a doctor to come along and offer him a reduced rate to join the expedition."

I knew that their brochure stressed that Marty and Tom would accept only the most skilled and checked-out canoeists for this dangerous trip. Safety was paramount. They would take along no duffers. I also knew I wasn't a great canoeist.

"Can I go, Tom?" I asked.

"You could go as a bowman in a guide canoe," he answered.

I felt relieved. Happy to know that at least I could go, I savored the assurance that there would be a place for me. For some, paddling as a bowman in a guide canoe might represent a reduced status, but I was not dismayed. I reveled in anticipation of someday running the Moisie, the river many consider to be the ultimate challenge of all canoe trips in eastern North America. No matter how old I was, or how prone I was to dumping, no one could surpass my desire to go there.

Again I would have enjoyed more campfire stories, but I heard the call of my sleeping bag and followed the dim light above the trees to my tent.

CANOEING THE JACK

Chapter 4

RUNNING BIG RAPIDS

Day Eight / Saturday, May 18, 1985
Fox Brook to Walker Brook

I woke up in the chill and rawness of the new morning. A threatening front had moved in during the night. The sky was dirty gray and the air seemed saturated with water.

At the cooking fire, Tom used his spatula to slice off chunks of butter to grease and re-grease the black skillet. White smoke rose into the cold air from the skillet. After breakfast of blue-berry pancakes, sausage, and coffee, there was no food left. Tom and Mark had packed the trip down to the last sausage link, and Sags ate that.

Eric had been consulting the foldout map and guide that discussed Big Rapids; it recommended a spray deck for the two-mile run.

"Tom, do we have spray decks?" Eric asked. "If we don't, then we can't go."

"You don't need a spray deck," Tom said.

"Are we having a prayer meeting this morning?" I asked. As we exchanged this little banter, we glanced toward the river. The five red canoes passed by on their way to run Big Rapids loaded with all their gear. We never saw them again.

Breakfast was over, and Charlie and others began loading the trailer with empty food boxes, rolled tents, and personal bags. When I carried my bag over, I told Charlie I hoped he wouldn't bury my bag at the bottom in case I needed dry clothes. "I won't put a cooler on top of your duffel," Charlie said.

I had made my decision. I would go. In the event I never came back to the St. John, I wanted to be able to look back on the experience with the satisfaction of having run every foot of water from put-in to take-out.

Don called me aside and said that he didn't want to run Big Rapids. His decision reflected common sense. The frequent kneeling on the trip had aggravated an old high school football injury. Lime on the sidelines had burned his shins many years ago. His scarred legs had required almost daily medication and bandaging on this trip. Just a year earlier, he had cut his shins while sawing wood, and subsequent ulceration had landed him in the hospital for five weeks.

"I need a ride," I said to Tom. "Can I go as a passenger?"

"We can't have three in a canoe," Tom said. "Maybe you can team up with someone."

I put on my life jacket and paced nervously as the last of the gear was being loaded. Tamara saw me as we were policing the area for forgotten equipment.

"Take off your life jacket," she said. "We don't leave for fifteen minutes."

"I'm just psyching myself up. Wearing this jacket convinces me that I'm really going."

The van and the trailer were loaded. Charlie was ready to drive downriver to the Walker Brook take-out. Sags and Don would go with him.

The group gathered around in the shroud of fog, which looked ugly. We expected a shower any minute, and isolated drops indicated a less-than-ideal situation for running rapids.

Jim then announced he would not make the run. "I can't fight this rain," he said. "Water on my glasses knocks me out. I can't see during rainstorms." His canoe was carried up to the trailer and racked.

Sharon decided against the run. I would team up with Walt. Walt and Sharon conferred. "I'm not going," Walt said, and their canoe was taken up and strapped on the trailer.

A Passion for Wilderness

Our casual talk about Big Rapids for the last week evidently had blown the risk out of proportion. Every day we imagined the addition of another rock or envisioned another drop in elevation so that Big Rapids had become the Niagara of Maine.

"This last run marks the highlight of the trip," Tom said. "Why would you want to miss it?"

"If we make it," I said, "we are going to give you such a razzing."

"We **are** going to make it," Tom said.

At the last moment, I found a partner. Steve would take the stern in **Lone Star,** and I would be the bowman. Our party split in two groups, some heading for the van with Charlie, and the rest to the waiting canoes. Steve and I checked over **Lone Star** and discovered that the bow seat was broken. If the seat were not fixed, I would have no place to sit during the flatwater stretches nor support and leverage while kneeling, during the whitewater sections. Tom performed makeshift repairs. Steve and I were ready.

I had no idea how well Steve and I would handle the canoe, since he had paddled solo thus far and a partner might seem strange to him. Would there be time to test the partnership before the rapids?

It was again exhilarating to back out and swing into the main current. We immediately ran Fox Brook Rapids, created by the incoming boost of water from that tributary.

Steve's legal training served him well. He was logical and methodical both as a lawyer and as a sternman, with each stroke placed precisely where he wanted it. We quickly formed a canoeing partnership.

Our group made excellent time in the duffel-free canoes. Tamara and Mark led and Steve and I ran second. Often we swung broadside and held out two canoes in the middle of the river, maintaining a slow drift downstream while the others came into sight. We even laid back against the seats.

In an hour, we felt thoroughly warmed up from paddling in the wintry chill. The rain squall passed over. All of us were glad we decided to make the run, no matter what happened ahead. The trip had taken hold of us compellingly. The onward flow of the St. John was addictive.

Tom went ahead and signaled us to close along the left bank. The bend ahead looked typical of those we had seen in the last week. We beached and scouted.

Big Rapids! As far as the eye could see, the big river roared down its gradient, over rocks and ledges and against the cliff wall on the left. Giant boulders on both sides compounded the difficulty of route finding. The river narrowed into a gorge perhaps an eighth mile across. The roar swept away the silence we had known in the flatwater sections. The scene both attracted and repelled me, on whether I should either shoot down on impulse or walk away by logic.

Tom stepped out on a rock, balanced himself, and pointed ahead.

"See that lone birch on the left? We'll head

for that and eddy out. Aim through these front rocks and then angle over to the left middle. And hit those standing waves head-on. We'll run Big Rapids in three sections and bail out each time."

Tom led. He bounded up and down, lifting up on the waves and dropping into the troughs. We watched silently, wondering if he could hang on. He took everything the river had to offer and then eddied out. We cheered him. Then he was standing, a tiny solitary figure beneath the birch, close to a mile away.

Steve and I said nothing to each other as we awaited our turn. We did not feel any need for prayer or thought or anything intellectual, just a physical instinct to keep the canoe upright and afloat. We raised our knees as high as we could against the inside gunwales and locked them. We were wearing the canoe.

Steve and I dug in and paddled as hard as we could. We would not let the current catch us and hurl us against the wall. "Paddle, paddle, paddle," my brain told me. "Paddle, paddle, paddle." My arms swung back and forth automatically. We shot down and held our preplanned route. Water splashed in at every trough, but we had no time to think of that. The cold splashes did not bother me, so fixed was my concentration on pad- dling ahead.

We hurtled past the last boulder and eddied out. Wedging the canoe through a rock channel, we hauled out on a ledge. I felt good beating this thing.

A Passion for Wilderness

Every canoe made a successful run. We all took on a lot of water and spent a few minutes bailing out. The landbound contingent of our group clambered over the ledges and rocks to join us. It almost seemed as if we hadn't seen them in a long time.

Now the sky was simply overcast and saving its rain for later on in the day. Jim and the others congratulated us. "I should have gone," Jim said.

All of us walked a quarter mile downstream to scout the next portion of the run. The river still had more of the same for us — boulders on both sides with tremendous whitewater and waves in the center. We picked out the most favorable spot in which to eddy out for the second leg. Far ahead we saw flatwater, the end of the third run.

I had the second run fixed in my mind and eyes. After walking back fifty yards or so, Tom turned around to view the same situation again.

"Look at that rock," Tom said, "and remember how we saw it just a minute ago. You have to view the water and rocks from so many angles." Tom was right; the new inspection revealed a totally different juxtaposition of rocks, water, and waves. For a moment I was lost.

The new alignment made me realize how complex route-finding can be. That section could be run in so many ways, depending upon such things as water level, velocity of the current, influence of rains, and new boulders toppled into the river by the last breakup. The St. John was changing constantly, especially during a heavy rain.

"The toughest part of this run," Steve said to me, "is getting out of here." We extricated the canoe from the channel, and swung upstream to avoid a few rocks.

The second section consisted of a straight run in the middle of the river, into the heart of that thrashing water. We had no choice, since drifting to either side meant the hazards of boulders and jammed logs. The debris of spring breakup was everywhere along the sides.

Steve and I paddled through the river's mountains and valleys. If a boulder lay ahead, hidden in the churning stacks, we would not have seen it until it was too late to maneuver. Paddle, slice through, paddle, hesitate a split second, splash into a hole, water in the face, paddle, buck through, spray on the arms. We rode through and pulled for the eddy pool. Again we did it, with a lot less water in the hull bottom this time.

We all made it, handily as it turned out. Tom walked ahead on another reconnaissance. We listened as he pointed out the route.

"These standing waves are the highest and strongest of the whole rapids. Watch out for the big white rock on the right bank. The river will take you into the wall on the left, so stay way inside of the wall. The best approach is to aim right, hold it, and once you approach the big white rock, swing out in the middle. And if you dump, just ride it out with your feet extended. This is a very rough section, and we may well swamp before reaching flatwater."

Big Rapids was emptying out of its gorge with all the power it could muster. The big white rock, sticking up like a smashed bullet slug, looked ominous enough to have bagged its share of canoe trophies over the years. Behind the rock was a yard-wide ridge of dirty snow, extending down along the bank about a quarter mile and interrupted occasionally with passes where the snow had melted. In the distance, the flatwater marked both the end of the rapids and the end of the trip.

Returning to our canoes to attempt the last stretch, we looked upstream and watched three canoes heading down, apparently intent to run the whole of Big Rapids nonstop. They were encountering all they could handle. Two were in the middle of the river, which we had run five minutes earlier. The third, however, was hugging the right bank, as its bowman and sternman evidently did not see the big white rock ahead.

"That guy on the right," Tom said, "ought to get out of there. He's got problems if he continues on that course."

The crews of the three canoes began backpaddling, slipped sideways into the main current, and ferried toward the left bank. They must have seen the dangers ahead. Within a minute, their fully loaded canoes beached near us for their own scouting.

Five of the six men were in their fifties or sixties. Their white beards and wire-rimmed glasses made them look distinguished. The sixth, perhaps their guide, was a muscular man in his thirties. Their outfit was impeccably roped inside their canoes, and it looked like an L. L. Bean or Eddie Bauer advertisement in a sporting magazine.

We exchanged the usual talk about where they had put in and how many days they had been on the river. Their manner was pleasant and courteous. Tom and their leader exchanged advice on running the last section. We went to our canoes, determined to demonstrate to the other party that we could run this hazardous stretch without dumping.

Tom led, aimed, swung left, and rode out the waves. No sooner had he started when we saw him raise his paddle in triumph after a rocket-fast run.

Steve and I angled into our preplanned route. I felt my heart pump wildly as we paddled like galley slaves. "If things start to go wrong," Tom had said, "the best course of action is to paddle forward." We did just that, barreled ahead, and caught the spot to the left of the big white rock. We shot past and maneuvered into the center and then slightly left, sweeping handsomely past the left wall. I sensed our friends standing on top of the wall onshore, cheering us on and snapping photographs. They got the pictures, but we had the ride.

My makeshift seat broke and I pitched backward momentarily. I grunted and yelled to Steve. There was no chance to fix it now. I leaned forward to regain a sense of equilibrium and kept paddling. With every wave jarring the canoe, the seat's collapse occurred at the worst possible time.

We broke through the last standing wave and settled into gently rocking water. We had run Big Rapids. I reflected that if I have done nothing else in my life, at least I have canoed the St. John and run Big Rapids. Even if it were for just a week, I was proud to be a canoe bum, a river rat. I looked ahead, anticipating new rivers.

Steve and I pulled toward shore. I could see the van and the trailer high on the bank at Walker Brook campsite. We beached the canoe and shook hands.

"With another case of beer," Steve said, "I could go on for another week."

Tom yelled over to me. "Dick, you must feel good to end the trip with such a great run."

Several people helped Steve and me lift **Lone Star** past a snow-drift ridge and up a steep bank to slide the hull forward on level ground. Within minutes, we were lifting all the canoes to the top of the van and strapping and lashing them securely for the long ride to Cathance Lake basecamp. The trip was over.

Within minutes, I became chilled, as I had lost most of my body heat from the strenuous paddle. Behind a tree, I changed into dry clothes and exchanged my boots for shoes.

The three tandem canoes passed below us. One gentleman waved to us. They were continuing down the great St. John. We felt sad watching them paddle onward. Within a couple of minutes, they were far downstream and about to round a bend toward rolling hills and long ridges. I watched them with a fixed stare before they disappeared from sight.

At that moment, Tamara gazed in their direction and uttered all our thoughts in a low voice.

"Take me with you," she whispered.

Richard E. Winslow III

EXPLORING VERMONT'S NORTHEAST KINGDOM

Should I be lucky enough to experience rein-
carnation, I hope to repeat my life as an outdoorsman and explore all the lakes and streams I
missed during my first existence. Although I am
not a professional limnologist, one of those
scientists who specialize in bodies of fresh water,
I am nonetheless a self-appointed inspector and
observer of lakes and ponds and all their inlets,
coves, islands, fishing holes and sand bars.

A Passion for Wilderness

I thought back to the thrills and pleasures of fishing and swimming in lakes I once experienced as a youngster, unaccountably seemed to forget for a long time, and now have found again. Finally I sorted out what was important from what was not. After the arid conventionality of obtaining an education, working at a professional career, and delivering myself to organizations and institutions that in turn cared little for me, I had paid my dues. I could no longer endure such suffocating conformity. It was time to go home spiritually to the lakes again. There I would be happy.

During the summer of 1984 I came to Vermont's Northeast Kingdom, a sparsely populated corner of the state bordering on Canada and well watered with streams and lakes.

Like a kid, I chafed with impatience to see and to do everything. Kids are the best and most animated explorers, jumping up and down with a can't-wait enthusiasm. I felt a return of this excitement when I approached Little Averill Pond.

As I walked, I thought of myself as a member of a movement which I had joined many years before. The rucksack revolution of the 1960s, which was long in the making before it caught the attention of the world, continues to spread unchecked into every valley and onto every mountain. My membership card was my day pack in which I was carrying crackers and a wedge of cheddar cheese for lunch. Raspberries and blackberries ripe on the bushes would be my dessert on the return route. I ate a few but suppressed the urge to strip the bushes completely as I came by.

My eyes at last caught the glimmer of a blue sheen through the trees. I suppressed a barbaric yell and the urge to sprint to the water's edge. I should not have.

As I hiked onward, a long sand beach stretched out before me and swung around to a point. Little Averill Pond itself, actually a good-sized lake, stretched back to the mountains, still a blue and hazy mass as the summer sun burned off the last of the lingering morning mist. The pond's irregular shoreline twisted and turned around points and into coves, shaped randomly by a retreating glacier as it rested, melted and dropped boulders and pulverized grit. The wildness of Little Averill seemed timeless, inviolate, but it is not. Presumptuous man has declared this sand beach for sale, for $250,000. It is hard to comprehend that some thousands of years of beach-making by the glacier and waves could have a price — and a fixed sum at that.

Waves rolled in a fixed cadence — pale blue rise, green crest, cream foam, a final kick of rushing water upon the gray sand, followed by a transparent sheet withdrawing to whence it came — a rhythm as measured as a creature's breathing. The pattern of the waves became almost a call that urged a response, so constantly did it affect my ears and eyes.

Out in the lake were two loons, one gliding along the surface and the other diving to sub-

A Passion for Wilderness

merge. There was beauty in their perfect syn-
chronizations as they took turns in their search
for fish. Each loon, during its time on the
surface, cast an alert eye toward me.

My hike brought me to a lake delta, where a
stream ran down from the highlands of Brousseau
Mountain, overflowed its banks into a bog, and
then cut a channel to the lake. The stream
pushed the sand aside at its mouth. The winds
of many storms had blown driftwood ashore and
pushed it ever higher onto a beach bench
ridge. Whole trees with gnarled branches and
massive root systems lay sprawled on the flats like
the skeletal remains of great fish. Spears of
grass emerged from the muck bottom and water to
bend in the wind. The stained and streaked cliff
face of Brousseau Mountain, gouged by the
glacier, had caught many a rain cloud to produce
more water for the stream.

This place was a natural campsite. To me,
lake and river campsites are the highlights of
wilderness experiences. You settle in and live,
eat, and sleep there for an extended period, far
longer than the time spent on a brief summit dash,
or a headlong run through rapids. Maybe someday
I would come back here to camp out for the night.
Of the many potential campsites I have "collected"
in my meanderings around the American continent,
this place with ample water, wood supply and wind-
swept air afforded itself as among the best I had
ever seen.

Clouds ambled across the sky, blocking the
sun at times to provide a shifting contrast of

bright sunshine and dark shadows. Leaving my lunch and outer clothing on a log of an immense driftwood tree, I waded into the water.

I trudged out on a submerged bar perhaps a quarter mile, until the water gradually crept up to my waist. Then I plunged in. Any lingering traces of tiredness and dispiritedness disappeared immediately. I dove deeper and entered a colder layer. Surfacing and returning toward shore, I headed for the stream channel. It was deep and the bottom was covered with leaves and their branches swept down and deposited by the stream. My feet felt nature's debris.

I dried off and returned to the log to eat my crackers and cheese. Blueberry bushes lined the sand ridge, but they were barren. The summer was drawing to a close.

I enjoyed this solitude — eating when I wanted, swimming when I wanted, and moving when I wanted — without having to react to anyone else's whims. Here I experienced an inner peace. The only gods were the sky, the water, and the mountains, all easy to see and to understand. There were no unfriendly deities demanding obeisance, nothing to clutter and confuse the mind. Here a long and satisfying life could ensue from swimming, paddling a canoe, catching fish, pitching a tent, and building a campfire.

The rest of those raspberries and blackberries were waiting for me on the hike back. I was happy to be a wanderer among the lakes and streams, judged on that alone if need be.

Ahead of me in the back country of the Northeast Kingdom were many more hikes to countless walk-in lakes and ponds with picturesque names: Cow Mountain Pond, South America Pond, Halfway Pond, Beaver Pond, Turtle Pond, and Unknown Pond. No matter what may happen in the next life, I am fully content to live out this one as a lover of lakes.

Richard E. Winslow III

SOLO

First Day / June 30

I am alone. My world is trees, snow, rock and sky. Beyond a spruce grove at timberline are snowfields, and then the sheer rock face of Chair Mountain, in the Elk Range of western Colorado. Here I will live for four days and three nights in the loveliest and loneliest place on earth. If it were not for an Outward Bound course, I would have never seen this magnificent place.

Just moments before, John, the Outward Bound

A Passion for Wilderness

patrol instructor, had turned toward me.

"Here is a good site, Dick."

"I don't see any level spot."

"Look around. You'll find one."

"All right."

For some minutes I keep hearing those words humming in my ears. Then there are only the sounds of flowing water, the snowmelt runoff raging ever more intensely as the sun climbs higher.

I follow Chair Creek upstream, skirting great tongues of snow. A waterfall dives down only to leap again in a series of cascades. Crossing is difficult. Everywhere great melting mounds of snow, left over from November, soak the ground.

After rejecting two or three campsites, I find the flat, dry area I am looking for. Three trees without hanging snags provide shade and shelter. Near the base of a cliff is a place for a fire.

I slip the straps on my pack and lay it on a log. I am not ready yet for decisions. Instead of setting up camp, I strip nude to sunbathe, lying half-asleep. For an hour, I experience the shock of loneliness.

For seventeen days our patrol of ten has shared everything — food, shelter, thoughts — in a total spirit of teamwork. Today John has dispersed us in designated zones below the snowbowl of Chair Mountain. We are all scattered on the seat of that chair with rock walls on three sides, the two arms and the back. The headrest is too high even for Paul Bunyan. The group effort is over; we are now on solo. Each of us will remain in his or her area without visiting one's neighbors and John is to check on us daily.

During the course, everyone lives without alcohol, drugs, or tobacco. Unconcerned with that anyway, I want to see things clearly and distinctly in a bright sky, not through clouds or fog. For the last two and a half weeks, we have heard no radio, read no newspaper, nor learned any news from the outside world. During solo, we are permitted no flashlights, candles, watches, or reading material, thus reducing our psychic link to civilization.

In years past no food or sleeping bags were allowed on solos. The idea was to improvise and survive the best way possible. This approach resulted in cases of exposure together with the virtual annihilation of the small animal population. With snares, traps, and crude bows and arrows, solo participants had wiped out almost all the squirrels and rabbits, much to the alarm of the local people in the village of Marble in the valley below. With John and several patrol leaders advocating reform, Outward Bound eliminated this Spartan aspect from its program.

John had told us that each individual had to decide how much food and equipment to carry to meet his own goals. I am soft. Given a choice, I elect comfort.

The sun reddens my skin. I dress. Intoxicated by the warmth of the sun, I have only two thoughts. One of my toes is puffy and swollen. Is it broken from a fall on rough talus three days ago? Is my camera's exposure mechanism damaged from a slip on a snowslope?

A Passion for Wilderness

I shake off my grogginess. Now it is time to set up camp. I level off the ground with the edge of my boot. As I kick some rotten yellow wood, it breaks up like a fragile honeycomb. For overhead cover, I stretch out my poncho and tie the four corners to branches and to a pole I pound into the ground. My ice axe becomes a secondary pole. With extra cord, I cinch the neck hole of the poncho tight to prevent leakage. Beneath the tarp I unroll a mat and a sleeping bag. I am ready for the night. Some rocks lying around, including a few I jar loose, soon become my fireplace.

I eat lunch — a few crackers, some dates, a grape drink to wash it all down.

Now I put my camp in final order. Each piece of equipment is in a specific spot. If I need something during the night, I will know exactly where it is. Normally I like to face my sleeping bag and the front of a tent eastward, Indian-style, to receive the first rays of the morning sun. Here, because of the setting and the slight tilt of the ground, the head of my bag is south. Other than that, I am satisfied.

A few feet away, chipmunks and squirrels dart about a fallen trunk, searching for seeds. Some birds peck persistently at the ground, looking for roots. They are happy and oblivious to my presence. Suddenly I remember D. H. Lawrence's comment: "I never saw a wild thing feel sorry for itself." If these animals are happy here, I should feel the same way.

During the afternoon I stretch out in the sun,

clothed with my hat plopped over my face. My mind buzzes from one idea to another — separate, jumbled, repetitious, as entangled as a gigantic forest blowdown, as choppy as the surface of a mountain lake in a chinook.

One recollection always returns, the climb we did the day before.

Yesterday we awoke to the stillness of a new day, clear and lovely. After breakfast, our patrol gathered at the campfire, our eyes riveted on the last orange flicks of flame as they perished into ashes and smoke. Ahead of us was the climb up Chair Mountain. There were few words, and none of the usual jokes. Everyone felt humble.

"If we are careful and use common sense," John had said, "we'll have a great climb."

As John spoke, we stood in a circle and then clapped hands, a ritual we performed each morning. Even after we released our grip, I felt the warmth in my fingers.

The mental conditioning for this climb began almost a month earlier when I looked up at Chair Mountain from the valley. Then it seemed such a spectacular, almost threatening, place. At the time I never thought I would be climbing up its slopes. Today as I looked up at the mountain I wasn't frightened, and I wasn't confident, just numb. The others didn't let on how they felt.

We hiked up into the snowbowl, past rust-stained boulders piled in long moraines. Snow ridges rolled like waves, with crests and troughs on the lower slopes. Above, in a black-

A Passion for Wilderness

On the trail to Chair Mountain

ened shadow, was a several-thousand-foot headwall, gouged by thousands of years of glacial action. On the summit ridge, arched cornices were cold blue underneath.

Our route was obvious. We had to gain the lower ridge by climbing the snowfields that sloped down the mountainside. Near the top, the snow clung at a steep angle, as if some mountain gremlin, perhaps none too trustworthy in his intentions, had plastered it on as a temporary patch.

A Passion for Wilderness

John stepped aside to let someone else lead the climb. Bonnie came to the front. She led. She always volunteered to be first. The rest of us followed her lead step by step on a traverse. Each person kicked the step a little larger and plunged his ice axe deeper so the next climber in line had an easier and safer foothold. I thought of Klondike gold seekers treading icy stairs over Chilkoot Pass, each locked in one rhythm. Ten people acted as one, with Bonnie's spirit and feet leading everyone onward and upward.

Alone, I would have turned back. The animal fear of slipping and tumbling made me alternately sweat and shiver in the cool air wafting from the snow. If anyone lost control for a second, it would make little difference after the first few feet. When our line stopped to let Bonnie kick the next step, I twisted back in a half turn, keeping my feet securely in place. The bottom was a long way down.

A wide snow thumb pointed up between two rock slabs. Bonnie angled her traverse to position us for a direct approach toward the ridge. Step, kick, dig the axe, breathe, step, kick, dig the axe, breathe. I kept going. The person behind me depended on me. I could not stop and delay those in the rear. The slope was at chest level. I was knee-deep in snow.

Bonnie and those in front of me bounded over to the rock ridge. They were safe, and turned back to watch the others still in line. At the top, Rick extended his hand and pulled me up the

A Passion for Wilderness

last step.   I burst over with a wild sucking
breath.   I made it.   It was like swimming
underwater for a long distance and surfacing with a
gasp.

We piled our ice axes together in a craterlike
gully and rested a few minutes.   The snow and ice
of the climb were behind us.   Ahead was the rocky
east ridge with the Tidritch Traverse, named for
an Outward Bound instructor, across the face to
the south ridge.

We bunched close together to reduce the hazard
from falling rock.   If we were spread too far
apart, someone might inadvertently dislodge a
boulder, which bouncing down and gaining momentum, could easily kill a person even wearing a
safety helmet.

"Loose rock," we cried, when we dislodged one.
At places we jumped across broad crevices, perhaps
two or three feet wide,   where alternate freezing
and thawing had split the solid rock.   It was as
if a giant had pried the ridge line apart with a
huge crowbar.

In case of emergency, Rick and Eric carried
climbing ropes, coiled and slung over their
shoulders.   Both kept up a string of jokes and
songs, with handkerchiefs covering their heads
in the tradition of the early voyageurs in Canada.
"Pierre" and "Jacques," as they called themselves,
were our Joliet and Marquette, our Lewis and Clark,
on this great adventure.

The traverse went well.   A few strategic hand
and toeholds brought us to the bony south ridge.
Here was all the exposure,   fresh air,   and scenery

we could want. On top, Rick and Eric received word from John to leave their ropes, which were not needed for the final assault. They cached them. Everyone was happy the dangerous part was over.

Soon we stood on the summit of Chair Mountain. All Colorado stretched to the horizon. To the east were the Maroon Bells, beautiful and treacherous with "rotten rock." Much farther eastward was the snowy Sawatch Range, the high but easy mountains where I had climbed twenty-two years earlier. To the south, the San Juans and the San Miguels stuck up like Spanish swords. We recognized the blades of Uncompahgre and Matterhorn Peaks.

My eyes dropped down to Buckskin Basin, its upper part all white. Two high lakes were still locked in ice, with deep blue crevasses of collapsed snow seemingly cut by a knife. Downslope the sun had freed two ponds, with their brown glistening shorelines kept wet by water trickling down from above. The lowest lakes, fifth and sixth in the basin, were among the trees, looking civilized and at home. None had a name.

When one of our group discovered the Colorado Mountain Club metal cylinder in a rock cairn, we all signed the register. That formality over, we were ready for lunch. Someone dug into his pack for a bag of gorp, the mountaineers' high-energy food of raisins, soy beans, peanuts, and M & M candies. For this special victory lunch, John gave each of us two strips of beef jerky. We passed around our canteens full of water or grape or lemon drink.

That was the way we lived. There was no holding back. After our first hour together on our first day, we had ignored any hygienic fastidiousness. Canteens were always passed around, with each person taking a hard swallow.

If someone had to urinate or defecate, it made no sense to hike away for maximum privacy, since the nearest tree or bush was often a mile away. One simply retreated a decent distance, turned away in the appropriate direction, and used snow, moss, pine needles, whatever was handy.

For every lunch on the trail or on a bush-whack, we sat in a circle, with the food in the middle — crackers, hardtack, plastic jars of cheese, peanut butter, and solid white honey, with cans of tuna fish, shrimp, and boned chicken. Most of us owned identical red-handled Swiss Army knives and we exchanged them inad-vertently during meals. After perhaps two or three days, the original was reclaimed after being recognized by a certain scratch on the blade or handle. It made no difference.

Some of us got sick. It was no disgrace to become ill at this high altitude; many had come straight from sea level to ten or eleven thousand feet in a few days without the proper time for acclimatization. Hypothermia, heat exhaustion, dehydration, and other mountain sicknesses affected many of us. Everyone had high-altitude headaches.

Once Margot stumbled and broke down on the trail, sobbing with frustration at the heaviness of her pack. Everyone comforted her and took a few items to lighten her load.

After one grueling day, two became ill with shivers and cold. John sent them immediately to their sleeping bags, while the strong and healthy set up camp and brought food to the disabled. When I had my bad day, the group stopped short of its objective to make an early camp. I went straight to bed, and my friends catered to my needs, bringing supper to my shelter. The next morning I felt perfect.

Scaling the cliff at Prospector's Park, we clambered up 5.2 and 5.4 class routes. "Keep going. You're almost at the top," shouted those above belaying from a rock seat. "Looking good," yelled those waiting at the bottom. "Move your right foot over and up about six inches." The psychological uplift from those encouraging voices kept us going beyond what we thought we could do. That happened a week ago.

As I lie here now alone, all this camaraderie is gone. Can I endure the next four days? Yes. But I still feel hollow and empty.

Why not slip away to visit Rick on the high ground above me? It would be so easy. We could talk the rest of the day. I resist the temptation. Rick looks like a mountain man, with blue eyes, blonde hair and moustache, and a self-reliant manner. Trapping, hunting, prospecting, and living off the land is the life for him. Sitting at a desk in a city office, shuffling papers, would kill him. Rick belongs in the mountains.

A Passion for Wilderness

Eric is also above me. How exciting it would be to sneak away and swap stories with him. Eric hiked the entire Appalachian Trail, and then the Pacific Crest Trail, the first time anyone had completed it end to end, oftentimes a bushwhack as the trail was unsurveyed and unmarked in places at the time he accomplished his feat. That hike was only a warm-up.

He then followed the Continental Divide from Canada to Mexico, 3,000 miles in five months. After his brother dropped out midway, Eric pushed on. The trek became more a mental than a physical battle.

A month before coming to Colorado, he and his crew survived the swamping of their scaled-down Viking boat replica off the New Hampshire coast. And his future plans include a solo transatlantic voyage in his own boat.

There is no recklessness in Eric, no Richard Halliburton melodramatic striving for popular acclaim. I had never before seen such a natural combination of physical stamina and common sense. "It's foolproof," Eric said, as he checked the ropes and slings for our hundred-foot rappel off a cliff or for a Tyrolean Traverse. He thinks out and plans everything.

Across the creek is Bonnie. A sociable person, she must feel the enforced isolation more than anyone else. Bonnie loves the water, and she earns her living as a sailing instructor. She must be quite a professional since she has competed in all kinds of international regattas in England and Europe. What is she doing here?

A Passion for Wilderness

Down in the valley is Ted.   He is most at home in a first-rate restaurant with the best food and drink.   For him, the Great Outdoors has its place.   Struggling with his heavy pack,   shortness of breath, and pain from an old football knee injury, he is waiting for all this to end.   The allure had long since left him.

We can't all be outdoor freaks.   I respect Ted for his honest assessment of this trek. During the past seventeen days, he would have much rather done something more productive to advance himself professionally — writing an article, or doing some important administrative work — than go through this foolishness.

Each of us had those moments, keeping it private, when we would have chucked the whole business.   I recognize those moods.   D. H. Lawrence had plenty of them down at his Kiowa Ranch near Taos, New Mexico, where I made a sort of pilgrimage last summer.

Again burning from too much sun,   I crawl under my shelter.   With my jacket bunched up for a pillow, I browse through Robert Ormes's **Guide to the Colorado Mountains**, a taboo item I smuggled with me.   There are fifty-two mountains over 14,000 feet in Colorado, and I've climbed eleven Fourteeners thus far.   The surveyors keep adding and subtracting from the list — the mountains grow or shrink with the later measurements.

Daylight dims as gray patches turn black and a stiff wind picks up.   A few drops fall.   Here a slight change in the weather determines every

A Passion for Wilderness

action. I put down the book and doze off.

When I awake, the sky has partially cleared, so I head for the creek to wash my face. I wash my clothes. I stroll. To keep active, I make every chore a game. With the passing days, I will repeat this ritual a half dozen or more times a day, simply to do something. To get a good night's sleep, I have to be physically active during the day.

With anticipation I take out my notebook. For several days I have neglected my journal: now I have the leisure to write. When I was with the patrol and seized a moment to scribble the briefest entry, I always felt guilty. As I would jot down the last word, someone inevitably would return from a creek with a Brilloed pot, or some firewood. I knew if I didn't write things down, I would quickly forget them. It wasn't fair to the others, but I justified it. Sometimes I was the one dragging in branches or fetching water, while someone else was writing.

Most field journals, it seems to me, are the tersest of documents. There is little time for them, as everyone is constantly busy — climbing, making a bivouac, lighting fires, cooking food, doing all the necessary things before sunset. We all hated making a dark camp, after pushing on or underestimating distances. Writing that journal, usually before our morning meeting, was pure luxury. With ten people, each dependent upon the others, there was no time to meditate under a tree about Thoreau or watch ants fight.

Now, with excess time, I write down everything.

A Passion for Wilderness

Where two or three words sufficed only days before, I now expand each idea to a paragraph or a whole page. Thoughts, lists, a daily calendar, a plan of things to do once the Outward Bound course ends, the momentous and trivial alike — all receive equal attention. Writing becomes an exercise, like washing my face.

Suddenly I realize that I have not spoken a word for hours. I ask questions but don't answer them. I begin to sing songs, some over and over again. Otherwise I think I might lose my voice.

This mountain solitude can be rationalized only so far. I knew about Jack Kerouac's experience as a fire lookout on Desolation Park in the Cascades in northern Washington in 1956. After sixty-three days up there alone, he ran out of things to write, to think about, and his brain went into a kind of summer hibernation. There was nothing to react or respond to. He was desolate.

I dream of those lakes in Buckskin Basin where this solo would have gone a lot faster. There I could fish a different lake every day. The upper lakes in their pocket craters appear fishless, and the water probably freezes solid in the winter. Perhaps the lakes below timberline shelter trout and grayling. Few people have ever hiked up into that country, as there are no trails. It is too steep for horses. There I could have everything all to myself. If the fishing were lousy, I could take daily hikes and yell at the cliffs for echoes. But here in my restricted area, I look at the same trees and rocks hour after hour.

A Passion for Wilderness

Even on this first day, I sense the time easily. It is pushing late afternoon, and I'm hungry. I build a fire for a canteen pot of instant chicken soup. I take a swig of grape drink. Dates are dessert.

I wonder how the old-timers ever explored and prospected this great land. Without matches, freeze-dried foods, goosedown or fiber sleeping bags, or topographical maps, many wore themselves out in this rugged country. We have it easy.

After washing my utensils in the creek, I fill my plastic jug in case I become thirsty during the night. I don't save the water very long. Dousing the smoldering coals, I stir up the ashes. The water hisses on the rocks. I watch the fireplace for a minute. Such things become automatic in camping.

Years earlier, I had worked with a bulldozer operator in Montana. Three of us were deep in the Lincoln National Forest. After lunch, I stamped out a cooking fire and walked away, joking to my other companion. Within seconds, the Montana man left the seat of his Cat, poured water on the coals, and kicked and stirred the remains of that fire for a few minutes.

"I've fought forest fires before," he said, "and I know how little it takes for one to get going. Not much."

An easygoing man always ready with a new joke or story, he wasn't serious very often — but he was very serious about half-put-out fires.

I have always remembered that incident. From that time I became a demon about fire safety.

A Passion for Wilderness

Perhaps it is trite to record that in a journal, but alone in the wilderness, one writes down the seemingly unimportant things that constitute the bulk of individual thoughts and worries.

With another hour of light left, I am restless. Why not explore a bit? Sidestepping my way up through the easy places to a ledge above, I spot a flat perch overlooking the valley to the north. I sit down on the hard Philosopher's Seat.

A few thousand feet below, beyond the spruces, meadows, and aspens, is the Crystal River. Its water glints white in the day's last sunlight. Gravel bars, with water swirling around them in channel, resemble the gold placers of Alaska and the Yukon.

Mount Sopris is to the north, straight ahead, with most of its snow gone since I first saw the mountain a month ago.

My eyes spot Capitol Peak, father to the east. The early surveyors insisted it was unclimbable; they were wrong, but Capitol is the toughest of the Fourteeners. It resembles the point of a huge gray arrowhead with a blood-gutter groove on one side. Perhaps an Indian god began to carve it, but unaccountably left it in place, unfinished in the range.

Down the Crystal River valley is the hamlet of Redstone, named for the nearby cliffs of that mining camp. I notice a few headlights weaving in and out of sight through the river canyon, as Route 133 follows it toward McClure Pass. Except for an overnight bivouac at the ghost town of

A Passion for Wilderness

Crystal, accessible by dirt road to the Outward Bound four-wheel drive vehicle for a resupply many days ago, this is my first glimpse of civilization since I began the course.

A purist of course would say the natural beauty is scarred by these signs of man's intrusion.

My thoughts drift back a dozen years to a campsite where I camped with another exploration geologist in Washington's Cascade Range. The Mount Buckindy area is still the most rugged, primitive place I have ever seen.

A helicopter pilot, not very happy at the prospect of landing there, found a rough site and left us on a meadow with tents and supplies. Every few days he returned with fresh food and the mail, and he took away our reports and mineral samples. Beside our camp was an alpine lake, but it was too cold for swimming. Everything indicated that no one had ever been or camped there.

Chick and I hiked and climbed around, searching for copper mineralization. For a week we lived there on this reconnaissance. We failed to discover any bonanza, but we enjoyed it in other ways. Once we surprised several adult mountain goats and their kids on a ridge.

Away from our campsite — through a mountain pass and across two or three ridges to the south — I noticed the work of loggers on a forest slope many miles away. Some of the area had been clearcut, with bulldozer Cat roads switchbacking up the side. It was a mess.

A Passion for Wilderness

Yet that sight and scar on the Cascade wilderness, as I gazed upon it, afforded me a sense of inner peace. "If I should stumble, break a leg, or fracture my skull, and die in this place before the copter could fly me out," I thought back then, "I will feel better seeing that slash in my last moments of consciousness." I would pass on, knowing that man has made his impression on earth, as crude and unsightly as it may look to others.

In a like manner, I felt the same emotions as I gazed down at Route 133. If I were to discard 20,000 years, and just lie naked near Chair Creek as I had earlier in the day, man would have gained nothing. After the 20,000 years since the Indians came to the Americas, we can enjoy and sanctify the wilderness, because we know we can always go back to hot showers, comfortable beds, books, medicine, even pizza stands and drive-in theatres.

In the unlikely event an Indian climbed up to this exact spot thousands of years ago, he undoubtedly cursed the cold nights and the snow before heading back downhill. Discovering the mountain passes, he wandered south for the sun and warmth of the mesas and buttes of what is now the Four Corners area.

I know I won't climb Capitol Peak this summer. I sympathize with the fisherman who grieves that the big one got away. He is determined to catch it the next year. I gaze at Capitol Peak with the same feeling. For a half hour I sit there, happier than if I were in the White House, Times Square, or Fisherman's Wharf in the company of captains and kings.

The sun is leaving. I must return to my camp-site. The smaller animals are returning to their burrows, and the deer, elk, and bear are seeking sheltered places for the night. Back at camp, I pour out the stale water, and dip the plastic jug in the creek again.

A few cold drops fall again from the black clouds swirling over me. Five minutes ago, the weather looked stable. I can still distinguish gradations of light in the dusk. A new weather front is moving in.

With the soupy conditions, I cannot find the Big Dipper or the North Star. Every time I camp out, I always enjoy spotting the North Star, perhaps for location, perhaps for superstition. Even if I become lost and must resort to a rough bivouac, I want to have a sense of direction before starting out the next morning.

I crawl into my bag fully clothed, comfortable in my goosedown jacket. Only my boots are off. I wear a winter wool cap and pull it down snug, another ritual I always perform so I won't wake up cold during the night. Outdoor experts say that about thirty per cent of one's body heat is lost when the head is bare. I also wear my wool mittens.

My last seconds of consciousness mingle with the music of that roaring creek, as it tumbles down from the snowfields.

•   •   •

A Passion for Wilderness

Second Day / July 1

During the night, I am vaguely aware of heavy showers. At times I stir for a few moments and instinctively move away from the edge of the tarp cover. Everything remains dry.

I awake in light. I empty the pools that sag my poncho roof.

The second day passes much as the first. Without human contact, monotony begins to set in. The only changes are in the weather and myself. Otherwise everything goes on as it has — and will — for thousands of years.

I hustle to remain active all the time, and repeat my chores. The second day goes much faster than the first. I am adjusting psychologically.

As the clouds burn off, I decide to write letters. I bask and burn in the sun. Before the day ends, I write to ten people. Most will not answer me, but I enjoy the activity of writing to them.

It is good to disassociate oneself from people and organizations. I don't need them all the time. Today I leave Outward Bound behind. For so long, all I have heard is talk about group dynamics, challenge, and interdependence. The patrol needs that. The one concept constantly repeated is the relationship to the group, the idea that an individual becomes literally a mechanical cog in a system of parts. If one part fails or doesn't carry its share of the load, the whole human machine might slow down or stop.

A Passion for Wilderness

With the repetition of the word, challenge, and the groping to go beyond what was thought possible, the mind becomes stretched like a pulled muscle. Even a simple thing, like pulling on boots in the morning, reaches the point of conditioning where it causes the reaction, "This is a challenge. I must do it." I become tired of the word.

"Too military," is the phrase one ex-Outward Bound instructor used when talking to me about the course. "I always approached the outdoors with happy anticipation," I said. "Can't there be a sense of humor?"

I agreed that it is sensible to discuss the day's activities and to plan for the next. But when this takes on the character of a briefing, complete with an instructor's manual and jargon, I rebel.

John wanted to share responsibility and to avoid assigning roles. He is too good an instructor for that. I also like him because he smokes his pipe and doesn't obey all the rules.

Another instructor delighted in his own individual style. To him, pushing a mile beyond the possible was not enough. He insisted on five or ten miles of hiking and climbing every day to the point of physical breakdown. To others, his group was known as "the push patrol." Just as a general always keeps his distance from his troops, this instructor tents and eats alone. It irritates him to see people sitting around a fire. A swift kick solves that.

A Passion for Wilderness

Our patrol didn't argue and we all got along. At day's end, we were tired, without any great thoughts. Writers must put those sublime conversations in their books, in the comfort and privacy of their studies, after the expedition is over.

Now it is refreshing to retrieve my individuality. Here no one can evaluate me with a pencil stub and little black book. To be free is exhilarating.

"I don't believe in anything. I'm not afraid of anything. I am free," is the self-chosen epitaph chiseled on the tombstone of Nikos Kazantzakis in Crete. Here below Chair Mountain there is no Marx, no Freud, no Camus, no Kazantzakis, no Outward Bound, no psychological belay or fixed rope, no piton to clip into, nothing except the self. I am philosophically naked and without shame. "I have nothing to prove to anybody. I have nothing to say to anybody. I am free," is my motto for the day.

During late morning, I do speak. John strolls by on his rounds.

"Everything all right?"

"Yes."

John nods and continues on, never breaking his stride. He is gone. How I wish he had stopped for a minute to tell me the latest news. I would have relished hearing the most trivial word.

After dates for lunch and a brief nap, I am anxious to move. Heading for my Philosopher's

A Passion for Wilderness

Seat, I notice that there is an even better lookout above it.

Scrambling to the top, I enjoy a little route-finding exercise. Now I'll have a superb view of the valley.

I am startled and jump back. There on the side of a rock is a pair of dungarees. My instant reaction is: A bear must have mauled a lone hunter here last fall and this grisly piece of evidence remains. What an isolated place to be attacked, and no one has ever known the man's fate until now.

My eyes dart around. Then I notice an orange climber's helmet and a bivouac. Glancing to one side, I spot Eric lying asleep, his back browning with the sun, on a pad on the ledge.

I restrain a yelp. Eric does not stir. I could awaken him, and we could talk all afternoon about backpacking. But since the Outward Bound solo credo permits no visiting, I respect his sleep. Without a noise, I manage to return to my own perimeter.

Again I collect firewood, have supper, and write in my journal. As I work, I feel inconsistent with my personality earlier that morning.

For so many days I have shared everything with nine other people, people who have helped me more than I have helped them. Having depended on them literally for life with a belay on a cliff, a check of a Prusik knot, or a sip of water, I now am lonely. Being on your patrol twenty-four hours a day builds a far closer relationship than that among colleagues on a nine-to-five job.

A Passion for Wilderness

I decide that I shall write Christmas cards to all of them. That simple vow makes me feel happy. I also pledge to myself to send copies of Bob Marshall's **Alaska Wilderness** to all of them.

A few years ago I was cramming for my comprehensive examinations in graduate school, and I was exhausted at the end of every day. A three-hour written exam each day for four days, with orals on the fifth, was a carryover from the medieval guild system. I was studying things that mean little to me now. Late at night, to clear my brain, I read a couple of chapters from Bob's book. I felt spiritually with him, exploring the Brooks Range in northern Alaska during the 1930s. It was like drinking cool water after a dusty hike.

Every sentence of that book radiates with the sheer joy and delight Bob felt at being in Alaska. The book became a religious experience for me, and it preserved my sanity during those hard times. Perhaps my patrol friends will enjoy it as much as I did.

For relaxation, I walk up to the Seat again. I glance up. Eric is standing. He sees me and waves. I wave back. We don't speak.

Capitol Peak is especially sharp in the clear evening air. Tomorrow will be another beautiful day.

After returning, I watch the sky. The stars pop out brightly. I locate the North Star. Now I am ready for sleep. Today has gone much better.

A Passion for Wilderness

Third Day / July 2

I jerk awake to the sound of a drenching rain. It is still dark. Soon the rain becomes hail; the hard pellets sting when I stick my hand outside. The rattling sound pings on in a summer snowstorm.

The poncho sags, lower and lower, and finally coming to rest with its accumulated weight on my legs and feet. It is miserable. I must do something.

With a violent wiggle, I am out of the bag, yanking on my boots, and stumbling out into the darkness. Brushing off the snow, I run my hand over the ground and find a few extra sticks to prop up my tarp. It's a makeshift shelter, but the best I can do.

I lie there, unable to sleep, and think. That's the trouble, I'm beginning to think too much. The previous summer, on August 16, some friends and I were caught in a snowstorm on Mount Sneffels, about one hundred miles to the southwest. "In five minutes," a Colorado native had told us, "it can become a whole new world out there." It's winter all year here if it wants to be.

Finally I get up for the day. Outside is a black grayness. With an instinct for distinguishing shapes, I stamp around.

The gray becomes white, then pink, diffusing throughout the void. I have watched sunrise many times, but today it is especially comforting. Although the air is raw and chilly, the sun offers psychological warmth. I must wait for the sun to melt the new snow and dry the rocks. Then I can lay out all my wet things to dry.

This morning I have other visitors besides the chipmunks and the birds. Mosquitoes, whole colonies of them, are out, stirred up by the storm. I'm their breakfast. Mine is a few dates.

Today I reflect more about myself. After exhausting the outdoor and routine thoughts over the last few days, I dwell on my own life. People and experiences I haven't thought about in years now concern me.

I don't want to think about myself that much. A friend who often visits Japan told me about his conversation on that subject with a Zen Buddhist monk. "After a while," the Zen Master commented about his long periods of enforced meditation, "you begin to hate yourself."

Recalling what I have done and said to people, I feel bad about mean and immature actions that I did out of spite. These incidents happened years ago. Undoubtedly, these people have long ago forgotten the matter, and have probably forgotten me. Yet here I am on the slopes of Chair Mountain, torturing myself. How needless it is. I begin wondering whether my fellow soloists are experiencing these same foolish emotions. But the moods do not last long.

I ponder the fact that many religious organizations demand a period of initiation. The hunger and privation of an initiation supposedly induces introspection, producing extraordinary

A Passion for Wilderness

visions in this strained mental state. When facing their ritualistic ordeals, primitive American Indians, including Carlos Castaneda's Don Matus, lapse from the conscious to the unconscious with a suspended state in between.

From biblical times to the present-day, man has wandered off alone in the wilderness and has come back holy. Whether or not he has returned holy or heroic, he has become dirty, tired, and spent. All I can think of now is a steak dinner, with no grandiose ideas of starting a new religious faith to shake the world.

Others, such as Mahatma Gandhi, the jailed Irish Easter Rebellion leaders, and Cesar Chavez use loneliness, fasting, and asceticism for political purposes. Somehow this self-inflicted experience is supposed to move the masses. Did they achieve their objectives? I have no political illusions about what I am doing. I live the experience for myself. Most Outward Bound soloists feel no need to say anything about it, let alone write an essay on it.

I think of Robinson Crusoe's real-life counterpart, Alexander Selkirk, marooned by choice on one of the Juan Fernandez islands. After an initial period of depression, Crusoe (and presumably Selkirk) erupted into great joy. He worked and whistled on his daily projects, frolicked with wild animals, and sang songs. I try to do the same.

Perhaps my happiness is artificial, but it is a way to cope with my situation. My penetrating thought is, "I'm here. How can I best exist with it?"

By now I am drowsy. There is no single sequence of thought patterns along a rational line. A hundred times during the solo, I mull over the same thought or memory. And I ignore other seemingly important matters, crucial to my life and future. In a single moment I experience the whole range of emotions — utter loneliness, exhilaration, boredom, happiness, and sadness. They are all mixed up like gorp.

I look up to the top of an Engelmann spruce. In the crown of the uppermost branches are shiny red seed clusters, vivid against the blue sky. Below the living green branches are dead white ones, brittle enough to snap off for firewood. Near the ground, great trunks are rotting, becoming part of the soil to grow trees again. Here is a whole natural cycle: birth, maturity, old age, and death.

Endlessly repeated is the sequence of dawn, noon, dusk, night, and dawn; or summer, fall, winter, spring, and summer. Man is a tiny part of nature going on timelessly.

I accept everything. There is no sense of history, of anything happening of importance. There is nothing to write down for the people in the outside world. It does not even seem alarming to think about falling asleep during the afternoon and never waking up. I have many plans, but death does not seem sad. I am in the endless cycle with the trees and seasons.

In this suspended state, I am shaken to my senses. My brain clicks into a conventional

A Passion for Wilderness

reaction. I am aware of something. Approaching by the same trail he used yesterday, John walks by.

"Any problems?"

"No."

That is the conversation for the day. He continues his pace. I feel cheated, as I had hoped John would exchange some news with me. I'm all right; that's all he needs to know. I am amazed at how much I have looked forward to that human contact.

I pass the afternoon just as I passed the morning. On my Seat, I notice smoke billowing like an Indian signal from Eric's campfire. Eric must have been adding more wood.

Coming down the slope from my Seat, I momentarily slip and jam my right foot against a rock. The foot hurts. It is the blistered one that had been infected. I flex it and believe the damage is slight.

Injuries are another law of the wild. Every day there is a new wound, a scraped arm, a half-sprained ankle, or a poke in the ribs from a snag. When the soreness leaves one injury, another appears. My hands are a matrix of fresh cuts, half-healed cuts, the scars of fully healed cuts, plus bruises and gashes, coated with ground-in dirt, sap, and Brillo pad gunk from scrubbing pots. It won't wash off.

My clothes are torn. My beard is scruffy. I don't care.

After supper, I dismantle my fireplace. After heaving the rocks away, I scrape up the ashes and

A Passion for Wilderness

scatter them in the bushes. With my foot, I smooth the ground and strew around branches and needles. All signs of the fire are gone. John is always dismayed by the sight of multiple fire rings, perhaps half a dozen around a lake where one would do, even in the remoteness of Alaska's Brooks Range, where he lived for months.

At my Seat, I notice Eric's fire again and look out over the valley. In a week, I'll be at the Redstone Inn, sitting down before a table-cloth, dishes, and a steak. It's difficult to analyze the past three days so I think about the future. Ahead of us, we have a three-day final examination, a twenty- or thirty-mile trek with-out our instructors. After all the groups rendezvous at Rustlers' Gulch, we will run a fifteen-mile marathon over 10,707-foot Schofield Pass to Lizard Lake, and back to base camp. To ensure that we leave healthy, the director has scheduled two days for classroom workshops and turning in of our gear. According to rumor, two live rams will be purchased from a local Marble rancher. The people in the course will then kill, skin, butcher, and roast the sheep for a farewell feast on the last night.

No one is talking about a post-camp mountain-eering jaunt. I had expected that a few of the diehard outdoor people would be planning and pro-moting an expedition to the Maroon Bells, the Crestones, or the San Juans. Then we could savor the mountains for a few more days.

But it turns out that virtually everyone is leaving immediately, to family, job, vacation,

342

A Passion for Wilderness

whatever.   The Colorado summer will end for them.

The same spirit prevails among the instructors, and the director too.   Only two or three of the staff will remain to lead another group through the next course.   They have only a single day of vacation between the two sessions.

I guess one can take the mountains only so long.   There are other things in life.

But there are a few exceptions.   Rick is heading for Jasper, Alberta, to explore the Canadian Rockies.   I have given him tips about that area.   John is also bound for Canada, but to the lakes and streams.   He will have a month of solitude with his canoe in the North Woods wilderness of Ontario's Quetico Provincial Park.

For myself, I am planning a rest day in Glenwood Springs for laundry, haircut, shave, and a long soak in the hot springs.   After that, I have scheduled a leisurely month's drive back East, with stops in Utah's Canyonlands, the Wind River Range, and the Black Hills.   But my emphasis will be on day hikes, not full-fledged assaults on the high peaks.

I dream again about the Buckskin Basin lakes and the Pierre Lakes, the latter located across the Maroon Bells-Snowmass ridge divide.   There I could have fished, and this solo would have passed much more quickly.   Except for that, the mosquito bites, and the jammed foot, I have no regrets.   But the solo is deliberately planned for thought and meditation, not fishing.   I leave my Seat for the final time.

A Passion for Wilderness

The whole night sky blazes. I checked the Big Dipper and North Star and go to bed.

Fourth Day / July 3

I sleep soundly and awake early. Outside it is gray, and I get up quickly.

Today I feel a rush of blood, a quickness in body and spirit I have not experienced for the past three days. I am leaving the woods. Perhaps Thoreau sensed this spirit at Walden Pond on his final day, leaving behind the old to go forward to the new.

I watch the red sunrise, as if a huge forest fire is burning over the mountains to the east.

My routine is ever the same. I eat the last of my crackers, a brand I hate (as do most of the others in the patrol), and the last dates. I wash and break camp. Soon my bivouac looks just as I found it four mornings ago. I walk around the area several times, to assure myself there are no leftover human traces.

To occupy my time, I check my feet and apply new patches of moleskin to the tender places. For a hiker, there is always another piece of busy work — with my knife, I dig out all the caked mud from the soles of my boots. I write some more.

What if John doesn't come by? It's his forty-sixth birthday today, and he wouldn't trick us. Or would he?   I wonder if I am so programmed

A Passion for Wilderness

and broken in that I simply would accept it as part of the solo and remain. Or would I pack out, round up my friends, and walk down to the Marble dirt road?

In the back of my mind, I recall reading the story about a New England prep-school headmaster meeting with his students on their solo survival exercise based on the Outward Bound model. After four foodless and bagless days of bivouac, the boys dragged in, dead on their feet.

"All right, men," the headmaster said, "let's say this is the real thing. Here's a candy bar apiece. Go back to your areas and I'll see you in twenty-four hours."

Somehow I have the distinct impression that the headmaster drove back to his home in a late-model car, to find his wife sitting in front of a cozy fire in the fireplace. After a cocktail, they were ready to eat a sumptuous dinner.

"That will take care of the kids for another day," he probably said. "Let's eat."

Yes, I could last another day, and another after that. But living as a hermit has no purpose. If the world collectively decided to go solo, there would be no exchange of ideas and man would go the way of the dinosaur.

Isolation can be experienced only periodically. A person would die if he lived indefinitely on the summit of Mount Everest. Robert E. Peary arrived at the North Pole, checked the readings on his instruments, and then headed his dog-sleds south. After a winter's solo on Ant-arctica, Admiral Richard E. Byrd returned to the

A Passion for Wilderness

United States to polish up his notes for his book, **Alone**. Alexander Selkirk soloed for four-and-a-half years, and then was picked up by a passing ship. No one stays on forever; all eventually come out.

I haven't changed much. A solo of four days and three nights isn't going to alter significantly a lifetime of established habits. At the age of forty-two, I realize I can never make my living as a mountain or big-game guide. During the course, I have struggled to keep up with people half my age. Yet I know I shall reflect on these four days more than I thought possible. They have been days of honest living without distractions.

After a few hours, I wonder why John isn't here. Perhaps we **are** extending another day.

I begin to think about my patrol, and all the others I've met and known these many days.

"Well, there ought to be a country preacher back at base camp," I had joked. "When we all trudge in, he'll gather us together for a mass wedding of twenty-six couples. We'll stay on in Marble, and hack it somehow. We can live in a commune, raise sheep, or run a ski resort, an Aspen without the frills."

The evening before the solo, our campfire gathering was euphoric. We all felt it. After our successful climb, we ate a fine supper. We discussed our hangups. Everyone passed around notebooks, and within minutes we had exchanged addresses and telephone numbers. From California to Massachusetts, from Iowa to Oklahoma,

we truly believed that someday we would be together again. Even separating for the solo, four
long days, was painful.

I have experienced those final partings many
times — a handshake, an embrace, sometimes with
tears — at prep school, college, the army, and
summer camp jobs, with addresses in booklets and
promises to keep.

In almost every case, no matter how deeply we
meant it then, our friendships died away. Everyone goes to a different place and resumes his old
life. Rarely, if ever, is one of these friends
heard of again, unless he or she becomes the
president, a sports or show business personality,
a political activist, an author, or a wanted
criminal.

Once I spoke with Dave Roberts, who has written
two mountaineering books about Alaska. About
ten or fifteen years ago, he and some buddies
climbed Mount McKinley. After weeks of grueling
hardships and dangers, the team staggered back to
its base camp, joyous over the ascent. Each made
a commitment, no matter what happened, to have
a reunion five years later. Those who were too
far away to make the party would telephone. They
would be friends forever. With each swig of
the victory brandy, they became doubly and
triply convinced that their gang would never
break up. After all they had gone through, how
could they?

One, two, three, four and finally five years
passed. There was no reunion, not even letters
or telephone calls. The critical survival bond

binding them together at over 20,000 feet on the summit of Mount McKinley, bolstered by the farewell party, pulled loose like a piton and snapped with the passage of time.

"I've lost track of half of them," Dave said. "I have no idea where they are. Many are out of climbing entirely."

Dave Roberts is probably right about these summer expeditions. Most of these three-week friendships dissolve as quickly as snow melted by sun.

It is with infinite sadness that I realize that in a week's time our patrol will be going off in private cars, chartered buses, and airplanes. In my head, I know it can't last; in my heart, I hope it will.

For everyone I wish the best. I hope Eric can backpack from Point Barrow, Alaska, south to Tierra del Fuego, tip to tip on the great American island. I think of Rick on an Alaskan hunt, bagging a Dall sheep with full-curl horn. Margot will buy a house soon. Bonnie might sail across the Atlantic in a regatta. John might go back to Africa, where he was a guide on Mount Kilimanjaro. I hope Ted gets his promotion.

I shall always remember that special place below Chair Mountain in the Elk Range. Here my memories can return for the rest of my life. Even when I am ninety years old, carrying a cane and unable to do the outdoor things anymore, I will be able to relive it and be as free as the animals.

I look up to see John standing with a smile

on his face. He opens his mouth to talk. The solo is over.

BIBLIOGRAPHY OF
WILDERNESS LIFE AND TRAVEL

In addition to the contributions of Henry David Thoreau, John Muir, Robert Marshall, Harvey Broome, Sigurd F. Olson, William O. Douglas, Edward Abbey, John McPhee, Edward Hoagland and others to the literature of wilderness writing, we include these kindred and meaningful accounts.

Books

Appalachian Mountain Club. **A.M.C. River Guide, Vol. 1, Maine.** Boston: Appalachian Mountain Club, 1980.

—. **The A.M.C. Massachusetts and Rhode Island Trail Guide.** Boston: Appalachian Mountain Club, 1964.

Barland, Hal. **Our Natural World.** Philadelphia: J. B. Lippincott, 1969.

Brady, John and White, Brian. **Fifty Hikes in Massachusetts.** Woodstock, Vermont: Back-country Publications, 1983.

Brower, Kenneth. **Earth and the Great Weather: The Brooks Range.** San Francisco, New York and Paris: Friends of the Earth, 1971. Essays: "Igikpak and the Arrigetch" by David S. Roberts.

Bueler, William M. **Roof of the Rockies: A History of Mountaineering in Colorado.** Boulder, Colorado: Pruett Publishing Co., 1974.

Calef, George. **Caribou and the Barren-lands.** Ottawa: Canadian Arctic Resources Committee, 1981.

A Passion for Wilderness

Choque, Charles, o.m.i. **Kajualuk.** Churchill, Manitoba: Churchill-Hudson Bay Diocese, 1985.

Cooper, David J. **Brooks Range Passage.** Seattle: The Mountaineers, 1982

Evans, G. Heberton III. **The Rupert That Was.** Cobalt: Ontario Highway Bookshop, 1978.

Frome, Michael. **Promised Land: Adventures and Encounters in Wild America.** New York: William Morrow and Company, Inc., 1985.

Garvin, John W. **Canadian Poets.** Toronto: McClelland and Stewart, Ltd., 1926.

Green Mountain Club. **Day Hiker's Guide to Vermont.** Montpelier, Vermont: Green Mountain Club, Inc., 1978.

Griffiths, Thomas M. **San Juan Country.** Boulder, Colorado: Pruett Publishing Co., 1984.

Hamlin, Helen. **Nine Mile Bridge: Three Years in the Maine Woods.** New York: W. W. Norton & Company, Inc., 1945.

Iowa Conservation Commission. **Iowa Float Trips.** Des Moines, Iowa: Iowa Conservation Commission.

Jenkinson, Michael. **Wild Rivers of North America.** New York: E. P. Dutton and Co., Inc., 1973.

A Passion for Wilderness

Kerouac, Jack. **Lonesome Traveler.** New York: Grove Press, Inc., 1970. Essay: "Alone on a Mountaintop."

Milton, John P. **Nameless Valleys, Shining Mountains: The Record of an Expedition into the Vanishing Wilderness of Alaska's Brooks Range.** New York: Walker and Company, 1970.

Miner, Joshua L., and Boldt, Jo. **Outward Bound U.S.A.** New York: William Morrow and Company., Inc., 1981.

Ormes, Robert M., with the Colorado Mountain Club. **Guide to the Colorado Mountains.** Colorado Springs: Robert M. Ormes, 1979.

Petersen, William J. **Iowa — The Rivers of Her Valleys.** Iowa City, Iowa: The State Historical Society of Iowa, 1941.

— **Steamboating - On the Upper Mississippi.** Iowa City, Iowa: State Historical Society of Iowa, 1968.

Roberts, David. **Deborah: A Wilderness Narrative.** New York: The Vanguard Press, Inc., 1970.

Rosebrough, Robert F. **The San Juan Mountains.** Evergreen, Colorado: Cordillera Press, 1986.

A Passion for Wilderness

Rutstrum, Calvin. **Back Country.** Pittsboro,
  Indiana: Indiana Camp Supply Books, 1981.

Sadlier, Ruth and Paul. **Fifty Hikes in Vermont.**
  Somersworth, N. H.: New Hampshire Publishing
  Company, 1974.

Short, Vaughn. **Raging River – Lonely Trails.**
  Tucson, Arizona: Two Horse Press, 1978.

Special Publications Division. **America's Wild
  and Scenic Rivers.** Washington, D. C.:
  National Geographic Society, 1983.

Terres, John K. **Discovery.** Philadelphia:
  J. B. Lippincott Co., 1961.

Warkentin, John. **The Western Interior of Canada.**
  Toronto/Montreal: McClelland & Stewart Ltd.

A r t i c l e s

Arnold, Tom. "The St. John River: A Personal
  Reminiscence." **Appalachia Bulletin Issue,**
  March 1982.

Baird, Irene. "Inuvik." **The Beaver,**
  Autumn 1960.

Brown, Bern Will. "The Hare Indians." **The
  Beaver,** Autumn 1974.

A Passion for Wilderness

Holn, E. O. "Anderson River and Fort." **The Beaver,** Winter 1963.

Hoyt, Austin. "Down the Back to the Arctic." **Sports Illustrated,** August 26, 1963.

Hyde, Stephen. "Notes from the Riverbank: Canoeing the St. John." **Habitat: Journal of the Maine Audubon Society,** March 1984.

Layton, Alfred W. G. "St. John River Canoe Trip." **Appalachia,** December 15, 1971.

Moffatt, Arthur R. "Man Against the Barren Grounds." **Sports Illustrated,** Parts I and II, March 9 and 16, 1959.

Sawyer, Fred R. "Through Unknown Maine: A Canoe Trip on the Upper St. John River." **Appalachia,** December 1949.

— "Upper St. John River, in Maine." **Appalachia,** December 15, 1956.

Skow, John. "Shame on the St. John." **Outdoor Life,** October 1979.

Tallmadge, John. "In the Mazes of Quetico." **Orion Nature Quaterly,** Summer 1984.

— "Into the Deeps." **Orion Nature Quarterly,** Winter 1986.

Wilderness Adventure Books
P. O. Box 968
Fowlerville, MI   48836

Please send the following books:

QUANTITY	TITLE	PRICE (U.S.)	AMOUNT
___	A Passion for Wilderness	$14.95	$ ___
___	One Incredible Journey	$16.95	$ ___
___	Lure of the Arctic	$10.95	$ ___
___	Cold Summer Wind	$13.95	$ ___
		TOTAL ENCLOSED:	$ ___

Postage will be paid by the publisher.
Send check or money order — no cash or C.O.D.

Mr./Mrs./Ms. _____

Street _____

City _____ State/Province _____ ZIP _____